The Girls and B
on Success

PARENTING
after
September 11, 2001

Also from Boys Town Press

For Parents

Common Sense Parenting® (also in audio and Spanish)

Common Sense Parenting Learn-at-Home Video Kit

Common Sense Parenting of Toddlers and Preschoolers

Parenting to Build Character in Your Teen

Angry Kids, Frustrated Parents

Boys Town Videos for Parents

Dealing With Your Kids' 7 Biggest Troubles

Parents & Kids Talking About School Violence

Unmasking Sexual Con Games: Parent Guide

Getting Along with Others: Activity Book

For Teens

Boundaries: A Guide for Teens

A Good Friend: How to Make One, How to Be One

Who's in the Mirror? Finding the Real Me

What's Right for Me? Making Good Choices in Relationships

One to One: Listening Tapes on Dating, Alcohol, Suicide and More

Unmasking Sexual Con Games: Student Guide

For a free Boys Town Press catalog, call 1-800-282-6657.

The Girls and Boys Town Book
on Successful Parenting

PARENTING
after
September 11, 2001

Val J. Peter
Executive Director, Girls and Boys Town

BOYS
TOWN
PRESS

Parenting After September 11, 2001

Published by the Boys Town Press
Father Flanagan's Boys' Home
Boys Town, Nebraska 68010

ISBN 1-889322-53-9

The Boys Town Press is the publishing division of Girls and Boys Town, the original Father Flanagan's Boys' Home.

10   9   8   7   6   5   4   3   2   1

Girls and Boys Town
National Hotline
1-800-448-3000

*Parents and children can call the
Girls and Boys Town National Hotline
for help with any problem,
24 hours a day, every day.*

Table of Contents

Introduction

A series of events have occurred in America that is changing the way moms and dads look at the responsibilities they have for their children. They all center around September 11, the day that symbolizes the end of the world as we knew it.

Before September 11, we as a nation were not focused on family. Our eyes were elsewhere: money, fashion, sports, Hollywood. Humor was cynical…nothing was sacred. But even in that age of cynicism and glamour, we were now and then shocked at how far we had strayed from what pundits called "family values." Two examples suffice.

- Some time ago, PBS's *Frontline* featured a documentary on a major outbreak of syphilis in Conyers, Georgia, with the core group being middle-class white girls, mostly under sixteen. It's a shock to hear a 14-year-old girl say she has had thirty or forty sex partners. Cynthia Noel, a nurse at the Public Health Department, told *Frontline:* "These girls were not homeless. They were not abused in any way. They were just normal, everyday, regular kids." These were kids whose parents were not parenting them. People were shocked, but most folks went about their business as usual.

- More recently in Chappaqua, New York, the *New York Post* exposed the story of a high school senior named Jeremy whose parents were right there at a party with lots of boys and girls present. The Westchester County District Attorney explains what happened: "This nude dancer, with the assistance of some of the high school students, was inserting objects into private parts of her body, as well as putting whipped cream on parts of her body that were then being licked by some of the students."

This story was enough to shock most parents but not enough to make any changes in their own parenting style.

Then came September 11 when the terrorist attacks radically changed our country and made countless parents pay attention and say: "How am I going to prepare my children for the days ahead?" What lies ahead? Years of terror and tragedy, courage and sacrifice?

- The torch of freedom is being passed to a new generation. And mom and dad know they need to prepare their children for whatever lies ahead.

- Family has become central to our lives again. So the question is: How do we parent after September 11?

Part of the answer is right in front of us. The National Center on Addiction and Substance Abuse (CASA) at Columbia

University issued research findings for 2000 which, in the wake of September 11, are being taken to heart by more and more parents.

Joseph A. Califano, Jr., CASA Chairman and President, listed twelve possible actions which parents could take with respect to their teenagers:

1. Monitor what their teens watch on television.

2. Monitor what they do on the Internet.

3. Put restrictions on the music they buy.

4. Know where their teens are after school and on weekends.

5. Expect to be told and are told the truth by their teens about where they really are going.

6. Are "very aware" of their teen's academic performance.

7. Impose a curfew.

8. Make clear they would be "extremely upset" if their teen used marijuana.

9. Eat dinner with their teen most every night.

10. Turn off the TV during dinner.

11. Assign their teen regular chores.

12. Have an adult present when the teen returns from school.

Then, based on how many of these actions parents actually take with their teens, CASA put parents into three categories:

- "Hands-on"
- "Half-hearted"
- "Hands-off"

Teens living in "hands-on" households, for example, have parents who regularly take ten or more of the actions listed above.

The survey found:

- Nearly one in five teens (18%) lives with parents classified as "hands-off," that is, parents who do not consistently have rules and expectations. These parents take five or less of the described twelve actions. Teens with "hands-off" parents are four times more likely to abuse substances than teens with "hands-on" parents.

- The survey found that 47% of teens living in "hands-on" households report an excellent relationship with their father. This compares to 13% of teens living in "hands-off" households.

- And a full 57% of teens in "hands-on" households report an excellent relationship with their mother. That compares to only 24% of teens living in "hands-off" households who report the same.

Mr. Califano says: "It is time for every parent to look in the mirror rather than to look outside to what someone else can do. Parents should ask themselves: 'Am I a parent to my teen, or a pal? Do I monitor what my teen watches on television or on the Internet, what music CDs he or she buys and listens to? Do I know where my teen is after school or on weekends? Have I made it clear I would be extremely upset if my teen used marijuana? Do I know how my teen is doing in school? Have I set a curfew for my teen? Do we have dinner together as a family almost every night – without the television on?' The more CASA examines teen risk of substance abuse, the more it becomes clear that parents have enormous power for good."

After September 11, these findings have even greater urgency.

This little book intends to help you, mom and dad, come back to the art of parenting that Father Flanagan and his boys and girls have never left.

CHAPTER 1

What's Wrong?

A strange phenomenon is occurring across our land. After September 11, 2001, more and more parents are asking what they need to do to better parent their children. And more and more children are discovering the days when they controlled their parents are fast disappearing. The results are pleasurable for moms and dads and beneficial for sons and daughters.

We are going to be sharing with you eight lessons in upbringing. They go back to Father Flanagan, himself. Yes, America is returning to the values Girls and Boys Town never left behind. Before beginning our lessons, let's start with the widespread phenomenon of parents not knowing how to parent. In many cases, it's not mom or dad's fault since they were never introduced to the art of "bringing up" children. It's more complicated than a simple lack of skills. It's the result, in many cases, of how we ourselves were raised. Let's start with some examples:

Here's a mother and father who learned from their immigrant parents who were too strict. They felt their parents raised them to be:

- too inhibited
- too guilt-ridden
- too uncreative
- too afraid to take risks
- too conventional
- too uptight

So this new mom and dad turned to the self-esteem movement for advice on how to parent. They read books on the new psychology of parenting and internalized one basic idea, namely, praise your child regularly.

- So they praise their children when they do well.

- They praise their children when they do not do well.

- They even praise their children when they are abysmal in their performance.

- One clear result is that their children are not uptight and guilt ridden like they were.

But there are other unforeseen results which mom and dad are not prepared for. Their son is now thirteen:

- He is skipping school.

- He is not following instructions at home.

- He is oppositional.

- He is defiant.

- When his parents try to discipline him, he effectively neutralizes their efforts by stating over and over again: "You don't love me. If you loved me you wouldn't do these things to me."

- They are troubled and offended by these stinging rebukes from their son.

What can these parent do, but give in and hope for the best?

As you'll see later, there is a lot these parents can do!

* * *

Then there is Amy, whose parents are divorced. Her father has custody of her. He is very mean and even beats her when he is drunk. There is no doubt about it. It is physical abuse. She runs away and comes to her mother. Mom has no custody rights because she has a cocaine problem. She gives her daughter hugs. The police come and take the daughter to a shelter. Her mother visits the shelter three days in a row and gives her a big hug each time. When she runs away, her mother gives her money to stay in a motel. Amy tells the judge she wants to go live with her mother who hugs her rather than her father who slugs her. The Girls and Boys Town counselor tells the mother: "You really can't have your daughter come and live with you because you have a drug problem and you will drag her down with you." Her response is: "Amy will think I'm a bad mom if I don't do this." What's a mom to do?

* * *

Here is a mom whose live-in boyfriend commits suicide. She calls Girls and Boys Town and says: "Could I please have Joey (her 13-year-old son) come home because I need him to console me during this time?" Whose needs are being met? Who is mothering whom?

* * *

One of Girls and Boys Town's well-loved senior pediatricians comes to lunch at the Village Visitors Center quite upset one day. As a pediatrician, he has been taking care of children for so long that he is now treating the grandchildren of the first children he saw as a young doctor so many years ago.

Why is he upset? Last week a mother came in with her 2-year-old daughter. The daughter had an earache. Doc gave her drops and said: "These will take good care of it. Please do this twice a day and come back and see me in a week."

The mother came back today, and her baby daughter was much worse. The mother said: "I am sorry, doctor, little Christina won't let me put the drops in her ears." Clearly mom is not parenting Christina.

* * *

Here is a mom and dad whose daughter, Marie, age 16, is totally out of control. Mom and dad try to discipline her but it doesn't work. "I tell all of my friends I have bad parents," Marie says. Mom and dad feel guilt ridden. They finally send their daughter to Girls and Boys Town.

Here she learns the self-help and self-discipline she needs. In her senior year, she strikes up a romantic relationship with a boy back home. Her mom and dad are very, very proud of her and her success here. So, on graduation day they present her with a brand new car and they put down six months' rent on an apartment so she can play house with her new boyfriend. They say she is "old enough to make up her own mind." Of course, Marie now declares them to be wonderful parents and not bad like they used to be. They are pleased.

These parents don't know the difference between being a parent and being a friend to their daughter.

* * *

Then there is a mother who allows the boyfriend of her 16-year-old daughter, Linda, to sleep over with her in their house. The mother isn't enthusiastic about it, but she allows it anyway because she is afraid her daughter will think her a "bad mom" if she doesn't.

* * *

Tommy's mom lets him have his tongue pierced in the seventh grade. She doesn't want to seem to be a bad mom. Lots of moms and dads succumb to their child's threats of blackmail: "I'll tell everybody you are a bad mom if you don't let me do this."

* * *

Mary, who is the seventh grade, is allowed to dress inappropriately because her mom thinks "it's cute" and she will be popular as a result. Mom is reliving her early adolescence through her daughter.

* * *

Tom and Cathy come from middle-class families. They both work and even though they know that home-cooked meals help bring a traditional sense of family, their children tell them that they would prefer to go to McDonald's. So they do…twice a week.

Who is training whom? Who is bringing up whom? These parents are missing the opportunity to provide the old-fashioned warmth they themselves experienced growing up.

* * *

A 10-year-old boy orders steak and lobster on a regular basis when the family goes out to dinner. Mom and dad can't really afford the costly meal, but don't want him to make a scene.

* * *

A young couple preparing for marriage, discuss the topic of children. The bride-to-be says: "I don't think we will have children because I don't know how to raise them." When I inquire whether her mom and dad were good at bringing her up, her response is: "Oh, no, they never raised me. I got whatever I wanted."

* * *

Then there is the 16-year-old girl, Gina, who is a sophomore and who has already been in three high schools. Gina comes from a wealthy family. After Thanksgiving her father announces the whole family will go to their ski lodge in the Colorado Rockies for the holidays.

She says she is not going. "I want to stay home and party with my friends." When dad says she needs to go because they are a family, she responds: "If you make me go, I will ruin Christmas for you."

Dad knows she is quite capable of ruining Christmas for her family. So, he lets her have her way. This is appeasement and will only lead to bigger problems in the future.

* * *

In all of these examples of parenting, something has gone wrong. And as a result, there is frustration and discouragement with the result that these parents don't like being moms and dads. At the heart of the problem is a profound misunderstanding of the parenting role and a corresponding lack of skills.

- None of the above parents are stupid.

- None of the above parents are simply immoral.

- Each is a mother or father who was never taught parenting skills or the art of "upbringing."

- No wonder they do not experience success.

- No wonder they do not enjoy parenting.

CHAPTER 2

The Art of Parenting

Lots of things are wrong in the examples given in the previous chapter. Let's start with one simple idea. Every one of these moms or dads is relying on feelings to tell him or her what to do with their children, and that is a bad idea.

Parenting should not be based on "feelings." Parenting should be based on clear thinking and good parenting skills.

Parenting or bringing up children is a role you play…a very specific role with very specific functions:

- It starts with understanding how to raise a child to be kind and caring and responsible.

- It's not about how you feel: wanting to be loved, or applauded, or relieved of guilt, or just left alone.

- Feelings are a notoriously unreliable guide to the role of bringing up children.

Children can manipulate our feelings easily. They know how to play on parents' feelings to their advantage: "I'll scream louder and louder until you give me what I want!" They learn to do so with skill from their youngest years.

Advertising takes advantage of the fact that little kids are easily trained. It coaches kids on how to manipulate mom and dad's feelings. Where does advertising begin? With a child's feelings:

- "You'll be a dork if you don't buy a certain product."

- Have it your way.

- Obey your thirst.

- Make your own rules.

- Just do it.

  So advertising:

- Encourages children to demand a product immediately.

- Admonishes kids to be dismissive of parents who aren't cool enough to appreciate that they have to have this stuff.

- Teaches them (through role modeling) to whine and holler until they get what they want.

- Hopes peers will make fun of kids who don't have this stuff.

Yes, advertising teaches your little child to be a whining, selfish, unattractive creature. Clear thinking and good parenting skills, however, can stop this and help your child become a giving, caring, sharing, attractive little child.

So, parenting should be the business of mom and dad:

- Gaining mastery over your own feelings.

- Not feeling guilty if you do not give in to your child's demands.
- Teaching them to value relationships over materialism.
- Teaching them to show empathy and respect for others.
- Teaching them to work to achieve goals.
- Teaching children self-control.

Advertising teaches kids how to nag their parents.

- It teaches them to play on mom's emotions.
- It teaches them how to whine.
- It teaches them to wheedle parents into buying them things.
- Advertising encourages children to think of "me first, now."
- Advertising tells our children they are valued for what they have.

Skillful parents can teach their children to value themselves for who they are…especially their relationships to brothers, sisters, mom, dad, grandparents.

A skillful parent needs to teach children to learn about self-control. Empathy. Moderation. Charity.

Here's a typical example of how a child tries to manipulate mom's feelings:

- Heidi, age 2, begs mom: "I want some M&M's...I want some M&M's." Mom says: "We are going to eat dinner in a few minutes, so you have to wait."

- Heidi screams more. Mom says no. Heidi screams louder.

- Mom finally gives in.

- What does Heidi learn from mom? You can get what you want from your mom by screaming and yelling and hollering.

- If she says no, you just have to scream, yell and holler louder and she will give in.

- Heidi learned from advertising how to nag.

- She practices this over a long period of time.
- She teaches mom to base her parenting on feelings, not on clear thinking and good parenting skills.

Advertising is competing with you in bringing up your child. You want to raise a kind, loving child. Advertising wants your child to be a proud, happy consumer. It says to your child: "You really need these M&M's. Do what it takes to get them." By giving in, mom, in this case, was trying to bring some peace. Of course she got some peace, but only for a very brief time and at a price.

The price she paid was greater frustration, opposition and perhaps outright warfare down the road.

If we are honest with ourselves, many parents come to realize they are trying to buy happiness for themselves and obtain love from their very small children by giving them what they want. But it doesn't work. If you give

Heidi what she wants, Heidi wants more and more. So the price keeps going up. And this makes us unhappy. After September 11, parents must be more willing to go head-to-head with advertisers for the sake of our little children.

Along comes adolescence and the advertisers and TV are now raising our children on a diet of sex and violence. When adolescence arrives, it is too late to try to buy happiness for ourselves and seek love from our children. Before September 11, the sitcoms advised us to just buy a little peace and quiet. In our heart of hearts, at this point we knew it was only appeasement. We realize now that the parenting role is not something we have exercised very well all these years. But sometimes we don't understand why. In this time of terrorism, most parents really would like to know how to be effective parents.

So let us look at eight lessons in clear thinking and good parenting. This is the way

27

America can return to the joys of parenting that Girls and Boys Town never left behind.

LESSON #1

The first lesson about your parenting role is this: *Children will love you no matter what you* do.

Little Heidi will love you no matter what you do. She will pout and complain. She will try to get what she wants. But she will love you. You need to know that up front.

- I have worked for years with little children who come from backgrounds of terrible abuse and neglect of all kinds.

- You know what? Even these children love their moms.

- They just wish they would act like moms.

- I have seen so many little girls abused by their dads.

- You know what?

- Even these children love their dads despite it all.

- They just wish he would act like a dad and quit doing these things.

- Little children want to love their parents.

- You may think they don't, but that is an adult view. That is not the way little children think.

- So you don't have to fear that your little child won't love you.

- We forget this lesson at our own peril.

LESSON #2

The second lesson is this: *Children of all ages want to be parented. They want structure. They want rules.*

Girls and Boys Town has listened to what kids are saying for more than 80 years. They are saying they want to be parented. They don't say it every minute of every day. But over eight decades, our kids say important things in moments of reflection and moments of wisdom. My children say:

- "I wish my parents had made the rules stick."
- "I wish my parents had not let me have my way."
- "I wish my parents had stopped me from doing drugs."

The boys and girls are telling us something very important.

- Many of them know their parents have not parented them.
- Many know their parents have acted like peers or buddies or friends, but not as parents.

If you think you are giving your kids love by always giving into them, you need to listen to our children here at Girls and Boys Town. Children need someone to parent them.

They will say they wish they had parents

who made more rules...they wish they had parents who would not let them have their way all the time...they wish they had parents who had stopped them from engaging in inappropriate sexual activity or drugs or alcohol.

What they are saying is that there is a particular way of loving that is part of being a parent. It involves providing structure and sticking to the rules.

In moments of whining and wheedling kids may say when they want something: "You are a bad mom...you are a bad dad...you don't love me because you won't give me what I want." Every parent has had their child say "I hate you" at some time. It goes with parenting.

But, mom and dad, you have to remember that in times of anger, your kids say these things to manipulate you. That's when you need to stick to your guns. Not give up and surrender.

When the going gets tough, tough (caring)

parents get going. And their kids get better.

LESSON #3

The third lesson is: *Children want parents to be parents, not friends or buddies.* The proper role of a parent is "upbringing." Bringing up a child is a special function.

There are stages of parenting:

- Parenting starts with the nurturing relationship during the dependency of childhood.

- It continues with the caring relationship as children grow into the independence of adolescence.

- But no stage involves being a buddy or friend.

If you have a garden, you know you need to prepare the soil in the spring, plant the seed, get rid of the endless weeds, trim and prune if necessary, watch out for and know how to get rid of beetles and the blight, as well as watering, cultivating and harvesting. If you grow a garden, you aren't reactive as much as proactive.

The same is true in raising children. A parent has to remember that it is his or her job to *bring children up* to be loving, caring, sharing, helpful, and happy people.

- The proper role of the parent, then, is to have the parent/child relationship based on upbringing.

- It's not a peer relationship. Building a peer relationship does not help a child learn the necessary skills or internalize important values or develop self-discipline. The peer relationship is more about simply having fun doing things together without teaching and without guidance. Peers hang out together. Parents bring kids up.

- Neither is the parenting relationship one of *just liking each other.* If your child has to like you all of the time, you can't possibly be a parent. If you have to like your child all the time, you can't possibly have fun as a mom or dad in the parental role.

- Neither is the relationship built on *friend-ship.* Although friendship is important, you are not just your child's friend. If you want always to be your child's friend, then you can't be his or her parent. Why? Because there will be times when you will have to act in a way that your child will perceive as not friendly at all. At times, a good parent says: "I will not give in to what my child wants to do. I will not give in to whim and fancy. I will not look the other way when you do very bad things. I will not act as your pal." Dad, this is not a relationship between Butch Cassidy and the Sundance Kid. Mom, this is not a relationship between two sisters.

- It is not a brother/sister relationship. Mom is not your sister. Dad is not your buddy.

- It is a parent/child relationship.

Sometimes an adolescent thinks that the parent/child relationship is a put-down. Of course it is not. A parent has to put up with more than they put down.

What are a child's wants and needs all about?

- I want to feel I can count on my parents.

- I want to feel they will be there for me.

- I want to feel I can predict their behavior.

- I need to learn discipline from them even if I object.

- I want consistency, clarity, and tough love.

- I want them to help each other and love each other.

- I am deeply attached to their relationship to each other.

- Divorce would be horrible for me because it would destroy that relationship they have with each other.

Parental behavior based on fear of being rejected or berated by your child is simple appeasement. It confuses roles and relationships. It works like this:

- I give into my kids…I give into their entreaties.
- I give them what they want and they rejoice…momentarily.
- Do my gifts do any real good?
- Yes, in the short run they buy a little temporary peace.
- In the long run, no, they don't do any good.
- The time of peace I buy gets shorter and shorter.
- Kids are not evil. They are opportunistic.
- They know how to get what they want from a parent who is filled with fear of being rejected by a child.
- They know how to get what they want from a parent who is tired of the relent-

less hassle that accompanies saying no.

What is the price of saying no? And how does it work?

Dr. Pat Friman, Clinical Psychologist at the University of Nevada at Reno, and Senior Fellow at the Boys Town Institute, uses the analogy of Elisabeth Kubler-Ross' five stages of dying to describe the process of moving a child from oppositional defiance to compliance. Listen to the language kids use toward their parents when they do not get their own way:

Stage One: Denial

Mom has said no and is sticking to her guns. Little Joey says: "I can't believe it. This isn't really happening. I must be dreaming. It must be a nightmare. Mom really can't be saying no and sticking to her guns."

Stage Two: Anger

Mom continues to refuse to give in and Joey says: "I know it really is happening and now I am really angry. I'll show her. Mom, I don't love you anymore. I never did. You aren't my real mother. If you were, you would not be doing this to me."

Stage Three: Bargaining

Mom continues to stick to her guns. Joey is saying: "Mom, I've seen the error of my ways. I will be good from this day forward. Just let me do what I want immediately. Can I get down from the chair, now, mom? You know how good I will be." When dad arrives, Joey pleads: "Daddy, you are my only hope. I love you so much. I want to hug you. Can I please get down from this chair?"

Stage Four: Depression

Mom and dad are still hanging in. Joey begins to say: "Not getting my way is worse than not existing at all...I might as well be dead...I feel awful...nothing is happening...I am depressed...I feel like an orphan...I am abandoned and neglected."

Stage Five: Acceptance

Mom and dad don't give in. Joey finally says: "I accept that you are in charge…I regret saying those things…I am ready to follow instructions."

At that very moment, mom must now give Joey a series of instructions to have her son put this newfound attitude into practice. If Joey follows those instructions, mom should give him a hug. If he doesn't, we are back to stage one.

This is what is called bringing up a child. This is what you call parenting or upbringing. You are bringing up your child to be an honest, upright, faithful, and playful young man or young woman.

The bottom line is this. Moms and dads, take courage. Stick to your guns and bring your children up. A dad said he used this method successfully with his daughter. But he said: "Because of this I have lost some of her trust."

My response was: "You have only lost inappropriate trust. If she trusts you less to get anything she wants, that is a step in the right direction."

LESSON #4

The fourth lesson is: *Follow your nature. You're a mom. You're a dad. It is natural for you to nurture and raise your children. It is rewarding. It will make you feel good.*

- If you view it as a duty or a burden, you will not give the positive side of parenting a chance.

- It is rewarding to nurture and raise your adolescent children as well. It will make you feel good.

- If your child approaches 12 or 13 and you say: "We are coming into the horrible years of adolescence," what you are really doing is conjuring up dread.

- Talking to other parents about how "bad" your kids are in their adolescent years is also conjuring up dread.

Yes, children change as they go into their teen years. But all we parents have to do is to adjust our parenting style so that it is age-appropriate for our adolescent. We'll see this in a further chapter.

CHAPTER 3

The Fun of Parenting

Sometimes kids get a very bad rap. Why? Because there are people who only think of the tough, unrewarding side of bringing up children. They neglect the great joys that a parent can have. Let's look at those joys starting first with our little children:

- It's fun to watch children share.
- It's fun to listen to the language children use when they play house in an affirming manner.
- It's fun to watch them be active and learn games such as jumping rope.
- It's fun to read stories to them.
- It's fun to sit down at the table and share ice cream and cake and not just serve it to them.

- It's fun to ask them questions like why they think rain comes down instead of going up, or why the sun comes up in the east instead of the west.

- It's fun especially to share nature with them.

- It's fun to collect leaves.

- It's fun to plant a garden and weed it and till it and watch it grow together.

- It's fun to share with them what you like, such as baking cookies and making pies.

- It's fun to do Thanksgiving things and Christmas things and Lenten things and Easter things and 4th of July things.

- It's fun to raise a little child.

Even when you have to say no to your child's unreasonable demands and stick to it, there can be a great deal of satisfaction involved for you. Why? Because you are bringing your child up to be a caring, sharing person: Someone with a great smile and with great hope and friendship skills.

- So when you say "No," don't take personally your child's insistence that this can't be happening.

- Don't take personally that "I hate you" and "I like daddy a lot better than you" and "I'll never love you again."

- You need to rejoice when you are successful with sticking to your "No" and you need to reward yourself because you are bringing your child up right and that is a joy in itself.

- When you go to bed at night, you have to say: "Thank you, Lord, that I stuck to my guns and did not give in. I am raising our child to be a friend and a husband or wife or mom or dad, and happy."

Parenting adolescent children also brings its own joy:

- Watching your daughter and her friends do all kinds of silly-gilly things.

- Watching your son or daughter develop as an athlete.

- Watching your son or daughter develop boy/girl friendship skills of sharing, politeness, and having fun.

- Taking your son hunting is a lot of fun.

- Taking your daughter shopping is a lot of fun.

- Helping your child learn dating skills.

- Helping your child deal with success and failure.

> "If you can dream
> And not make dreams your master
> If you can think
> And not make thoughts your aim
> If you can meet
> With triumph and disaster
> And treat these two imposters
> Just the same."
>
> – RUDYARD KIPLING, *IF*

The difficult times of adolescence occur mainly through the ignorance or stubbornness of your children who are playing with dynamite and don't realize it.

- Saying no and making it stick in adolescence is difficult because on one hand you can't be too strict, and on the other hand, you can't be too loosey-goosey.

- Your adolescent children will learn quickly from MTV, rap music and games that it is "cool" to flip the bird to parents. You cannot tolerate this, even though you know it is going to happen.

- When you stick to your guns, rejoice and congratulate yourself. Get down on your knees and thank God for the strength to help your son or daughter to be brought up properly.

- Girls and Boys Town's *Common Sense Parenting*® gives a solid list of behavioral rules and appropriate consequences to put into practice in your family.

47

- It's a great achievement. You will feel very good inside yourself.

LESSON #5

The fifth lesson: *If you are bored with life, your child will be bored with life. If you are bored with your child, your child will be bored with you. If you are excited about life, your child will get excited about life.*

- You can get your child excited about something by getting excited about it yourself.

- If you act excited about fishing, your child will probably act excited about fishing.

- If you act excited about reading, your child will start to act excited about reading.

- If you act excited about baseball, your child will probably imitate you and want to be excited about baseball.

Share your excitement with your child.

LESSON #6

The sixth lesson: *If you share your happiness and sadness with your child, they will share their happiness and sadness with you.*

- There is a sadness when your friends and family get transferred to another town. Share that with your child.

- There is happiness in loving your spouse and having a good time together. Share that with your child.

- There is sadness over the loss of your mom and dad. Share that with your child.

- There is happiness over the successes of your brothers and sisters. Share that with your child.

- There is happiness looking at your Christmas tree. Share that with your child.

- There is sadness in taking it down. Share that with your child.

LESSON #7

The seventh lesson: *When raising children, it is good to recall the old tune "There's No Business Like Show Business." You need to "smile when you are low."*

- This may sound like a contradiction to what was said above, but it really isn't.

- You need to share more joys than sorrows if you want your child to grow up with a smile.

- If you go around acting like a victim, you will teach your child someday to do the same.

- It is good to say: "Yes, son and daughter, we have troubles, but we know how to deal with them."

- "Look for the silver lining when a cloud appears in the blue."

- "Pack up your troubles in your old kit bag and smile, smile, smile."

CHAPTER 4

The Parenting Role

The parenting role can be divided into five basic components. Each one of these components comes in many shades and many colors, but these five are essential to the role:

- Teaching skills
- Inculcating values
- Teaching self-discipline
- Engaging in play
- Passing on a sense of "eternal purpose"

Teaching Skills

The parenting role is a teaching role. This is most clearly seen when we first become a parent. A mom teaches a baby all kinds of skills. The fun skills are laughing, playing, having fun, and speaking. The tougher skills are walking, potty training, and sharing.

The imparting of skills grows as a child develops. Let's take TV as an example. As our children begin to watch TV there are two skills that we need to impart quite quickly:

- The skill of delaying gratification as opposed to what the ads say, namely, demand a product and get it immediately.

- Showing empathy and respect for others instead of what advertising does, namely, mocking those who don't have the right toys or the right clothes or who look funny.

We also pass on to our children skills which we don't intend to pass on to them and which we don't even know we are passing on to them:

- how to make a cake

- how to make a fuss

- how to throw a ball

- how to throw a fit
- how to laugh
- how to cry
- how to "hold 'em"
- how to "fold 'em"

Inculcating Values

The second component of parenting is inculcating values. Let's continue with an advertising example. Advertisers are also trying to raise our children instead of us doing the job. They want our children to embrace the values of "have it your way" … "obey your thirst" … "make your own rules" … "just do it." These are the values of consumption.

We want our children to value themselves for who they are and not what they have. We want our children to value their friends for who they are and not what they have. We want our children to value our family for who we are and not what we have.

- Children do what you do (by and large)…not what you say.

- When learning moral values, your child is more likely to embrace your moral values if you have a good relationship with him or her.

- So work on your relationship and then make your values clear.

- Teach your children to put balance into their lives…just as you role model this balance in your life.

- Then your teaching will be from real life experiences that can be shared.

We want our children to be brought up to be honest, decent, caring people. We want them to be filled with faith, hope, and love. We want them to appreciate and follow the Ten Commandments. We want them to be filled with compassion and also courage. None of these values are instincts. All of them must be passed on through a process of teaching. The more a mom and dad see their roles as teaching or inculcating values, the easier it is to correct our children when they lie, cheat, or steal.

Moms and dads who practice "upbringing" skills greatly reduce the risk of their children misusing drugs, alcohol, and sex. Upbringing is the most underutilized tool in drug prevention. The National Center on Addiction and Substance Abuse's research shows that parents of seven out of ten adolescents set few if any rules. Not surprisingly, these seven kids are four times more likely to get into serious drug problems.

If I want my son to be an honest person, and he has just taken something from the store that does not belong to him, I have a marvelous opportunity to teach without being overly punitive. It's a great time to go back to the store with my son and explain to the manager that the boy has taken this candy bar without paying for it. It is important that my son feel guilty when he lies, cheats, or steals. That is appropriate guilt. It is healthy and maturing. This is the beginning of conscience formation in our little son or daughter. It is quite critical. Without it, our children will grow up without a moral conscience.

For example, parents who lie, cheat, or steal quickly pass these negative practices on to their children. The other day here at Girls and Boys Town, a 14-year-old boy gave me this explanation for his shoplifting the day before at K-Mart: "My dad says stores make a 10% allowance for shoplifting so we just want to get our share."

Above all, we want our children to value relationships over materialism. Advertising stresses "me first now." You and I can teach our children just the opposite.

Here are three values to teach our children so they value relationships over materialism: empathy, moderation, and charity.

- **Empathy.** Empathy is just the opposite of making fun of kids who don't have the right jeans or the right shoes or who live on the wrong side of the tracks. Empathy is not a matter of making fun. It's just the opposite. It's a matter of helping, sharing and caring.

How do you develop empathy? Let me tell you a story. Tony, age 15, is one of our boys. He comes from a very wealthy family in New England. He learned all the values of consumerism from his mother, who had money for him, but never any time. He began to believe that a person's importance is based on what he has, and he had a lot...just about everything that MTV told him he had to have "to be cool." The many difficulties in his life brought him to us. On Christmas evening I happened to be present when he called his mother to complain. I found out later that he had sent her a list of Christmas gifts that she "needed to buy" for him, valuing about $2,600. The phone call was to let her know he did not appreciate receiving only $600 worth of items from that list. Remember, this is Christmas night, a time when you should feel grateful, peaceful, hopeful and happy. He was ungrateful, angry, envious and unhappy.

One of the best ways we know at Girls and Boys Town to help a lad like this is to teach him the value of empathy. He really doesn't care about anybody else other than himself.

A key insight hit me the day he told me that as a little boy he loved the puppy they had. And his father, in a fit of anger, took the puppy away and never brought it back. It was perhaps the last time Tony ever cared for anyone or anything except himself.

We tried three strategies to teach Tony empathy. In other words, we set up occasions for learning to occur.

The first was assigning him a job at our small animal farm. He became attached to our bucket calves (those that need to be fed by a bottle with a nipple, morning and night). But what he really attached himself to was the barnyard cats…there are four of them and they are "in charge" of the barns. They walk around like foremen. But what really touched him was the stray cats. Yes, people dump their throw-away kitties at our barn, expecting us, of course, to care for them. Caring for the cats helped Tony a lot.

Another strategy was to spend more time with Tony doing things together. Tony claimed at first he didn't care. But he did!

A final strategy was to ask Tony to be a mentor to a 4th grader in his house who came to us not knowing how to read. The little boy quickly attached himself to Tony. Tony rejected the friendship for quite a while. But then they became good friends.

Tony is now much more empathetic than he used to be. Praise the Lord for that.

- **Moderation.** Moderation means not too much and not too little.

Advertising tells us that we really need to be one of the first people in class to have the newest style or the most up-to-date game, or the most expensive shoes.

Advertising tells us that we should "super-size" just about everything, even if we can't possibly use it. We should super-size at McDonald's to the point where we couldn't possibly eat everything.

Moderation means just the opposite. It means being satisfied with what we have. Not to be satisfied with what we have oftentimes makes children look like spoiled brats.

It is the value of moderation that makes us feel good when we can say, "No, I won't take more than my fair share." Or, "I won't eat to the point of bursting at the seams."

Usually a few days after Christmas we have a big pizza party for our kids at Sortino's, one of the best pizza places in the Midwest. A very generous benefactor pays for this marvelous holiday outing. Everyone is in the Christmas spirit. We get all dressed up. And with regard to moderation, there is a curious phenomenon that takes place. A boy will go up to the counter and if not instructed to stop, will take an extra-large pizza and go over in a corner all by himself, not sharing it with anyone…letting half of it grow cold…it's plain old hoarding. I always go up to the lad and say: "Mikey, you need to give me that pan of pizza and come over and join the other kids. Here at Girls and Boys Town we take only one piece of pizza at a time. We eat the crust and we learn to share so that every boy and girl gets hot pizza and there's enough to go around." First you get a grumble or two, but by the end of the night, Mike comes up and says: "Thanks, Father, I had a great time." Lesson learned.

Remember how inspiring it is to see a little 2-year-old break his or her doughnut in half and share it with a friend. That's what we're trying to teach. Advertising's message is just the opposite: "Me," "Mine," "Now."

- **Charity.** If we can teach our children the value of charity or generosity, it will be so, so very helpful in the lives of our children. They will be much happier. They will be more loved. And they will bring goodness into the world.

Charity or generosity is one of the first indicators of a happy person. The message we would like our kids to take to heart is: Giving is better than receiving.

Many years ago, I was assigned to a parish with a priest who is one of the most spontaneously generous people I have ever met in my life. He gives with a smile. He gives and does not count the cost. He does not do so for selfish purposes. He gives because giving is better than receiving. He doesn't give after reflection. He just gives spontaneously. I learned spontaneous giving from him.

Teaching Self-Discipline

Helping your child learn self-discipline is the third component of our parenting role. As America becomes a target of terrorism, the need for self-discipline grows enormously.

No parent simply wants his or her child to grow up and follow whatever Hollywood says. Every parent knows that the direction the media takes is often the direction of whim and fancy. These are not good guides for our children or for adults.

That is why helping your child learn self-discipline is an important task. Sometimes people think that inculcating self-discipline is always negative. Of course it's not.

It is true that self-discipline means not lying, not cheating, not stealing. It means developing self-restraint in all of these areas.

But if you lived with us here at Girls and Boys Town, you would discover quite quickly that there is a huge, huge area of self-discipline that is positive, not negative. Our children come here crippled by fear, anxiety, disappointment, abandonment, abuse, and neglect.

For us, self-discipline requires that we make sacrifices enough to move beyond these negative influences of our lives. That means self-discipline requires that a child learn:

- To discipline oneself against fear (of abandonment or abuse or neglect or mental illness) so you are not controlled by it.

- To discipline oneself against terror (chemical or biological elements like anthrax or bubonic plague) so it does not paralyze you.

- To discipline oneself against disappointment (my dad promised he would call for my birthday and he never did) so it does not destroy you.

- To discipline oneself against an over-burdening sense of duty (my mom is sick and I, a 14-year-old, need to go home and take charge of the house).

- There are times when it takes self-discipline to give yourself permission to throw caution to the wind and to play sports with great vigor. This is a time to be fully passionate.

- A boy or girl without self-discipline is not likeable. They have a hard time making friends. They are selfish. They are petulant. They are a nuisance. They are a pain. And therefore, they are hard to love.

In other words, self-discipline means impulse control:

- Learning how to respond to terror in a constructive fashion.

- Discovering what the triggers for cynicism or despondency are in our lives and learning how to channel them appropriately.

- Anger management is so important. Advertising says: Get angry if you don't get what you want *immediately.* Yet delaying gratification is the pause that refreshes us into human kindness and warmth.

Engaging in Play

The fourth component of the parenting role is play. Playing with our children is one of the most fun things we can do.

- Mom plays peek-a-boo with her baby. They both smile, laugh and have fun.
- Dad and his 4-year-old son play hide and seek.
- Mom and her 6-year-old daughter tell fanciful stories about how the family puppy is carrying on conversations with them and how the birds outside are playing tag and having meetings and planning vacations.
- Dad teaches his 8-year-old son how to fish and his 7-year-old daughter, too.
- Mom teaches her 11-year-old daughter how to cook and her 12-year-old son, too.

All of this is play. All of it is fun. And it is part of the parenting role. One of the things I like most about Girls and Boys Town is all of the fun we have together.

- The picnics
- The roller-skating

- The football and basketball games
- The volleyball and soccer games
- The Christmas play
- The Tuesday high school caucus
- The daily opening exercise at our middle school
- The walks around the lake
- The geese in the fall
- The sleigh riding in the winter
- The Easter egg hunt in the spring
- The 4th of July fireworks in the summer

If you don't think bringing kids up is fun, you have really missed something.

So when your son or daughter turns 11 or 12, don't listen to the people who tell you: "Oh, the horrible years are coming now. You will hate every minute of it." That can be a self-fulfilling prophecy. But it doesn't have to be. It can be a time of great fun.

A Sense of Eternal Purpose

The fifth component of our parenting role is passing on a sense of "eternal purpose." We all come from the hand of God. We are made for a purpose. We are on a mission...each of us.

No one is a random isolate. Passing this sense of the "eternal purpose" on to our children is something our children most frequently cite as a precious gift when we have gone home.

So pass on to your children that sense of purpose so important in living.

Every one of those moms and dads who died in the New York and Washington and Pennsylvania tragedies was put on this earth for a purpose:

- Each had a song to sing and if it was not sung, the world is the lesser for it.

- Each had a message to deliver and if they did not deliver it, something important was lost.

- Each had a love to bring and without it

the world is less loving.

The same is true of their children. It is also true of you and me. So let's get going on our "mission."

Summary

There is a wonderful family I know living out in the Nebraska Sandhills. Their nearest neighbor is about 20 miles away.

The mom told me the story of her 16-year-old-daughter who, in a rebellious mood one day, said: "Who do you think you are that you can tell me what to do?" The mother, who truly understands her parenting role replied: "I will tell you who I am. The Lord made me a woman. He made me a wife and a mother. He gave me you as a daughter. He told me my mission was to bring you up as best I could and to inculcate the values of the Ten Commandments. I need to carry out that mission. The Lord gave me this job to raise you properly. I plan to do the Will of the Lord. Do you understand this?"

On the following Mother's Day, the daughter thanked her mom for "helping me understand by being such a good mom." Case closed.

Oftentimes, a daughter or a son won't be so quick to thank you. But it is only a matter of time…even if it takes ten, twenty or thirty years…but it won't take that long…your son or daughter will thank you for parenting.

So, in summary, the parenting role has to avoid two extremes. The one extreme is to think of yourself simply as a drill instructor or disciplinarian. This is to be avoided. The other extreme is to think of yourself as someone who just loves your son or daughter. That, too, is to be avoided. We can't bring our children up successfully by embracing either of these two extremes.

CHAPTER 5

Friendship Skills

Above all, teach your children friendship skills. After all, friendship is the basis for all successful marriages and family life. Because of that, friendship skills should be a major focus of teaching our children as they grow up:

As very little children, the first set of friendship skills they need to help them develop are learning how to play with each other:

- Saying "Hi."
- Saying "Welcome."
- Saying "Would you like to play with my toys?"
- Sharing games.
- Riding the merry-go-round together.
- Being on swings.

- Going down the slippery slide.
- Listening to stories.
- Picking up toys together.
- Having fun.

Let's look at some negative behaviors of little children…behaviors not helpful to friendship…which we have to help our children "unlearn":

- Grabbing a toy from your friends.
- Refusing to play with your friend.
- Saying bad things to your friend.
- Not sharing.
- Seeking too much attention.
- Crying when you don't get your way.
- Pouting to show anger.
- Throwing temper tantrums.
- Hitting.

These negative behaviors are hard to unlearn. Wouldn't it be better for parents to get ahead of the game early on by teaching positive skills?

Parents have to shift gears as children grow into adolescence. If we are to bring our adolescents up right, we need to teach them certain specific skills.

Conversation skills:

- This is an especially fun time when you can teach your son or daughter how to talk to kids of the opposite sex.
- Talk about schoolwork.
- Sports.
- Current events.
- Movies.
- Fun things.

Relationship skills:

- Showing how a boy and girl can become friends.
- Teach your child how to dance. Most parents don't do this anymore. But it's

really important and really fun. You may have to learn new dancing yourself. But teach it.

- Teach your adolescent to get involved in extra-curricular activities with both boys and girls. It's a way for your child to discover their talents and develop their skills.

- Teach them to remember as little children how they shared and they can share now, too.

- Teach them courting skills – polite language and polite behavior.

There are also negative skills your children will learn from others and you have to help them avoid these:

- Intimidating language
- Sexual harassment
- Being pushy
- Being a bully
- Girls experiencing the power they have over boys and manipulating this

- Boys and girls only being friends with "good looking" members of the opposite sex

- Playing one person off against the other

- Becoming a jealous or possessive young woman

- Boys saying lewd things to girls (they learn it from CDs)

- Imitating soap operas

- Or even imitating pornographic films

If you have been teaching your son or daughter all along, it is not a tough transition to do this in adolescence.

Pre-teach your adolescents in advance with clear, positive and negative consequences and never, never announce consequences that you cannot carry out.

- Teach your children to express their feelings appropriately, not just to you, but to their friends.

- Teach your adolescent that friendship means sharing and caring, but it does not mean you possess the other person and it does not mean that your friend's body is an amusement park. They are a temple of the Holy Spirit just as you are.

We also need to teach our children the kinds of language which adolescents should avoid if they are to build genuine friendships:

- Player language *(yo baby, you know you want it)*
- Ho language *(I got what you want)*
- Possessive language *(my woman…my man)*
- The language of rap
- The language of sexual harassment
- The language of domination, subjugation, subordination
- The language of exclusion

Teach your adolescent to be slightly counter-cultural – that's right, teach them to say no to at least some of the things which their friends want to do or the music tells them to do or "everybody does."

- To be slightly counter-cultural means that you are the kind of friend that won't misuse others.

- You are the kind of friend who will not lead others into harm's way.

- You are the kind of friend who tells your pals what they need to hear and not what they want to hear.

- You are the kind of friend who won't say lewd things to act cool.

- You are the kind of friend who won't shoplift to act cool.

Teach your adolescents that if they are not to be overpowered by drugs, sex, and alcohol, that they need to have a personal relationship with the Lord, whose power is far greater than the power arrayed against them. This includes the power of advertising which is clearly not on their side. In a personal relationship with the

Lord, there are friendship skills that help your son and daughter realize that their value does not depend on what they have, but on who they are…their relationships.

The wider range of interests your son or daughter can develop helps build friendships.

- The reason so many kids get into drugs, sex and alcohol is because they have few interests.
- Their lives are boring.
- They haven't learned anything in school.
- They haven't gotten excited about their world.

Conclusion

Prophecies about raising adolescent children are self-fulfilling. If you tell yourself it is going to be gosh-awful and start believing it, it will come true. It will be gosh-awful. You will be miserable and so will your children.

If you tell yourself it will be fun and interesting, and yet different from childhood, that will come true provided you bring your adolescents up and not let others do so for you.

CHAPTER 6

Giving Gifts or Buying Love

The U.S. Department of Labor estimates about 60% of mothers today are working and their children are in day care.

This is a relatively new way to parent in America. It has both pluses and minuses. Traditionally, moms have stayed home to raise their children. Large numbers of them have regularly reported a high level of satisfaction in doing so.

But now so many have moved into the workplace. And there are lots of reasons for having done so. One is the simple straightforward reason that they have talents which they would like to share with others in the workplace. Another is that their husbands have walked out on them and have abandoned the family financially and every other way.

It is a happy event to note that many mothers can handle the job of a working mom very well.

LESSON #8

The last lesson is: *Give gifts to your children out of a straightforward love for your child and not out of guilt.*

The kind of gift giving that is based on guilt is easy to spot.

- Dad gets drunk…he beats his son…and then the next day he buys his son a gift. This father/son relationship has been harmed and there is no repair of the relationship by this kind of gift giving.

- A boy forces sex on his girlfriend and the next day he buys her a gift. The relationship between this boy and his girlfriend has been horribly harmed and a gift is no repair of the relationship.

There is another kind of gift giving out of guilt that affects especially working moms. Working moms often feel guilty for spending time away from their child. Ask any day care worker about that. They will be happy to give you many examples.

Sometimes moms give into their guilty feelings and ply their day-care children with gifts. Let's see how this works in a child's mind:

- Mom comes to day care and gives her child a gift.

- The child says: "Mom shows up always giving me stuff."

- "Thanks, mom, it shows you love me and I really want you to bring me more stuff tomorrow when you come for me."

- And sure enough, mom comes and brings "more stuff."

  Watch what is happening here:

- These rewards are not rewards contingent on behavior.

- They are not based on the parenting role of teaching skills or inculcating values.

- They are operant acts on mom's part to reduce her own anxiety.

- Of course, they increase her anxiety instead.

Let's take the example of business trips. Lots of working moms have to travel. So do dads. They bring gifts in compensation. It's equivalent to saying: "There was a debt incurred because I was away doing my job and not being here as a mom or dad should be for you."

Here again, the child says: "Dad is showing up after a trip dying to give me stuff. I think I'll ask for more stuff whenever he goes on a trip." These rewards are not contingent upon the child's behavior. The traveler is trying to reduce his own anxiety. The result, of course, is that the anxiety is increased and not reduced. And that makes a child to be a spoiled brat…always demanding "more, more, more.

There are two categories of gift giving when coming back from a trip. We have just described one of them. It is gift giving out of guilt.

There is another kind of gift giving when coming back from a trip. It's "mysterious." Because mom or dad went to a "far away place."

Here the idea is not give me, give me, give me, give me. The idea is: "Your mom traveled to an exotic or unknown place (for example, Cedar Rapids, Iowa). She wanted to share a bit of that exotic place with you. So she brought home something that actually had been in that exotic place. Maybe it's just a postcard from the motel room. Note here, it doesn't have to be expensive. You don't even have to purchase it. It could be something free.

The idea is to make traveling part of a world of fantasy and adventure. The motive is for mom and child to share an adventure and to

..ve fun together. This does not take away guilt. It simply increases the child's supply of fun.

Here at Girls and Boys Town's elementary school, we provide small, inexpensive prizes for good work in reading and spelling and even for not being sent to the office.

Where do these prizes come from? All my kids know the answer:

- Father Peter has a good Chinese friend, whose name is Charlie Chan.

- Charlie is a merchant trader who lives in Katmandu, Nepal.

- Charlie travels to Kuala Lampur on a regular basis to do business with Father Peter.

- They always meet on the corner of the Streets of the Seven Happinesses and the Flaming Dragon.

- This is where they strike many deals.

- This is where the riches (trinkets) of the Orient pour out.

- And come all the way back to our little elementary school.

- We even have a Katmandu newspaper which from time to time prints articles about these negotiations going on in Kuala Lampur.

- Such a mystic approach is referred to as "the willing suspension of disbelief."

- Our kids don't call it that.

- They call it fun.

It's always fun to bring a smile to our children's faces. But let's not get rid of our anxiety by buying them gifts. If we do, they will simply demand more. And we will discover our anxiety did not go away, but only increased.

Grandparents or, for example, a favorite aunt, don't occupy the role of a parent. They can always bring candy and the kids love it. Their role is different. They are not parents. Their job is not to bring the kids up.

85

Many of us today learned the love and candy approach from our own moms and dads. We have a confused role of parenting:

- We think parenting means having the kids always love us.

- We think parenting means to relive our childhood.

- We think parenting means showing off our kids to the neighbors.

- We think parenting means your children can always stay at home no matter how much they violate the rules with drugs, sex, alcohol, truancy, and stealing.

- We think that parenting means I will always stand by my children and even lie to the school principal or to the police to get them off the hook.

These things are not parenting. What do our children learn from parents who act as love buyers?

- They learn it's okay to ruin their parents' lives.

- They learn it's okay to be selfish, over-demanding and self-indulgent.
- They learn to be brats.
- They help their parents learn to hate the role of parenting.

  Do you ever feel trapped like this?

- You don't know what to do.
- You are fearful the kids won't like you.
- First you start giving in.
- Then you start gift giving.
- This is gift giving out of fear of being bad parents.
- Giving in out of fear of not being loved.
- Giving in out of fear that your children will be unhappy.
- This is unfortunately neurotic behavior: Engaging in behavior out of fear and the behavior increases the fear.
- We need to avoid this emotional parenting trap.

Please notice that these parents are not engaging in behaviors meant to destroy the family.

- They are not drunks.
- They are not drug addicts.
- They are not physically, sexually, or emotionally abusing their children.
- They are love buyers.
- They are parents who don't understand the role of parenting.
- Consequently, they do not engage in the parenting role.
- Consequently, they do not like being parents.

Yet none of this has to be. We can learn parenting skills ourselves. We can learn the art of gift giving. We can find joy in being moms and dads.

CHAPTER 7

A Tribute to Mothers

I had the meanest mother in the world. While other children could skip breakfast, I had to have cereal and toast. While others had Cokes and candy for lunch, I had to eat a sandwich. As you can guess, my supper was different from other children's, also. My mother insisted on knowing where we kids were all the time. You would think we were on a chain gang. She even had to know who our friends were and what we were doing.

She insisted on our following her rules. She kept saying it was "her house." What a dictator! Oh yes, I know she praised us a lot, but who cares about praise from someone who thinks she is the "boss of everything?" Can you imagine, she even had to approve what clothes we wore? So we always looked old-fashioned. She would not even let us go to the drive-in movies. How could she be so mean?

My mother actually had the nerve to break the Child Labor Law. She made us work. We had to make beds, wash dishes, learn to cook, and all sorts of cruel things. I believe she lay awake at night just thinking of mean things to do to us. She always insisted upon our telling the truth, the whole truth, and nothing but the truth, even if it took us hours and hours to do so – and it often did. She embarrassed us by insisting that she personally meet our dates. How humiliating.

She insisted on taking us to church every Sunday without exception. She did not care how late we were out at night. We got up with her and went to church. As you can see, my mother was a complete failure. Because she was so mean, none of us kids have ever done drugs or been arrested or been involved in violence. Some of us did our time in service to our country. All of us do community service. And whom do we have to blame for the terrible way we turned out? You're right, our mean mother. She forced us to grow up into kind, sharing, thinking, honest adults.

Using this as a pattern, I am trying to rear my own children here at Girls and Boys Town. I stand a little taller and am filled with pride when my children call me "mean."

CHAPTER 8

These Fallen Fathers Were At-Home Heroes

BY JANE GROSS

Jeannine McIntyre's husband, Donald, a Port Authority police officer, planned to join the Parent-Teacher Association in New City, N.Y., even if he was the only man. He often surprised his 5-year-old daughter with "hair pretties," as she called barrettes. He had saved enough overtime for a month-long paternity leave when his third child was born in December.

Dr. Nichole Brathwaite-Dingle's husband, Jeffrey, a high-tech executive, was a stay-at-home father during her medical residency, in charge of bedtime and bath time, school bus schedules and spelling words. He planned to take his 9-year-old son and 3-year-old daughter trick-or-treating on Halloween, while his wife was on call, had he not died in the Sept. 11 attack on the World Trade Center.

Mr. McIntyre and Mr. Dingle, both in their 30's, are among the hundreds of dead and more than 5,000 still missing, most of them men, in the worst terrorist attack in American history. Some were gallant rescue workers, hailed for their courage.

But many more were heroes only to their wives and children. Now the world is hearing their stories, and taking a revealing look at a generation of men who defy cultural stereotypes of absent or work-obsessed fathers largely missing from their children's lives.

"This gives the lie to so much that we talk about," said David Blankenhorn, the founder of the Institute for American Values, a nonpartisan organization doing research on family issues that has focused on the growing number of fatherless children in America. "We've been thinking of men essentially as a problem in this society for a long time."

Mr. Blankenhorn, the author of *Fatherless America* (Basic Books, 1995), took some blame for the attention paid to men who either abandon their families or play marginal roles, leading to an epidemic of single-parent families. "The thing people like me didn't say clearly enough," he said, "is that the current generation of in-the-home, love-the-mother fathers are the best we've ever had. And their children are lucky, compared to other kids in this generation, but also historically."

At times of disaster like these, relatives recount the best about their loved ones, setting aside their faults and frailties. But the involvement of these men in their children's lives is compelling in its detail, hard to dismiss as gauzy sentiment.

There was John Robinson Lenoir, a senior vice president at Sander O'Neill & Partners, who wore a pink tutu at his daughter's ice-skating party, playing Dad the Dancing Bear. There was Richard Prouty, a firefighter, who slept for a week on his daughter's college dormitory room floor to help her through final exams when she was ill.

There was Ronald C. Fazio, an accountant at the Aon reinsurance company, who participated in planning every detail of his 30-year-old son's wedding scheduled for this month, including choosing a florist and reception hall. There was Andrew Alameno, a trader at Cantor Fitzgerald, who brushed the hair of his 2-year-old daughter's Barbie doll, played endless rounds of junior Monopoly with his 5-year-old son and skipped dinners with clients to hurry home to Westfield, N.J., by 6 o'clock.

And there was Andrew Kates, a senior managing director at Cantor Fitzgerald, who took his three children ice-skating or to the library every weekend even if it meant passing up a golf game. "It wasn't just me nagging him," said Emily Kates, 38, Andrew's wife, the mother of Hannah, 5, Lucy, 3, and Henry, 1. "Men are aware now that that's the deal. There's an expectation of equality."

The emergence of the involved father, an equal partner in the raising of children, has made headlines for at least a decade, one of many social changes wrought by the women's movement. But for most of that time, according to Judith Wallerstein, founder of the Center for Families in Transition in Northern California, model fathers were the exception, not the rule; more wishful thinking than reality.

"Hailing fatherhood, until very recently, was just a gleam in someone's eye," said Ms. Wallerstein, author of *The Unexpected Legacy of Divorce* (Hyperion, 2001). "But these men we're hearing about now are not just crazy guys who went to Antioch. This has become mainstream."

Mr. Blankenhorn recalled a time when fathers shook their sons' hands but would not dream of hugging them, when they defined their own responsibilities as "bringing home the bacon," being faithful, and "being the disciplinarian."

Richard Lynch had a toddler and was looking forward to a houseful of kids, just as his father had. But the elder Mr. Lynch did not do the wash.

"A lot of these young men stepped up to the plate, even though their parents didn't," said Jan Mackell, Mr. Lynch's mother-in-law.

These days, Mr. Blankenhorn said, men who are in the focus groups he conducts as part of his research into what constitutes a good father still say their "prime imperative is to provide for the family."

But, after listing that as their No. 1 priority – "If you don't do that, you're not a man," he paraphrased – they want to discuss, at length, "how they feel about the day-to-day nurturing of their children."

It is this mundane nurturing that permeates the memories of widows and children.

Ron Fazio Jr., who is to be married on Oct. 14, said he comes up blank each time an interviewer asks his father's hobbies. "His true hobby was his family," Mr. Fazio said. That meant camping trips in the Poconos, leading Boy Scout Troop 64 in Closter, N.J., and cooking pasta and red sauce for Sunday dinners. But it also meant activities rarely associated with men, such as planning the details of his son's wedding and spending the entire Labor Day weekend furniture-shopping for the young couple's new home.

Mrs. McIntyre, a stay-at-home mother to Caitlyn, 5, and Don, Jr., 3, said her husband cooked dinner most nights. He also shopped for his children's clothes. "It sounds like I'm making it up," she said. "The other men used to say, 'You're making us look bad.' But he was really in touch with his feminine side. Everyone used to say that."

Mrs. Alameno attributed her husband's eager participation to the fact that his father, a surgeon, and hers, a lawyer turned judge, were devoured by "building careers" when their children were young.

"Andy liked his work," Mrs. Alameno said. "It was challenging. But he didn't consider himself a worker bee. That's not how he defined himself. If you'd have asked him, he'd have said, 'I'm a father.'"

When Dr. Brathwaite-Dingle, a pediatrician at St. Barnabas Hospital in the Bronx, set out to plan a memorial service for her husband, she listed the lessons he had taught her and their children, Jassiem, 9, and Nia, 3. High on the list, she said, was the way he had "redefined gender roles" in their family.

When Jassiem was 4, Mr. Dingle got a job in Washington while his wife stayed in New York to begin clinical training. Her hours made it impossible for her to care for the child, the couple decided, so Jassiem lived with his father, who chose a school, hired a nanny and arranged play dates.

After Nia was born and the family was reunited in the Bronx, Mr. Dingle, studying for an M.B.A., was the full-time parent: cooking, doing laundry, going to parent-teacher conferences. Even after he returned to work, at Encompys, a high-tech company, Mr. Dingle made the pancakes every Saturday morning, baked Christmas cookies and went to see the Pokeman movies his wife despised.

He sounds too good to be true, Dr. Brathwaite-Dingle agreed ruefully.

"He did everything," she said, "except bathrooms."

Epilogue

At the beginning of this little book, we talked about research done by Columbia University's National Center on Addition and Substance Abuse (CASA). The message of Father Flanagan to parents was that they should bring their children up and not simply be friends or bystanders to their children. That is the same message repeated in 2001 by the President of CASA: "The loud and clear message of this survey is this: Moms and dads should be parents to their children, not pals."

The CASA study gives the following examples of how a teen's risk for substance abuse increases when parents fail to:

- **Monitor their teen's television and Internet viewing, and restrict the**

music CDs they purchase. These teens are at twice the risk of those teens whose parents monitor these activities.

- **Know where their teen is after school and on weekends or expect their teen to tell them where they are going at night or on weekends.** Teens whose parents do not keep track of their whereabouts are at twice the risk of teens whose parents do.

- **Impose a curfew.** Teens without a curfew are at one and a half times the risk of teens who have one.

- **Have dinner with their teens most every night.** Teens who do not regularly eat dinner with their families are at one and a half times the risk of teens who have dinner with their parents nearly every night.

- **Closely monitor their teen's academic performance.** Teens whose parents are "very unaware" of how their teen is doing at school are at nearly three times the risk of teens whose parents are "very aware" of their teen's schooling.

- **Give their teen a clear message about marijuana use.** Teens whose parents would "not be too upset" about their teen's pot use have teens at more than triple the risk of teens whose parents would be "extremely upset." (Statement of Joseph A. Califano, Jr., February 21, 2001)

Parents who take five or less of the twelve actions listed below are called "hands-off" parents because they regularly fail to set rules and monitor their teen's behavior. What are those twelve actions again?

1. Monitor what their teens watch on television.

2. Monitor what they do on the Internet.

3. Put restrictions on the music CDs they buy.

4. Know where their teens are after school and on weekends.

5. Expect to be told and are told the truth by their teens about where they really are going.

6. Are "very aware" of their teen's academic performance.

7. Impose a curfew.

8. Make clear they would be "extremely upset" if their teen used pot.

9. Eat dinner with their teen most every night.

10. Turn off the TV during dinner.

11. Assign their teen regular chores.

12. Have an adult present when the teen returns from school.

Since September 11, family life seems so much more important. We have all seen pictures of some of the children (more than 1,400 in all) who now have no dad or no mom. These parents said goodbye to their kids in the morning and never came home that night: firefighters and police officers whose heroism is an inspiration to their orphaned sons and daughters… business men and women of all kinds whose love and guidance will be an everlasting legacy to their families. We all share the tragedy of their lives. And their loss (and our sharing of it) more than anything else is the reason we want to better love and parent our beloved children. In the end, they are all we have…God Bless America.

Cover Design: Stacy Oltmans
Page Layout: Anne Hughes
Production: Mary Steiner

111-19-0095

NUnit
Pocket Reference

NUnit
Pocket Reference

Bill Hamilton

Beijing · Cambridge · Farnham · Köln · Paris · Sebastopol · Taipei · Tokyo

NUnit Pocket Reference
by Bill Hamilton

Copyright © 2004 O'Reilly Media, Inc. All rights reserved.
Printed in the United States of America.

Published by O'Reilly Media, Inc., 1005 Gravenstein Highway North,
Sebastopol, CA 95472.

O'Reilly books may be purchased for educational, business, or sales
promotional use. Online editions are also available for most titles
(*safari.oreilly.com*). For more information, contact our corporate/
institutional sales department: (800) 998-9938 or *corporate@oreilly.com*.

Editor:	Brian Jepson
Production Editor:	Sarah Sherman
Cover Designer:	Ellie Volckhausen
Interior Designer:	Melanie Wang

Printing History:

August 2004:	First Edition.

0-596-00739-6
[C]

Contents

NUnit Pocket Reference

Introduction

I was inspired to write *NUnit Pocket Reference* because I was frustrated with the lack of documentation for NUnit—an excellent, indispensable tool for unit testing software. My aim was to write a book that my colleagues and I would find useful—a short, concise reference for installing, using, and extending NUnit.

Unit testing software started with xUnit—a testing framework developed by Kent Beck and Erich Gamma to test Small-Talk code. Test frameworks now exist for most programming languages—for example, JUnit for Java, CppUnit for C++, and NUnit for .NET.

NUnit is a port from JUnit. NUnit is similar to JUnit but is for the .NET Framework development. Unlike JUnit, NUnit is language independent, and can be used to test C#, VB.NET, and J# programs as well as most other programs developed using the .NET Framework. You can write a test in a different language from the code being tested and use NUnit to test projects that use multiple languages.

NUnit Version 2.2 supports Microsoft .NET Framework Versions 1.0 and 1.1, and Mono—an open source version of the Microsoft .NET development platform that runs on Unix, Windows, and Mac OS X. This book has been written with the .NET Framework version in mind; however, most of the information applies equally to the Mono version. For details about Mono, see *http://www.mono-project.com/*.

The examples in this book are written in C#, but NUnit can be used with any .NET language—I just happen to prefer C#. Regardless of your programming language preference, you should find the short examples easy to understand and adapt.

Conventions Used in This Book

Italic is used for filenames, URLs, and to introduce new terms.

Constant width is used for code and to indicate keywords, parameters, attributes, elements, arguments, methods, constructors, switches, and other code items within text

Constant width bold is used to highlight code.

Using Code Examples

This book is here to help you get your job done. In general, you may use the code in this book in your programs and documentation. You do not need to contact us for permission unless you're reproducing a significant portion of the code. For example, writing a program that uses several chunks of code from this book does not require permission. Selling or distributing a CD-ROM of examples from O'Reilly books does require permission. Answering a question by citing this book and quoting example code does not require permission. Incorporating a significant amount of example code from this book into your product's documentation does require permission.

We appreciate, but do not require, attribution. An attribution usually includes the title, author, publisher, and ISBN. For example: "*NUnit Pocket Reference* by Bill Hamilton. Copyright 2004 O'Reilly Media, Inc., 0-596-00739-6."

If you feel your use of code examples falls outside fair use or the permission given above, feel free to contact us at *permissions@oreilly.com*.

Acknowledgments

Thanks to everyone who has helped to develop NUnit and to the rest of the NUnit community for creating a great open source framework that makes it much easier to produce quality software.

I'd like to thank my editor, Brian Jepson, who is not only diligent, but a pleasure to work with, and my technical reviewer, Brad Merrill, for his helpful feedback.

Finally, I'd like to thank Molly, my family, and the usual suspects for their support and humor.

Unit Testing

This section provides an overview of software testing, describes unit testing and its place in the testing cycle, provides an overview of test driven development, and recommends best practices for unit testing.

Testing Software

Software testing measures the performance of software against both functional and nonfunctional acceptance criteria. Unit testing ensures that software does what it commits or is expected to do.

Successful unit testing starts with *acceptance criteria* that you identify during the requirements analysis; the acceptance criteria and the requirements are specified together. Acceptance criteria must be measurable—a statement such as "the software must perform well" is not enough. You must identify each combination of inputs and the expected output, and the final state for each based on the starting state.

Testing is approached from two different but complementary focuses:

White box
> Tests the unit, component, or system by looking at what happens within the code. Tests are determined based on how functionality is actually implemented. The flow of both control and data within the code is tested. In addition to verifying inputs and outputs, you can examine all code paths, and see exactly how the code processes the inputs to generate the outputs, how errors are raised and propagated, and the internal state of the code after it has been executed.

Black box
> Examines the behavior of a unit, component, or system from a functional perspective—this is why such tests are sometimes referred to as *functional tests*. These tests evaluate whether the system performs successfully from an external perspective. In a black box test, you supply inputs to a piece of software—method, component, etc.—and verify that the outputs are what you expected without looking at the inner functioning of the software. You cannot directly inspect how the inputs are processed, how the outputs are generated, how resources are handled, or how errors are handled or propagated. You cannot look within the code, so you cannot ensure that you are testing all branches of the code.

A successful testing strategy, including unit testing, uses both black box and white box testing

Software testing is typically broken down into five phases:

Unit testing
> Tests the smallest testable element of software to verify that it performs according to its specification both internally and externally. This is often, but not necessarily, a single method. The biggest challenge in unit testing is to understand exactly what the software is supposed to do and to develop all tests needed to verify the actual behavior.

Component testing

Tests the constituent components or subsystems of the entire system.

Integration testing

Tests combinations of components in the target environment that make up the system to assess their interactions and behavior.

System testing

Tests the end-to-end functioning of the fully integrated software at its external boundaries to ensure that it functions as expected. These tests are designed to test the system from the end user's point of view. These tests often map to and are derived from use cases. Additionally, system testing addresses nonfunctional requirements such as:

- Stress and load
- Memory management
- Reliability
- Recovery and disaster recovery
- Security
- Interoperability
- Compatibility
- Installation
- Data conversion

Nonfunctional criteria are often specified outside of requirements—for example, in UML supplementary specifications.

Acceptance testing

Performed by the end user of the software or a representative to show that the software meets the end user's needs. Successful completion of this phase signals that the software is ready for deployment or release.

Figure 1 shows the relationship between the testing phases and focus.

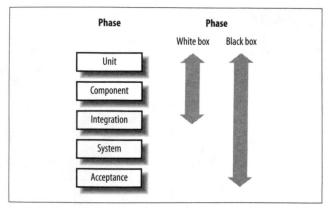

Figure 1. Testing phases and focus

There are two techniques that keep the number of test conditions manageable while ensuring adequate coverage:

Equivalence sets

A set of input values that are processed in an equivalent fashion and produce qualitatively the same behavior to make a test succeed. Equivalence sets partition the complete range of possible input values into a manageable, representative subset. Use a single value from the equivalence set as input to the test case to effectively test all values within the equivalence set. Equivalence set testing allows you to test across the complete range of possibilities while minimizing the number of test cases.

Boundary values

A set of input values that are used to test conditions where system behavior should or might change. This includes smallest negative value, largest positive value, zero, both positive and negative near-zero numbers, and typical negative and positive values. Boundary value testing complements equivalence set testing, because defects tend to cluster around boundary conditions.

Software testing ensures applications are of the highest quality and bug-free when they are delivered. Unit testing:

- Helps find defects early when they are easiest and cheapest to fix.
- Builds quality into the software by forcing developers to do their part in the testing process. (Developers understand best how to test the software and can inspect the code more directly than quality assurance.)
- Allows quality assurance personnel to focus on testing the entire product thoroughly rather than identifying issues that should have been recognized and fixed during development.

If developers do not unit test, they will not be able to deliver bug-free components that behave correctly in integration testing. This makes it difficult for quality assurance personnel to complete testing in a reasonable timeframe.

What Is Unit Testing and Where Did It Come from?

This book is about unit testing, specifically about using NUnit with the Microsoft .NET Framework.

Unit testing defines a collection of automated tests that you run continuously during the software development phase to ensure the code performs as required, and to identify when changes or new development introduce bugs. The entire collection of unit tests must execute successfully. If a test fails, the developer must make corrections until all tests pass before continuing development.

Unit testing is the ongoing process of stabilizing code during the development cycle; identifying and removing defects earlier is faster and less expensive than later in an application's life. Unit testing reduces both integration and system testing efforts, which results from bugs that the developer should have caught and fixed much earlier in the development cycle. Integration and system testing become more effective and less expensive, and higher quality code is the result.

Using unit testing as the sole measure of whether development is complete and ready for integration or user-acceptance testing is not as simple as it sounds: the unit tests have to be good, and writing good tests is difficult.

If you stabilize code during development, it allows you to spend more time and effort on the creative aspects of programming. Programming becomes more enjoyable as software quality improves.

Unit testing is often associated with test-driven development, discussed in the next section. However, unit testing can be useful regardless of the software development methodology you use.

An unit testing framework like NUnit makes it simple to:

- Create and organize tests
- Run all tests or a subset of tests
- Review test results that include details of any failures

There are three techniques for identifying and executing unit tests within your code:

Manually
    The programmer codes and invokes each test.

Reflection
    A testing framework locates and executes tests defined using both inheritance from testing framework classes and naming conventions. This is how NUnit 2.0 and JUnit work.

Reflection with attributes
    A testing framework locates and executes tests identified by attributes. This is how NUnit 2.1 or later works.

Test-Driven Development

Test-driven development is the iterative process of designing and building software one unit test at a time. The objective of test-driven development is to build the software that is actually required instead of the functionality that the developers think is required. Here is the typical sequence of steps:

1. Write a test for a new piece of functionality. At this stage, the test will fail because the functionality is not yet implemented.

2. If necessary, implement a stub or mock object to make the code compile. At this point, the test still fails.

3. Replace the stub with the least amount of code required to make the test pass.

4. Run the test. If it fails, keep working until it passes adding only the minimum code required to make it pass.

5. Refactor as necessary, ensuring that all tests still pass.

TIP

Refactoring is a systematic approach to restructuring code without changing its external behavior.

---

6. Start again at step 1 with a new test.

Whether you do a lot of refactoring (as is generally the case in test-driven development) or you rely on good design up front and refactor only when dictated by nonfunctional testing or unanticipated requirements, unit testing assures you that changes have not broken the code.

This does not mean that unit testing is only useful as part of test-driven development. You can just as easily write tests from the use cases that you utilize to develop and design software. Instead of using unit tests to drive development, the tests ensure that the software meets the requirements specified by the use cases as you build the software.

Whether you believe in test-driven development, unit testing is a valuable process. NUnit provides the framework and tools that make unit testing easy so that developers do not have an excuse not to use it.

Test Harness

A *test harness*, also called a *test fixture*, provides an infrastructure to hold related tests. It contains the logic to set up and tear down the collection of tests in the harness, as well as for each of the individual tests. This includes activities such as instantiating and cleaning up resources and initializing state. Setup and teardown functionality isolates code that is run for each test or test fixture from the actual test code. Setup and teardown code eliminates redundant test code, which improves maintainability. This functionality also improves performance for resource-intensive operations by performing them once before all tests are run and cleaning them up after all tests are run.

Setup and teardown processes can be complex and must be designed carefully so that they do not introduce errors or unnecessary test interdependencies.

Unit Test Design and Development Overview

The design and development of the unit test suite for an application typically follows a simple series of steps:

1. Identify functionality to be tested
2. Identify and set up preconditions for the test
3. Write a unit test to test a piece of functionality
4. Within the unit test, define one or more assertions to verify that the software works correctly by checking actual outputs against expected post conditions
5. Clean up after the test
6. Repeat steps 1 through 5 for each piece of functionality

Best Practices for Unit Testing

Some general guidelines to effective unit testing follow:

- Write unit tests that are fine-grained, independent, and test one piece of functionality at a time. This approach allows you to isolate and identify problems quickly and keeps you from having to examine complex interactions between components.

- Keep tests simple; decompose complex tests into a series of simpler tests.

- Create a separate test method for each test. When a test fails, isolating and identifying the problem will be easier. Adding complex logic in test methods can also introduce errors within the test.

- Ensure your tests provide complete coverage of functionality that needs to be tested. This is equally important whether you are using test-driven development or doing design-first development based on analysis such as use cases.

- Run regression tests often: the earlier you identify problems, the easier they are to fix.

- Refactor your code continuously to make it more efficient, easier to use, and easier to understand. Through a series of small changes, refactoring adapts code to meet new requirements, and serves to simplify code and improve its design. This is especially important in test-driven and iterative development. Refactoring is easier to do and more effective when done frequently. Unit testing gives you the confidence to refactor continuously.

- Make assertions self-explanatory so that you and other developers can easily understand what you are testing.

- Use meaningful names for your test methods. This will make the tests self-documenting.

- Group tests into logical, related groups using test fixtures, and group tests further into test suites.

- Provide an optional argument to assertions that describes what a failure means.

- Write tests before or while writing the application code. This will allow you to remember the intent of the code and will result in much more effective tests.

- Do not check your code into a version control system in a distributed development environment until all tests succeed.

- Write one test at a time and make it pass before moving on to the next test.

What Is NUnit?

NUnit is an easy-to-learn, open source framework built using Visual Studio .NET 2003 and the .NET Framework 1.1. NUnit automates unit tests for all .NET languages.

NUnit facilitates unit testing by providing a framework to support test development and test runners to run the tests and assess their results. NUnit includes test runner executables with both GUI and command-line interfaces. The command-line interface is particularly useful for automated build and test environments.

NUnit tests are easily repeatable by anyone with access to the code and test assemblies. This allows you to test the impact of your changes on the work of the entire development team in a distributed development environment. Verifying your code against the entire project maintains the integrity of the overall build.

How Does NUnit Work?

The NUnit framework provides a collection of base classes and attributes to support unit testing. Unit testing code is organized into tests, test fixtures, and test suites, as described in "Setting Up NUnit."

.NET reflection lets you dynamically examine and modify code at runtime. Reflection queries metadata in the portable executable (PE) file (i.e., a DLL or EXE) using services in the System.Reflection namespace. The Common Language Runtime (CLR) allows you to add descriptive declarations called *attributes* to annotate programming elements, such as methods, fields, properties, and types. These attributes are saved with the metadata. Attributes are used both to describe code and affect application behavior at runtime. The .NET Framework supplies built-in attributes, and you can also define your own.

NUnit 2.1 or later uses attributes to identify tests and to specify testing metadata within the test code. NUnit scans the attributes to identify tests, and then uses reflection to locate and execute all of the tests in an assembly.

NUnit loads a copy of the code being tested into its own *application domain*—a unit of isolation that prevents an application from interfering with other applications running within the same or different process. This allows NUnit to check for changes to assemblies you are testing and automatically reload them as necessary without restarting to ensure you test the latest assembly. NUnit will not automatically recompile code that has changed, however.

Setting Up NUnit

This section describes how to get, install, and configure NUnit, and explains what is included in the installation.

Prerequisites

NUnit 2.2, the fourth major release of NUnit, runs on Windows 98, ME, NT, 2000, 2003, and XP (as well as Linux, Unix, and Mac OS X). If you are running Windows 98, ME, NT, or 2000, you might need to download the Windows Installer from the Microsoft Download Center *http://www.microsoft.com/ downloads*. This will allow you to install the NUnit *.msi* file.

Select Windows Installer from the Products/Technology drop-down menu, and pick the installer for your operating system.

Programming Languages

NUnit supports all .NET programming languages and works across all .NET languages. For example, you can write unit tests in VB.NET to test C# code.

NUnit supports testing assemblies written in any .NET language. Support is limited to C#, VB.NET, J#, and C++ if you intend to open Visual Studio .NET projects and solutions directly rather than open the compiled assemblies.

Getting NUnit

The official NUnit site is *http://www.nunit.org*. At this site, you will find download instructions, documentation, and contact information for the developers.

You can download the most recent version of NUnit from the Files section of the SourceForge.net project page at *http://sourceforge.net/projects/nunit/*. The site has discussion groups about NUnit, as well as add-ins for NUnit that are discussed later in "Extending NUnit." Discussion groups are located at *http://sourceforge.net/forum/?group_id=10749*.

Installing NUnit

The NUnit download is either a Windows Installer package or a zip file for Linux, Unix, and Mac OS X versions of Mono. On Windows, double-click on the file to begin the installation. The installer copies the files to a directory structure and installs shortcuts in the Start menu. On Linux, Unix, and Mac OS X, extract the zip file and follow the instructions in the *doc* subdirectory.

On Windows, NUnit installs files in the directory *%SystemDrive%\Program Files\NUnit x.y*, where *x.y* is the version number, as in *c:\Program Files\NUnit 2.2*. The installer also creates three subdirectories:

bin

Contains the class libraries, test assemblies used to build NUnit, and both the GUI and console-based test runners and configuration files

doc

Contains a quick start guide called *QuickStart.doc*, a brief user manual called *ReadMe.pdf*, and a document outlining the changes from the previous versions

src

Contains the NUnit source code, samples in C#, VB. NET, and J#, and the Visual Studio .NET deployment project for NUnit

The installation program creates entries in the Start menu under the *NUnit 2.2* folder, which includes links to the NUnit program (a shortcut is also placed on the desktop), the documentation, and the samples.

The developers of NUnit created a collection of tests that they used during the building of NUnit. These tests are in the assembly *nunit.tests.dll* in the installation subdirectory *bin*. You can load and run these tests to ensure that NUnit is correctly installed. Launch the NUnit test runner GUI by selecting NUnit-Gui from the NUnit start menu. Select File→Open... from the menu to open the Open Project dialog. Open the *bin\nunit.tests.dll* file, and then press the Run button on the test runner GUI. If NUnit is installed correctly, all of the approximately 600 tests will run and succeed, and the status bar will be green.

The developers of NUnit also created timing tests—long-running tests that check whether the test runner handles remote timeouts correctly. These tests are in the *timing-tests.dll* assembly in the installation subdirectory *bin*. The timing tests might take as long as ten minutes to run. While they are running, there is no indication that they are doing anything, so be patient.

The *Samples* subdirectory contains sample tests written in C#, VB.NET, J#, and managed C++.

Configuring NUnit

NUnit uses a configuration file to control the test runner and provide configuration settings for testing. There are two files—one each for the test runner GUI and console—called *bin\nunit-gui.exe.config* and *bin\nunit-console.exe.config*.

The NUnit configuration files are separate from regular project configuration files that store application-specific configuration settings; by default, these configuration files are named *application.config* for executables and *web.config* for ASP.NET applications.

The NUnit configuration files allow NUnit to run on systems with multiple versions of the .NET Framework (i.e., 1.0 and 1.1) installed. Configure this in the startup element of the configuration file:

```
<startup>
  <!-- Prefer .NET 1.1 if present - if you want
    to run under 1.0 on a machine with both
    1.0 and 1.1 available, change the order of
    the following statements. -->
  <supportedRuntime version="v1.1.4322" />
  <supportedRuntime version="v1.0.3705" />
  <requiredRuntime version="v1.0.3705" />
</startup>
```

Within the startup element of the configuration file for either the test runner GUI or console, the order of the supportedRuntime elements indicates the version of the .NET Framework to use: NUnit tries to use the .NET Framework versions in the order in which they appear. The runtime element contains the binding redirections required for NUnit to work with .NET Framework 1.0.

Unlike previous versions, NUnit 2.2 no longer requires different configuration files to support different versions of the .NET Framework.

The appSettings element in the configuration file has an apartment key. The line is commented out by default. To uncomment the line to run test threads in a single-threaded apartment (STA) instead of defaulting to the multithreaded apartment (MTA):

```
<appSettings>
  <!-- User application and configured
    property settings go here.-->
  <!-- Example: <add key="settingName"
    value="settingValue"/> -->
  <add key="toolTip.ShowAlways"
    value="False" />
  <add key="shadowfiles.path"
    value="%temp%\nunit20\ShadowCopyCache"
  />

  <!-- Uncomment the following line to
    run tests in the STA -->
  <!--  <add key="apartment"
    value="STA" /> -->
</appSettings>
```

Manual Installation

Follow these steps to manually install NUnit.

1. Copy the following files to the target directory:
   - *nunit.core.dll*
   - *nunit.framework.dll*
   - *nunit.extensions.dll*
   - *nunit.uikit.dll*
   - *nunit.util.dll*
2. Run Administrative Tools→Microsoft .NET Framework 1.1 Configuration, select Assembly Cache from the tree view, click Add an Assembly to the Assembly Cache, and add both *nunit.framework.dll* and *nunit.core.dll*.

To use the test runner console, *copy bin\nunit-console.exe* and *bin\nunit-console.exe.config* to the target directory.

To use the test runner GUI, copy *bin\nunit-gui.exe* and *bin\ nunit-gui.exe.config* to the target directory.

Navigating the Source Code

If you're interested in hacking on or learning from the NUnit source, it includes the complete source code. NUnit 2.2 is built using Visual Studio 2003 and the .NET Framework 1.1, and you will need these to open the solution and project files. The NUnit solution file is *nunit.sln* in the *src* subdirectory of the installation directory. The solution contains projects for the NUnit framework, console and GUI test runners, tests, and samples.

The project for the test runner GUI is *nunit-gui.csproj*, which is located in the *src\nunit-gui* subdirectory.

The project for the NUnit console test runner is *nunit-console. csproj*, which is located in the *src\nunit-console* subdirectory.

The project for the NUnit framework is *nunit.framework.dll. csproj*, which is located in the *src\framework* subdirectory.

You can identify other projects in the solution by opening the NUnit solution file *nunit.sln* and examining it in the Visual Studio .NET Solution Explorer.

Unit Testing with NUnit

This section discusses the different elements of the NUnit framework and how to use them to create unit tests and test structures. Figure 2 shows the relationship between the NUnit elements.

In the simplest case, NUnit requires only test cases and one or more test fixtures. Each test must contain at least one assertion. A description of these elements follows.

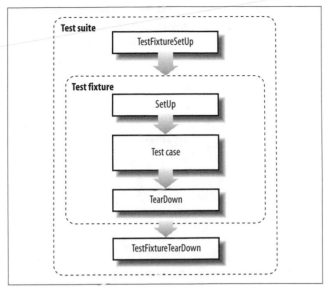

Figure 2. NUnit test elements

Test cases

A test is the lowest building block of unit testing and tests a single piece of software functionality. Programmatically, a test corresponds to a method in the unit test code.

You identify a test by decorating a method with the [Test] attribute. For example:

```
[Test]
public void Test1()
{
    // test case implementation
}
```

A test method must be public (so that the test runner can locate it using reflection), returns void, and take no arguments.

A unit test performs one or more assertions that determine whether the functionality being tested works properly. An assertion simply tests an actual post-condition against the expected post-condition required for the test to pass. Assertions are described later in "Assertions."

The [Test] attribute has an optional argument named Description that defines the description that appears in the test properties dialog in the test runner GUI. For example:

```
[Test (Description = "MyTest")]
```

WARNING

For backward compatibility with earlier versions of NUnit, a method is automatically identified by NUnit as a test if the first four characters of the method name are "test"; this identification is not case sensitive.

Test fixtures

A test fixture is used to group and run multiple tests that test a logical collection of functionality. Programmatically, a test fixture corresponds to a class that in turn contains unit tests as methods of the class.

A test fixture class must have either a public default constructor or no constructor, which implicitly creates a public default constructor. Identify a class as a test fixture by decorating it with the [TestFixture] attribute. For example:

```
[TestFixture]
public class Class1Test
{
    // test fixture implementation
}
```

In addition to unit tests, a test fixture contains any setup and teardown code for both the test fixture and for the tests within the test fixture. Setup and teardown code is optional and is described later in "Other Testing Elements."

Creating a Test

The following steps outline how to create a solution that contains two projects—a project being tested and an NUnit test project:

1. Open the Visual Studio .NET IDE and create a new blank solution called NPR.

2. Add a new Visual C# class library project called MyApp to the solution. This is the project you'll be running the tests against.

3. Rename Class1 to MyMath. Change the class declaration to read:

   ```
   public class MyMath
   ```

4. Add a single method called Add that takes two integer arguments and returns their sum. The completed class follows:

   ```csharp
   using System;

   namespace MyApp
   {
       public class MyMath
       {
           public int Add(int i, int j)
           {
               return i + j;
           }
       }
   }
   ```

5. Add a new Visual C# class library project called MyAppTest to the solution. This is the project that will contain the NUnit tests. It is a good idea to use a name that allows the test project to be easily identified—for example, use the name of the project being tested with the suffix Test.

WARNING

It is generally best to compile application code and test code into different assemblies. This makes it easy to build a release executable that does not contain any unit tests.

---

6. Add a reference to the NUnit framework to the test project MyAppTest; select Project→Add Reference from the Visual Studio .NET IDE menu. In the Add Reference dialog, double-click on *nunit.framework* in the listbox on the .NET tab and click OK. (See Figure 3.)

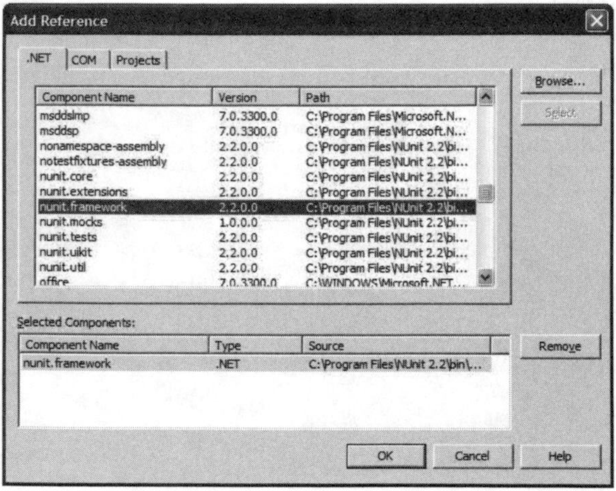

Figure 3. Add a reference to NUnit framework

7. Add a reference to the project being tested: MyApp to the test project MyAppTest. Select Project→Add Reference. In the Add Reference dialog, select the Projects tab. In the listbox, double-click on the project you are testing. Click OK. (See Figure 4.)

8. The Solution Explorer now appears as shown in Figure 5.

9. Add the NUnit.Framework types to the test class Class1:
   ```
   using NUnit.Framework;
   ```

10. Add the MyApp types to the test class Class1:
    ```
    using MyApp;
    ```

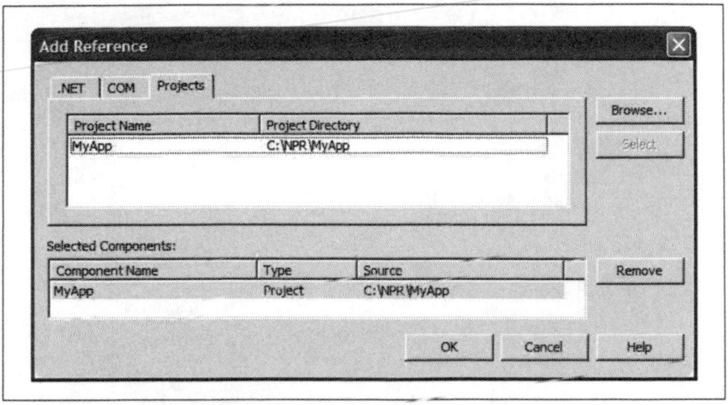

Figure 4. Add an NUnit project reference

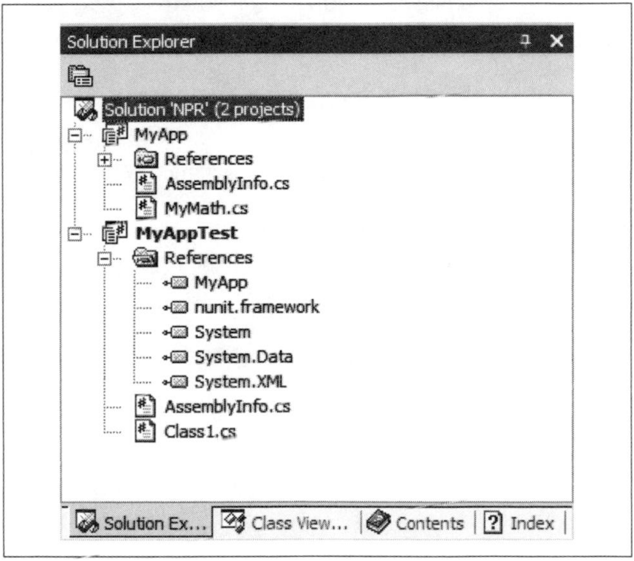

Figure 5. A Solution Explorer with references

11. Add the [TestFixture] attribute to the test class Class1 to indicate that the class contains test code. So far we have:

```
using System;
using NUnit.Framework;
using MyApp;

namespace MyAppTest
{
    [TestFixture]
    public class Class1
    {
    }
}
```

12. Create test method MyAddTest in the test class. Remember that this method must be both public and void, and take no arguments. Identify the test method by decorating it with the [Test] attribute:

```
[Test]
public void MyAddTest( )
{
}
```

13. Write the test. In this case, test the Add method in MyMath:

```
[Test]
public void MyAddTest( )
{
    MyMath m = new MyMath( );
    Assert.AreEqual(m.Add(2, 3), 5);
}
```

The completed test class follows:

```
using System;
using NUnit.Framework;
using MyApp;

namespace MyAppTest
{
    [TestFixture]
    public class Class1
    {
        [Test]
        public void MyAddTest( )
        {
            MyMath m = new MyMath( );
```

```
                    Assert.AreEqual(m.Add(2, 3), 5);
                }
            }
        }
```

14. Compile your code.

15. Run the test as described in the next section "Running a Test" (open the test assembly *MyAppTest.dll* in the *NPR\ MyAppTest\bin\debug* directory from the test runner GUI). Figure 6 shows the test runner GUI after running the test.

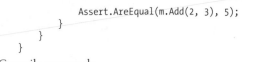

Figure 6. An NUnit test runner GUI results

Running a Test

The *test runner* is an application that locates tests within an assembly, runs them, and organizes the test results. NUnit provides both GUI and console test runners.

The NUnit test runner executes each test once. Before executing each test, test-level setup code is executed. After executing each test, test-level teardown code is executed. SetUp and TearDown are described later in "Other Testing Elements."

The following steps outline how to run tests using the test runner GUI:

1. Launch the NUnit test runner GUI.

2. Click File→Open and select the DLL built by the test project. In our example, this is *MyAppTest.dll* in the *bin\ Debug* folder for the project.

3. The test runner GUI displays all test fixtures, and the tests each fixture contains are visibile in the tree in the left pane.

4. To run all tests, select the topmost node in the tree view. Alternatively, to run a subset of tests or a single test, select any node in the tree view.

5. Click the Run button. If the tests pass, a green bar will display; otherwise, the bar will be red. Colored dots next to the tree view nodes indicate the success or failure of tests, test fixtures, and test suites.

Assertions

Assertions test whether the program is behaving as expected by verifying that an actual post-condition matches the expected post-condition. Programmatically, these conditions are tested using static methods of the Assert class that return either true or false, indicating whether the condition is met.

If you have multiple assertions in a test case, the test case stops executing as soon as one assertion fails, and subsequent assertions do not run.

Although there is no limit to the number of assertions that you can put in a single test case, a large number might suggest that the test case should be broken into smaller test cases to make it easier to identify code that causes the test to fail.

WARNING

The Assert class replaces the Assertion class found in NUnit versions prior to 2.1. Use the Assert class because there is no guarantee that the Assertion class will be supported in future versions of NUnit.

The NUnit framework provides the assertions as shown in Table 1.

Table 1. NUnit Assert methods

Assertion	Description
AreEqual	Succeed if the two double, int, float, or object arguments are equivalent; the two arguments must be the same type
AreSame	Succeed if the two object arguments are references to the same object
Fail	Always fail
Ignore	Dynamically ignore the test or suite at runtime
IsFalse	Succeed if the argument is false
IsNotNull	Succeed if the argument is not null
IsNull	Succeed if the argument is null
IsTrue	Succeed if the argument is true

Except for one form of the Fail method, each Assert method uses some of these arguments:

expected
 The expected value

actual
 The actual value

delta
 The maximum acceptable difference between the expected value and the actual value

message
 The message to display if the expected and actual values are not equal

parms
 Object array that is output as part of the message text using formatting information in the message string.

condition
 The evaluated condition

anObject
 The object being tested

The prototype for each Assert method follows:

Assert.AreEqual

```
Assert.AreEqual(object expected, object actual)
Assert.AreEqual(object expected, object actual,
    string message)
Assert.AreEqual(object expected, object actual,
    string message, object[] parms)

Assert.AreEqual(int expected, int actual)
Assert.AreEqual(int expected, int actual,
    string message)
Assert.AreEqual(int expected, int actual,
    string message, object[] parms)

Assert.AreEqual(decimal expected, decimal actual)
Assert.AreEqual(decimal expected, decimal actual,
    string message)
Assert.AreEqual(decimal expected, decimal actual,
    string message, object[] parms)

Assert.AreEqual(float expected, float actual,
    float delta)
Assert.AreEqual(float expected, float actual,
    float delta, string message)
Assert.AreEqual(float expected, float actual,
    float delta, string message, object[] parms)

Assert.AreEqual(double expected, double actual,
    double delta)
Assert.AreEqual(double expected, double actual,
    double delta, string message)
Assert.AreEqual(double expected, double actual,
    double delta, string message, object[] parms)
```

The AreEqual assertion method supports core data types, as well as arrays having the same or compatible data types and the same number of elements.

Assert.AreSame

```
Assert.AreSame(object expected, object actual)
Assert.AreSame(object expected, object actual,
    string message)
Assert.AreSame(object expected, object actual,
    string message, object[] parms)
```

Assert.Fail
```
Assert.Fail()
Assert.Fail(string message)
Assert.Fail(string message, object[] parms)
```

Assert.Ignore
```
Assert.Ignore()
Assert.Ignore(string message)
Assert.Ignore(string message, object [] parms)
```

Assert.IsFalse
```
Assert.IsFalse(bool condition)
Assert.IsFalse(bool condition, string message)
Assert.IsFalse(bool condition, string message, object[]
parms)
```

Assert.IsNotNull
```
Assert.IsNotNull(object anObject)
Assert.IsNotNull(object anObject, string message)
Assert.IsNotNull(object anObject, string message, object[]
parms)
```

Assert.IsNull
```
Assert.IsNull(object anObject)
Assert.IsNull(object anObject)
Assert.IsNull(object anObject, object[] parms)
```

Assert.IsTrue
```
Assert.IsTrue(bool condition)
Assert.IsTrue(bool condition, string message)
Assert.IsTrue(bool condition, string message, object[]
parms)
```

Example 1 shows how to use each method of the Assert class.

Example 1. Using the Assert class

```
[Test]
public void Test3()
{
    bool b = true;
    Assert.IsTrue(b);
    b = false;
    Assert.IsFalse(b);
```

Example 1. Using the Assert class (continued)

```
    object o = null;
    Assert.IsNull(o);
    o = new object();
    Assert.IsNotNull(o);

    int i1 = 1;
    int i2 = 1;
    Assert.AreEqual(i1, i2);

    double d1 = 1.0;
    double d2 = 1.0;
    Assert.AreEqual(d1, d2);

    float f1 = 1F;
    float f2 = 1F;
    Assert.AreEqual(f1, f2);

    String s1 = "abc";
    String s2 = "abc";
    Assert.AreEqual(s1, s2);

    Object o1 = new object();
    Object o2 = o1;
    Assert.AreSame(o1, o2);

    Assert.Fail();
}
```

The tests in Example 1 pass, with the exception of Assert.Fail, which always fails. Assert.Fail is useful for testing error handling—for example, where a specific line of code should not be reached if the software is designed correctly.

Custom assertions

Custom assertions, although not part of the NUnit framework, simplify test code and make it easier to maintain with application-specific assertions you use repeatedly. For example, you might need to assert that a number or all numbers in an array are odd. The following code defines a class that has an overloaded custom assertion that does this:

```csharp
using System;

using NUnit.Framework;

public class CustomAssert
{
    public static void AssertOdd(int i)
    {
        int[] a = {i};
        AssertOdd(a);
    }

    public static void AssertOdd(int[] a)
    {
        for(int i = 0; i < a.Length; i++)
        {
            Assert.IsFalse(a[i] % 2 == 0);
        }
    }
}
```

The following code uses the custom assertion:

```csharp
[Test]
public void Test1()
{
    CustomAssert.AssertOdd(1);

    int[] a = {1, 3, 4};
    CustomAssert.AssertOdd(a);
}
```

In this case, the second call to the custom assertion fails, because the last member of the array is even.

Other Testing Elements

In addition to the fundamental elements described, the NUnit framework provides other elements that allow you to write more sophisticated, efficient, and maintainable tests.

Setting up and tearing down

SetUp and TearDown code allow you to segregate and reuse common initialization, and clean up code across tests. This simplifies test coding and ensures consistency.

NUnit provides four attributes (two for tests and two for test fixtures) that can be used to mark methods that provide SetUp (initialization) and TearDown (cleanup) code:

- The [SetUp] attribute specifies a method that contains common initialization code for test cases in a test fixture. This code is run prior to each test in the fixture, except for ignored tests. A test class can contain only one SetUp method.

- The [TearDown] attribute specifies a method that contains common cleanup and shutdown code for test cases in a test fixture. The code is run after each test in the class, except for ignored tests. A test class can contain only one TearDown method.

- The [TestFixtureSetup] specifies a method that contains code that runs only once per fixture, before any tests in the test fixture are executed. A test fixture can have only one TestFixtureSetUp method.

- The [TestFixtureTearDown] specifies a method that contains code that runs only once per fixture, after all tests in the test fixture have executed. A test fixture can have only one TestFixtureTearDown method.

Each of the four methods must be public, return void, and take no arguments.

Example 2 shows the relationships among the four methods.

Example 2. SetUp and TearDown code

```
using System;

using NUnit.Framework;

[TestFixture]
```

Example 2. SetUp and TearDown code (continued)

```csharp
public class Class1Test
{
    [TestFixtureSetUp]
    public void FixtureSetup()
    {
        Console.WriteLine(
            "Class1 TestFixture setup");
    }

    [TestFixtureTearDown]
    public void FixtureTearDown()
    {
        Console.WriteLine(
            "Class1 TestFixture teardown");
    }

    [SetUp]
    public void TestSetUp()
    {
        Console.WriteLine(" Test setup");
    }

    [TearDown]
    public void TestTearDown()
    {
        Console.WriteLine(" Test teardown");
    }

    [Test]
    public void Test1()
    {
        Console.WriteLine("    Test1 start");

        Class1 c1 = new Class1();
        Assert.IsTrue(true);

        Console.WriteLine("    Test1 end");
    }

    [Test]
    public void Test2()
    {
```

Example 2. SetUp and TearDown code (continued)

```
        Console.WriteLine("    Test2 start");

        Class1 c1 = new Class1();
        Assert.IsTrue(c1.Method1() == 100);

        Console.WriteLine("    Test2 end");
    }
}
```

Running the example generates the following output to the test runner GUI Console.Out pane:

```
Class1 TestFixture setup
  Test setup
    Test1 start
    Test1 end
  Test teardown
  Test setup
    Test2 start
    Test2 end
  Test teardown
Class1 TestFixture teardown
```

SetUp and TearDown methods are inherited from base classes and will be called before executing the test method in the inheriting class. To add to the base class functionality, create the SetUp or TearDown methods in the inheriting class and call the appropriate method in the base class.

Testing expected exceptions

An *expected exception* is an exception that a test must throw in order to pass. This lets you test exception handling.

The [ExpectedException] attribute identifies a test that you expect to throw an exception. The [ExpectedException] attribute takes two arguments. The first is mandatory and indicates the exception that you expect to be thrown in the test method. The second argument is an optional string message describing the reason for the exception.

The following code throws a System.Exception. The [ExpectedException] attribute indicates that this exception is expected for the test to run successfully:

```
[Test]
[ExpectedException(typeof(System.Exception)]
public void TestException1()
{
    throw new System.Exception();
}
```

If you specify a message, it must match exactly. The test will succeed if the message argument is not included in the attribute and the exception has a message, but will fail the other way around. For example, the test in the following example succeeds:

```
[Test]
[ExpectedException(typeof(System.Exception))]
public void TestException1()
{
    throw new
        System.Exception("Exception reason.")]);
}
```

The test in the following example fails:

```
[Test]
[ExpectedException(typeof(System.Exception),
    "Exception reason.")]
public void TestException1()
{
    throw new
        System.Exception("Another reason.");
}
```

If the specified exception is not raised in the test case, the test fails. Exceptions that inherit from the specified exception also fail.

Ignoring tests

It is sometimes useful to exclude tests from a test run when the functionality is not yet implemented or to facilitate debugging. NUnit makes it easy to exclude individual tests or entire test fixtures.

The [Ignore] attribute specifies that tests or test fixtures should not run. The [Ignore] attribute takes a mandatory string argument that describes why the test is ignored. For example:

```
[Test]
[Ignore("The reason why test is ignored.")]
public void Test2()
{
    Class1 c1 = new Class1();
    Assert.AreEqual(c1.Method1(), 100);
}
```

You can specify multiple attributes together. The following code ignores an entire test fixture:

```
[TestFixture, Ignore("The reason why test
    fixture is ignored.")]
```

The test runner GUI identifies ignored tests with a yellow dot in the tree view. If there are ignored tests in the run, the success bar will be yellow instead of green if all unignored tests pass.

Using the [Ignore] attribute is better than temporarily removing, commenting out, or renaming tests that you don't want to run. Ignored tests are compiled with the code, and the test runners indicate that those tests were not run.

Test categories

Test categories allow you to define custom groups of tests and test fixtures. You associate a test or test fixture with a category by decorating it with the [Category] attribute. For example:

```
[Test]
[Category("MyCategory1")]
public void Test1()
{
    // test case implementation
}
```

You can combine the two attributes in the preceding example:

```
[Test, Category("MyCategory1")]
```

Tests and test fixtures can be associated with one or more categories:

```
[Test, Category("MyCategory1"),
    Category("MyCategory2")]
```

Categories can be included or excluded when running tests. In the test runner GUI, select the categories to include or exclude using the Categories tab as described in "Test Runner GUI," later in this book. In the test runner console, use the /include and /exclude switches to include and exclude categories as described later in "Test Runner Console."

The Explicit attribute is used together with the Category attribute to control when tests that belong to a category are run. For example:

```
[Category("MyCategory1")]
[Explicit]
```

Or more simply:

```
[Category("MyCategory1"), Explicit]
```

By default, a test run includes all tests that do not belong to a category as well as tests that belong to a category without an Explicit property or with the Explicit property set to false. Setting the Explicit property to true indicates that the test will not run unless you explicitly specify the category. This might be useful to exclude long-running or resource-intensive tests, for example.

Test suites

A test suite is a collection of test cases, test fixtures, and possibly other test suites. Test suites let you create logical groupings of related tests, test fixtures, and other test suites. You can identify a test suite using a namespace.

You can define test suites in NUnit Version 2.1 and later using namespaces. Do this by assigning all of the classes in the test suite to the same namespace. The name of the test suite is the same as the name of the namespace. The classes can be in the same file or spread across different files. Test suites are optional.

Prior to NUnit Version 2.0, test suites were defined using the [Suite] attribute. NUnit Version 2.2 continues to support the [Suite] attribute for backward compatibility.

Limitations

You can only load assemblies that you have permission for under code access security. By default, you cannot load assemblies from a Uniform Naming Convention (UNC) path, which is a standard way to access network shares. You can change this behavior with the .NET Framework Configuration Tool. You should do this only if you completely understand the security implications. For more information about the .NET Framework Configuration Tool, see MSDN.

Test Runner GUI

NUnit provides two test runner interfaces—GUI and console. Both interfaces provide similar functionality. The test runner GUI is most useful for testing code while you are developing. The test runner console is useful in automated testing environments.

The test runner GUI can be launched using either the shortcut that is created when NUnit is installed or from the command line, as discussed later in this section.

This section describes the test runner GUI. Examples use the *nunit.tests.dll* assembly that the NUnit developers use to test NUnit; this assembly installs with NUnit into the *bin* subdirectory.

User Interface

The following sections describe the different parts of the test runner GUI.

Test tree view

The test tree view displays on the Test tab at the left side of the test runner GUI. It displays the hierarchy of test suites, test fixtures, and tests in the assembly.

The success or failure of each test is shown in the tree view— a green dot indicates success, a red dot indicates failure, and a yellow dot indicates that a test was not run. The tree view also allows you to selectively run single tests or groups of tests.

Figure 7 shows the test runner GUI.

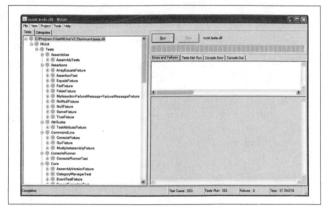

Figure 7. A test runner GUI without checkboxes

You can display checkboxes for each node in the tree view, allowing you to select tests to run. Select or deselect the menu item View→CheckBoxes.

Figure 8 shows the test runner GUI with checkboxes.

Select multiple checkboxes and click the Run button to run the tests for the checked nodes. All child tests of a checked parent are run.

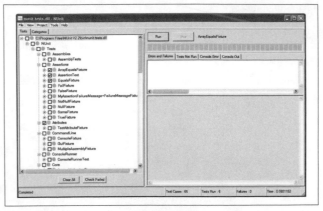

Figure 8. Test runner GUI with checkboxes

The Clear button deselects all checkboxes. The Check Failed button selects only the tests that failed in the last run.

You can right-click on any node in the tree view and select Properties from the context menu to find out what the node represents and information about the node. Figure 9 shows the properties for a test case.

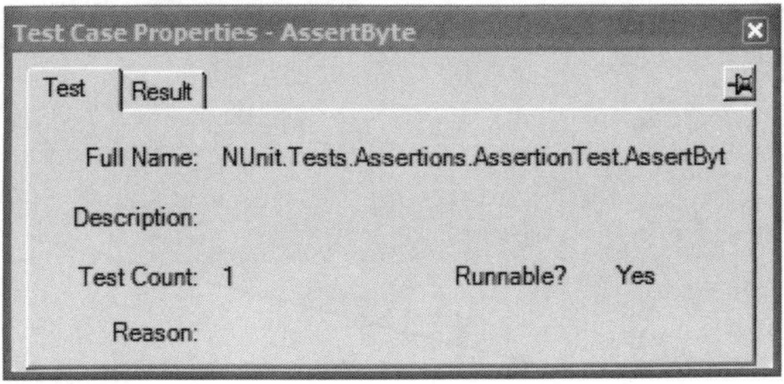

Figure 9. The Test Case Properties dialog's Test tab

The Test tab displays the following information:

Full Name
Fully qualified name of the test.

Description
Description of the test as specified by the optional Description argument of the [Test] attribute.

Test Count
Indicates the number of test cases contained, either directly or indirectly. The test count for a test case is always 1.

Runnable?
Indicates whether the test can be run. Tests marked with the [Ignore] attribute display "No." Tests that are not coded correctly—for example, tests marked private—also display "No."

Reason
Indicates why the test is not runnable (see Figure 9).

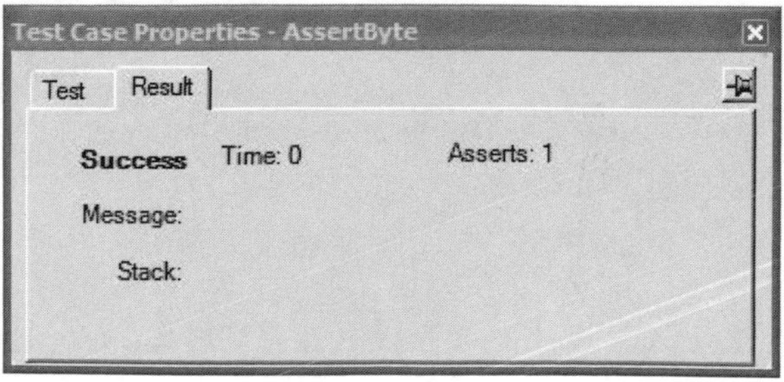

Figure 10. The Test Case Properties dialog's Result tab

The Result tab shown in Figure 10 displays the following information:

Status
"Success" if the test passed and "Failure" if the test failed

Asserts
> The count of assertions in the test case

Time
> The time to run the test in seconds

Message
> The error message, if the test failed

Stack
> The stack trace at the point of failure, if the test failed

The Result tab is not available before the test case runs.

If any field is too short to display the complete information, putting the mouse pointer on top of the field shows a tooltip that displays all of the information.

The properties for both a test fixture and a test suite have a Test tab, as shown in Figure 11 and Figure 12, that displays the same information as the Test tab of the Test Case Properties dialog.

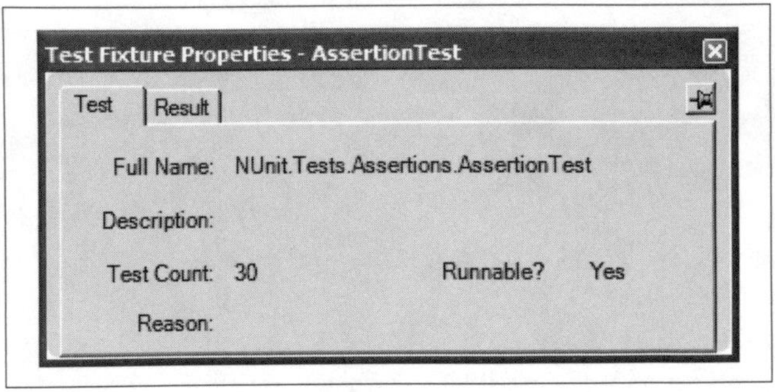

Figure 11. The Test Fixture Properties dialog's Test tab

The properties for both a test fixture and a test suite have a Result tab, as shown in Figure 13 and Figure 14, that displays the same information as the Result tab of the Test Case Properties dialog. In both cases, the Result tab is not available before running tests.

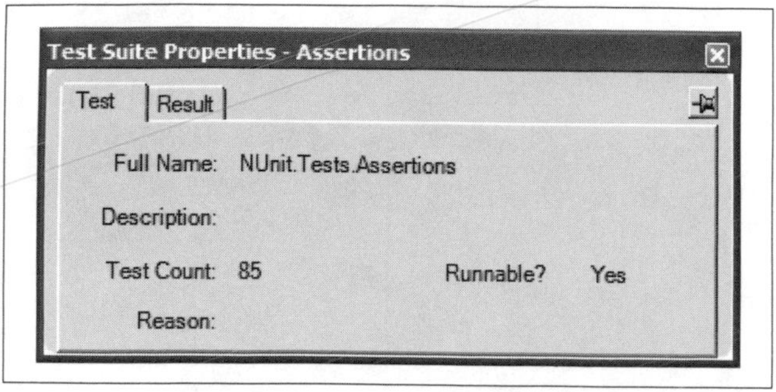

Figure 12. The Test Suite Properties dialog's Test tab

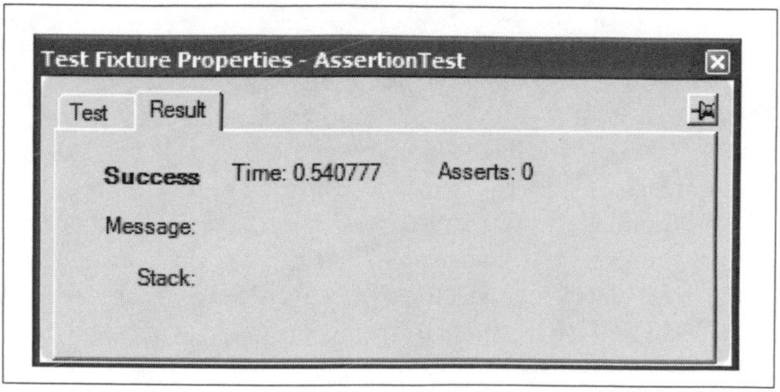

Figure 13. The Test Fixture Properties dialog's Result tab

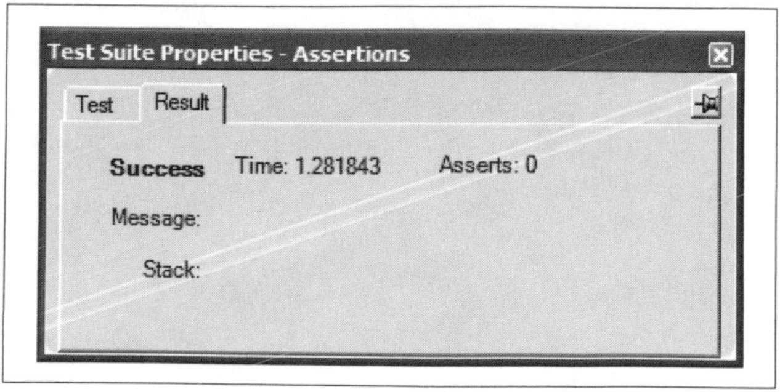

Figure 14. The Test Suite Properties dialog's Result tab

In addition to the Test tab that displays the tree view, the test runner GUI has a Categories tab, as shown in Figure 15.

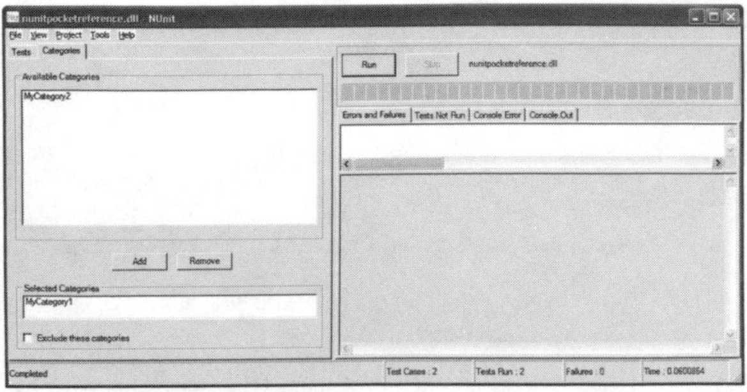

Figure 15. Test runner interface Categories tab

The Categories tab has two listboxes: the top displays available categories and the bottom displays selected categories. The Add and Remove buttons select and deselect categories. Below the Selected Categories listbox, the "Exclude these categories" checkbox specifies whether tests and test fixtures in the selected categories run or are excluded when you click the Run button.

The Categories tab is the same whether or not checkboxes are displayed in the tree view.

Progress bar

The progress bar shows the relative number of tests that have run and remain to run. Once all tests have run, the bar will be one of three colors:

Green
    All tests succeeded

Yellow
    At least one test was ignored as directed by an [Ignore] attribute or an Assert.Ignore() method call; all other tests succeeded

Red
> One or more tests failed

The dots next to the individual nodes in the tree view are also marked according to this color scheme.

Test results

The test runner GUI has a tabbed output window below the progress bar. The output window displays tests results in four tabs:

Errors and Failures
> This window is divided into two halves. The top half lists all the tests that have failed, and the bottom half shows the stack trace for the failed test selected from the list in the top half.

Tests Not Run
> Displays a tree view containing all tests not run and the reason they were not run. If the test is marked with the [Ignore] attribute, the information in the string argument for the [Ignore] attribute is displayed as the reason. If the test cannot be run for any other reason—for example, the test method is marked private—an error message is displayed.

Console.Error
> Displays test code output directed to the output error stream using static methods of the Error property of the Console class. The following code shows one way to do this:
> ```
> Console.Error.WriteLine("This is sent to the
>     Console.Error window.");
> ```
> If the test fails before the output error command executes, the test ends immediately and there is no output.

Console.Out

Displays test mode output directed to the output stream using static methods of the Console class. The following code shows one way to do this:

```
Console.WriteLine("This is sent to the
    Console.Out window.");
```

If the test fails before the output command executes, the test ends immediately and there is no output.

Menu

The File menu has commands for handling NUnit project files as described in Table 2.

Table 2. NUnit GUI File menu commands

Command	Description
New Project...	Opens a New File dialog, which allows you to create a new NUnit project. If a project is open and you have made changes to it since it was last saved, you are prompted to save it before it is closed.
Open...	Opens a File Open dialog, which allows you to select and open a NUnit project that you have previously saved. If a project is open and you have made changes to it since it was last saved, you are prompted to save it before it is closed.
Close	Closes the open project file. If a project is open and you have made changes to it since it was last saved, you are prompted to save it before it is closed.
Save	Saves the open project. If you have not previously saved the file, a File Save dialog is opened, which allows you to specify the name of the project file and where it will be saved.
Save As...	Opens a File Save dialog, which allows you to specify the name of the project file and where it will be saved.
Reload	Reloads the open file using the most recent versions of assemblies being tested.
Recent Files →	Displays a list of most recently opened NUnit projects, .NET assemblies, .NET projects, and .NET solutions. You can control the number of items in this list using the Tools→Options dialog.

Table 2. NUnit GUI File menu commands (continued)

Command	Description
Exit	Closes NUnit. If a test is running, you are asked if you want to continue or cancel the test. If you have made changes to the current project, you are given the opportunity to save it.

The View menu has commands for managing aspects of the project tree view as described in Table 3.

Table 3. NUnit GUI View menu

Command	Description
CheckBoxes	Optionally displays checkboxes for the nodes in the tree view as shown in Figure 8.
Expand	Expands the selected node in the tree view. This command is not available if a node is not selected.
Collapse	Collapses the selected node in the tree view. This command is only available if a node is selected.
Expand All	Expands all nodes in the tree view.
Collapse All	Collapses all nodes in the tree view.
Expand Fixtures	Expands all test fixture nodes that are visible in the tree view to reveal the contained test cases.
Collapse Fixtures	Collapses all test fixture nodes that are visible in the tree view.
Properties	Displays the properties for the node selected in the tree view.

The Project menu contains commands for managing the current NUnit project as described in Table 4.

Table 4. NUnit GUI Project menu

Command	Description
Configurations→All available configurations	Selects the configuration to test (such as Debug or Release).
Configurations→Add...	Opens a dialog, as shown in Figure 19, which allows you to create a new configuration based on an existing configuration.

Table 4. NUnit GUI Project menu (continued)

Command	Description
Configurations→Edit...	Allows you to remove, rename, or add a new configuration, and to select the active configuration (i.e., will be tested). Figure 18 shows the dialog. Configurations are discussed in more detail in "NUnit Projects."
Add Assembly...	Opens a File Open dialog, which allows you to select and add an assembly to the active configuration of the open project. Adding assemblies is discussed in more detail in "NUnit Projects."
Add VS Project...	Opens a File Open dialog, which allows you to select and add a Visual Studio .NET project to the open project. Each configuration in the project is added to the respective configuration in the open project. New configurations are created in the open project if necessary. This menu item is only available if Visual Studio support is enabled. Adding a new project is discussed in more detail in "NUnit Projects."
Edit	Opens the Project Editor dialog as shown in Figure 17. The project editor is discussed in more detail in "NUnit Projects."

The Tools menu has commands for managing the output of the test results, viewing exception details, and controlling the operation of NUnit as described in Table 5.

Table 5. NUnit GUI Tools menu

Command	Description
Save Results as XML...	Opens a File Save As dialog, which allows you to save the test results to an XML file. Saving test results as XML is discussed later in "NUnit Projects."
Exception Details...	Displays a dialog with the complete stack trace for an exception raised while trying to load, unload, or run a test.

Table 5. NUnit GUI Tools menu (continued)

Command	Description
Options...	Opens the NUnit Options dialog, shown in Figure 20, which allows you to control the operation of NUnit. NUnit options are discussed in more detail in "NUnit Projects".

The Help menu has commands to return help and version information for NUnit, as described in Table 6.

Table 6. NUnit GUI Help menu

Command	Description
Help	Opens NUnit help.
About NUnit...	Displays version and other information about NUnit and a link to the NUnit home page.

Status bar

The test runner GUI status bar displays results from the most recent test run. Information is presented in five panes and includes the current status of NUnit GUI or the test currently running, the number of test cases in the project, the number of tests run, the number of failures, and the time in seconds to execute the tests. As tests are run, the status bar is updated to show the test currently running and the number of tests completed.

While tests are running the status bar displays the name of the test being run in the leftmost pane. Once the tests are run, the status bar displays "Completed."

NUnit Projects

An NUnit project is defined by a file with the extension *.nunit*. The file contains information about one or more assemblies or Visual Studio .NET projects that should be loaded and tested.

The NUnit project file is in XML format and specifies available configurations (i.e., Release and Debug), the active configuration, and the full paths to each assembly contained in the project for each configuration. An example follows:

```
<NUnitProject>
  <Settings activeconfig="Debug" />
  <Config name="Debug" binpathtype="Auto">
    <assembly path=
      "bin\Debug\NUnitPocketReference.dll" />
  </Config>
  <Config name="Release" binpathtype="Auto">
    <assembly path=
      "bin\Release\NUnitPocketReference.dll" />
  </Config>
</NUnitProject>
```

The root element of the *.nunit* file is always NUnitProject.

The Settings element defines the active configuration by naming one of the following configurations using the activeconfig attribute. In this case, the Debug configuration is active.

One or more Config elements define the configurations available in the project. The name attribute defines the name of the configuration. The binpathtype attribute is set to Auto, indicating the directory paths are generated automatically from the assembly locations. An appbase attribute specifies the ApplicationBase directory, while the binpath attribute lets you manually specify a semicolon-delimited list of directories.

Each Config element contains one or more assembly elements that identify each assembly in the configuration by specifying the full path to the assembly in the path attribute relative to the directory containing the *.nunit* file.

The Project Editor dialog

The Project Editor dialog lets you modify and create NUnit projects. The editor contains a common area and an area with two tabs.

The common area contains:

- A label showing the full path of the project.
- A dropdown list that lets you select the project to edit.
- An Edit Configs button that launches the Configuration Editor dialog. This is described in "Selecting, Adding, and Editing Configurations."

The Project Editor has two tabs below the common area—the General tab is shown in Figure 16 and the Assemblies tab is shown in Figure 17.

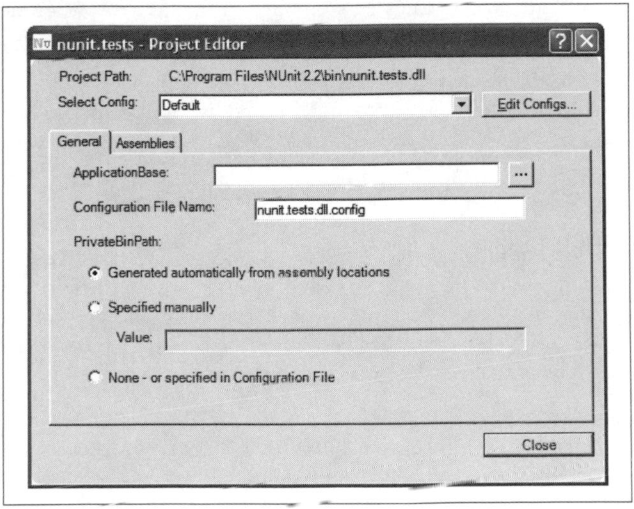

Figure 16 The Project Editor dialog's General tab

The General tab lets you set options for the configuration selected in the dropdown list. The General tab controls the following settings:

ApplicationBase
Defaults to the directory containing the assembly for the active configuration. All assemblies in the project must be located in or under this directory.

Configuration File Name
> Specifies the file that contains configuration settings for the NUnit project. It defaults to the name of the test project with the extension *.config*.

PrivateBinPath
> Is combined with the ApplicationBase to specify directories to probe for private assemblies. There are three options:

> *Generate automatically from assembly locations*
>> Automatically sets to the semicolon-delimited list of directories for all assemblies in the active configuration.

> *Specify manually*
>> Specifies a semicolon-delimited list of directories.

> *None (or specified in configuration file)*
>> Allows the directories to be specified outside of NUnit.

The Assemblies tab lets you select and manage the assemblies in your project. A listbox contains the assemblies in the project. A checkbox next to each assembly allows you to indicate which assemblies contain tests. The four buttons to the right of the listbox manage the assemblies in the project:

Add Assembly
> Displays a File Open dialog that allows you to add an assembly to the selected configuration.

Add VS Project
> Displays a File Open dialog that allows you to add a Visual Studio .NET project or solution to the project. Each configuration in the project is added to the respective configuration in the open project. New configurations are created in the open project if necessary.

> Visual Studio support must be enabled through the Tools→Options dialog.

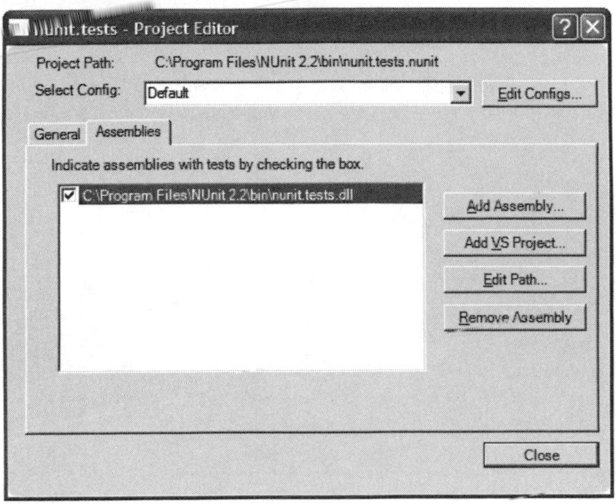

Figure 17. The Project Editor dialog's Assemblies tab

Edit Path

Opens a dialog that lets you change the path for an assembly in the selected configuration.

Remove Assembly

Removes the selected assembly from the specified build configuration.

Selecting, Adding, and Editing Configurations

A Visual Studio .NET project automatically creates separate configurations for Debug and Release, the builds for debugging and for final release distribution. You can also specify custom configurations (see Figure 18).

The Configuration Editor dialog shown in Figure 18 lets you manage the different configurations in the test project. The description of the functionality of the buttons on this form follows:

Figure 18. A Configuration Editor dialog

Remove

Removes the configuration selected in the listbox from the project. If the configuration is active, the next item in the list becomes active. If you remove the last configuration, you will no longer be able to load the test project until you add a configuration.

Rename

Opens a dialog that lets you rename a configuration.

Add...

Opens the New Configuration dialog, shown in Figure 19, that lets you create a new configuration based on an existing configuration.

Make Active

Makes the configuration selected in the listbox active.

Close

Exits the Configuration Editor dialog.

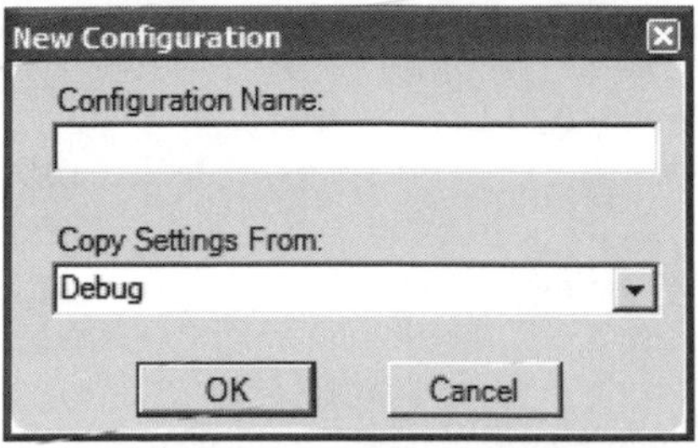

Figure 19. A New Configuration dialog

The Options dialog

Figure 20 shows the NUnit Options dialog.

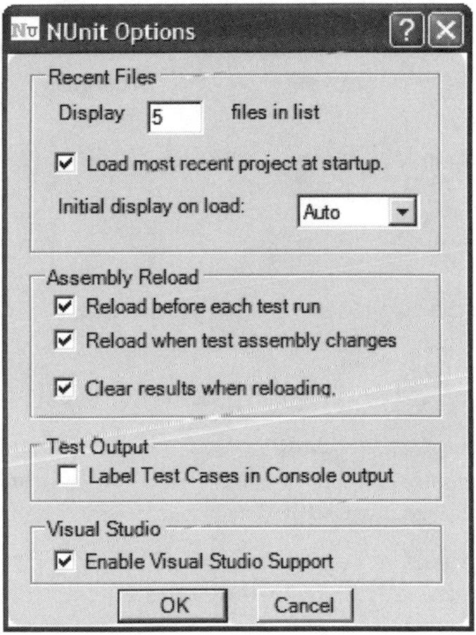

Figure 20. An NUnit Options dialog

You control the following aspects of NUnit through the Options dialog:

Display N files in list
Lets you specify how many entries are displayed in the File→Recent Files menu.

Load most recent project at start-up
If selected, loads the last NUnit project when NUnit is started. If the test runner GUI is launched from the command line, a command-line switch specifying a file to open—assembly, .NET project, or NUnit project—or the /noload switch takes precedence.

Initial display on load
Controls how much the tree view expands when tests are loaded. The four choices are:

> *Auto*
> Selects one of the other options based on how the tree view best fits in the available space.
>
> *Expand*
> Expands all nodes.
>
> *Collapse*
> Collapses all nodes.
>
> *Hide Tests*
> Expands all nodes except test fixtures.

Assembly Reload group
Three checkboxes control how assemblies are reloaded:

> *Reload before each test run*
> Assemblies are reloaded each time tests are run whether the assemblies appear to have changed or not.
>
> *Reload when test assembly changes*
> Assemblies are automatically reloaded when changed. This feature is disabled when NUnit is run on Windows 98 or ME.

Clear results when reloading
> Results for tests are cleared when assemblies are reloaded either manually or automatically; otherwise, results are retained.

Label Test Cases in Console output
> If selected, test names are included in the test runner console output.

Enable Visual Studio Support
> If selected, Visual Studio projects and solutions (as well as assemblies) can be opened and added to existing projects.

Opening Visual Studio projects

If you enable Visual Studio project support in the Tools→Options dialog, you can open supported types of Visual Studio .NET project files. NUnit supports C# (*.csproj*), VB.NET (*.vbproj*), J# (*.vjsproj*), and C++ (*.vcproj*) project types. NUnit reads the project file to locate the assemblies for the different configurations (e.g., Debug and Release). NUnit loads the first assembly configuration that it finds in the Visual Studio project file, which is usually the Debug configuration.

When NUnit runs tests on a Visual Studio project, the default location for the NUnit configuration file is in the directory containing the Visual Studio project file rather than the directory containing the assemblies in the Visual Studio project. This applies whether you are using the runner GUI or console.

Opening Visual Studio solutions

If you enable Visual Studio project support in the Tools→Options dialog, you can open Visual Studio solutions (*.sln* files) as well as Visual Studio projects. If all of the projects within the solution are located in the same directory structure—in the directory of or a subdirectory of the solution—all assemblies for supported project types will load, allowing you to run all tests in the solution.

If the projects within the solution are in different directories, you will be able to open the solution; however, an exception will be raised. This is a limitation of NUnit. To run tests within the solution, use the Project Editor to remove assemblies from the NUnit project, leaving only assemblies that are in the same directory tree. This allows you to test that subset of the projects in the solution.

Adding Visual Studio projects

You can add Visual Studio projects to an NUnit project using the Project→Add VS Project... command. As with the Visual Studio solution, all projects that are opened must be in the same directory or a subdirectory of the first Visual Studio project that is opened or an exception will be raised—the order in which the projects are opened and added to the NUnit project matters.

Running Tests

You have several ways of selecting which tests to run in the test runner GUI.

- To run all tests, select the topmost node in the tree, and either press the Run button or right-click the topmost node and select Run from the context menu.

- To run the tests for a test suite, test fixture, or a single test case, select the corresponding node in the tree, and either press the Run button or right-click the node and select Run from the context menu. You cannot select multiple items to run using the Control or Shift key.

- If checkboxes are displayed in the tree view, check the tests, text fixtures, and test suites that you want run and click the Run button. If you check a parent node, all tests in the child nodes are run whether checked or not.

Tests execute in the order they appear in the tree view. The status bar indicates the progress while tests are running.

Once test execution is complete, the results are displayed in the tabbed window below the progress bar.

In all cases, click the Stop button to cancel test execution.

Debugging from the Visual Studio .NET IDE

You can set the test runner GUI to open your test assembly when you select Debug→Start or press the start button on the toolbar. This will allow you to use the debugging capabilities of the Visual Studio .NET IDE (Integrated Development Environment) on both test and application code. The following steps show how:

1. Open the Project Properties dialog by selecting Project→*myprojectname* Properties from the menu, or by right-clicking the project in Solution Explorer and selecting Properties from the context menu.
2. Select Configuration Properties→Debugging in the left tree view pane.
3. Change Debug Mode to Program. Click the Apply button. The Start Application option will become available.
4. Select the Start Application field and click the ellipsis (...) next to it. Locate and select *nunit-gui.exe* (in the *bin* directory of the installation folder). Press Open.
5. Enter the name of the test assembly (*.dll*) in the Command Line Arguments field.

Figure 21 shows the completed Project Properties dialog.

1. If you have a solution with multiple project files, set the project that you have just configured to be the startup project: right-click the project in Solution Explorer and select Set as StartUp Project from the context menu.
2. Set your debug breakpoints.
3. Press the Start button on the IDE toolbar or select Debug→Start from the main menu. The GUI test runner will open. Click the Run button to run your tests.

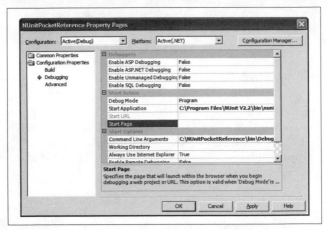

Figure 21. A Project Properties dialog for debugging

Results in XML format

NUnit allows you to save results in XML format from both the test runner GUI and console. This section discusses the XML schema and output. See the test runner GUI and console sections for information on how to generate the XML output file.

The file *src\core\results.xsd* defines the schema used to format the XML results output.

Example 3 shows an excerpt of the XML output for the tests in *nunit.tests.dll*.

Example 3. TestResult.xml for nunit.tests.dll

```
<?xml version="1.0" encoding="utf-8"
  standalone="no"?>
<!--This file represents the results of
  running a test suite-->
<test-results
  name="C:\Program Files\NUnit
  V2.2\bin\nunit.tests.dll" total="605"
  failures="0" not-run="0" date="7/1/2004"
```

Example 3. TestResult.xml for nunit.tests.dll (continued)

```xml
   time="11:13 PM">
  <test-suite
    name="C:\Program Files\NUnit
    V2.2\bin\nunit.tests.dll" success="True"
    time="37.5139424" asserts="0">
    <results>
      <test-suite name="NUnit" success="True"
        time="37.3336832" asserts="0">
        <results>
          <test-suite name="Tests" success="True"
            time="37.1634384" asserts="0">
            <results>
              <test-suite name="UiKit"
                success="True" time="1.6423616"
                asserts="0">
                <results>
                  <test-suite
                    name=
                    "AddConfigurationDialogTests"
                    success="True"
                    time="0.6909936"
                    asserts="0">
                    <results>
                     <test-case
                     name="NUnit.Tests.UiKit.
                     AddConfigurationDialogTests.
                     CheckForControls"
                     executed="True"
                     success="True"
                     time="0.401" asserts="8" />

<!-- ... -->

                     <test-case
                     name="NUnit.Tests.UiKit.
                     AddConfigurationDialogTests.
                     TestComplexEntry"
                     executed="True"
                     success="True"
                     time="0.050" asserts="2" />
                     </results>
                  </test-suite>
```

Example 3. TestResult.xml for nunit.tests.dll (continued)

```
<test-suite
  name="ProgressBarTests"
  success="True"
  time="0.2603744"
  asserts="0">
  <results>
    <test-case
      name="NUnit.Tests.UiKit.
      ProgressBarTests.
      TestProgressDisplay"
      executed="True"
      success="True"
      time="0.260"
      asserts="12" />
  </results>
</test-suite>

<!-- ... -->

              </results>
            </test-suite>
          </results>
        </test-suite>
      </results>
    </test-suite>
  </results>
</test-suite>
</test-results>
```

The XML output is straightforward. The test-suite element identifies both test suites and test fixtures. The test-case element identifies test cases. Identifying information, statistics, and results are stored as attributes of those elements.

The number of tests that fail or are ignored is displayed by the failures and not-run attributes of the test-results element:

```
<test-results
  name="C:\NUnitPR\bin\Debug\
  nunitpocketreference.dll"
  total="5" failures="1" not-run="1"
  date="4/25/2004" time="11:22 PM">
```

If a test fails, the success attribute of the test-case element and all parent test-suite elements is false. The failure element contains the details about why the test case failed in a message element and a stack-trace element. The code for the test case follows:

```
[Test]
public void Test1()
{
    Assert.IsTrue(false, "Test 1 failed");
}
```

The corresponding test-case element from the test output follows:

```
<test-case name="MyTestSuite.Class1Test.Test1"
  executed="True" success="False" time="0.010"
  asserts="1">
  <failure>
    <message><![CDATA[ ]]></message>
    <stack-trace>
      <![CDATA[    at
      MyTestSuite.Class1Test.Test1() in
      c:\nunitpocketreference\class1test.cs:
      line 41]]>
    </stack-trace>
  </failure>
</test-case>
```

If a test is ignored, the executed attribute of the test-case element is set to false. The reason element contains a message element that indicates why the test was ignored. The code for the test case follows:

```
[Test]
[Ignore("My reason for ignoring test 2.")]
public void Test2()
{
    Assert.IsTrue(true);
}
```

The corresponding test-case element from the test output follows:

```
<test-case name="MyTestSuite.Class1Test.Test2"
  executed="False">
```

```
<reason>
  <message>
    <![CDATA[My reason for ignoring test 2.]]>
  </message>
</reason>
</test-case>
```

Running the Test Runner GUI from the Command Line

You can run the test runner GUI from the command line and specify arguments to control its behavior. There are two ways to run NUnit from the command line.

You can switch to the directory containing the *nunit-gui.exe* program. The default directory is *c:\Program Files\NUnit V2.2\ bin*. With this option, you must specify the full path to the assembly you are testing.

Alternatively, you can add the directory for *nunit-gui.exe* to the environment path by selecting Control Panel→System, selecting the Advanced tab, and clicking the Environment Variables button. Select Path in either the user or system variables, and append the directory containing *nunit-gui.exe* to the path. Separate the path from any other entries with a semicolon. If you launch the test runner GUI in this way, you can execute *nunit-gui.exe* from the assembly directory, which eliminates the need to type the assembly path. The examples in this section use this method.

Use the command nunit-gui.exe (or simply nunit-gui) from the command prompt to start the test runner GUI with the most recently loaded project:

```
nunit-gui.exe
```

Testing an assembly

You can specify an assembly to test on the command line:

```
nunit-gui.exe NUnitPocketReference.dll
```

Alternatively, you can specify the name of a .NET project or solution file. NUnit loads the assemblies specified in the .NET project definition:

```
nunit-gui.exe NUnitPocketReference.csproj
nunit-gui.exe NUnitPocketReference.sln
```

You can also specify the name of an NUnit project file:

```
nunit-gui.exe NUnitPocketReference.nunit
```

You control the test runner GUI with the following optional switches:

/fixture

Specifies the test fixture or test suite for which to load tests. You must specify the full name of the test fixture or namespace. The name of the test fixture is case sensitive. For example, the following command loads all tests in the test fixture Class1Test in the MyTestSuite test suite:

```
nunit-gui.exe NUnitPocketReference.dll
    /fixture=MyTestSuite.Class1Test
```

The following command loads all tests in the test suite MyTestSuite:

```
nunit-gui.exe NUnitPocketReference.dll
    /fixture=MyTestSuite
```

You can also use this to load an assembly, .NET project file, .NET solution file, or NUnit project.

/config

Specifies the build configuration (for example, debug or release) to test:

```
nunit-gui.exe NUnitPocketReference.csproj
    /config=Debug
nunit-gui.exe NUnitPocketReference.csproj
    /config=Release
```

You can specify a custom build configuration in the same way:

```
nunit-gui.exe NUnitPocketReference.csproj
    /config=myBuildConfig
```

/noload
>   Opens the test runner GUI without loading the last
>   project:
>
>    ```
>    nunit-gui.exe /noload
>    ```

/run
>   Runs all tests automatically:
>
>    ```
>    nunit-gui.exe NUnitPocketReference.nunit /run
>    ```

/? or /help
>   Displays a dialog with brief help about test runner GUI
>   switches:
>
>    ```
>    nunit-gui.exe /help
>    nunit-gui.exe /?
>    ```

Test Runner Console

The test runner console is text-based and not interactive. It is
most useful in automated testing environments where you
use an automated build tool, such as NAnt, to run NUnit
tests automatically as part of the build cycle.

The test runner console has a number of options in addition
to those available in the test runner GUI. The console interface outputs test results to an XML file. By default, the file is
named *TestResult.xml* and is placed in the working directory. This XML file is overwritten without warning if it
already exists. The schema and contents of the file are
described earlier in "Results in XML format."

To use the test runner console, add the directory for *nunit-
console.exe* (the default directory is *c:\Program Files\NUnit V2.2\
bin*) to the environment path by selecting Control
Panel→System, selecting the Advanced tab, and clicking the
Environment Variables button. Append the directory containing *nunit-console.exe* to either the user or system path. Separate
the path from any other entries with a semicolon.

Test an assembly by specifying its name on the command line:

```
nunit-console.exe NUnitPocketReference.dll
```

The output includes:

- Output that you have directed to the console in the tests. This output is the same as that sent to the Console.Out window in the test runner GUI.
- Statistics about the tests run including the number of successes, failures, tests not run, and the time it took to run the tests.
- A list of tests that failed.
- A list of tests that were ignored.

Figure 22 shows a test runner console run.

Figure 22. A test runner console

There are several other ways that you can specify the tests to run—for example, you can specify the .NET project name. NUnit loads the assembly specified by the .NET project definition:

```
nunit-console.exe NUnitPocketReference.csproj
```

You can also specify a .NET solution file with the same result:

```
nunit-console.exe NUnitPocketReference.sln
```

Finally, you can specify an NUnit project file:

```
nunit-console.exe NUnitPocketReference.nunit
```

Run a test in multiple assemblies by adding the names of all assemblies to the command line:

```
nunit-console.exe MyAssembly1.dll MyAssembly2.dll
```

You cannot specify multiple .NET projects, .NET solutions, or NUnit projects on the command line.

Control the test runner console with the following optional switches:

/config

Lets you control the build (for example, Debug or Release) that is tested:

```
nunit-console.exe NUnitPocketReference.csproj
    /config=Debug
nunit-console.exe NUnitPocketReference.csproj
    /config=Release
```

You can load a custom build configuration the same way. For example:

```
nunit-console.exe NUnitPocketReference.csproj
    /config=myBuildConfig
```

/fixture

Specifies a test fixture or test suite in which all tests will be run. You must specify the full name of the test fixture or namespace. The name of the test fixture is case sensitive. For example, to run the tests in the Class1Test test fixture within the MyTestSuite test suite:

```
nunit-console.exe NUnitPocketReference.dll
    /fixture=MyTestSuite.Class1Test
```

To run the tests in the MyTestSuite test suite:

```
nunit-console.exe NUnitPocketReference.dll
    /fixture=MyTestSuite
```

You can specify a test fixture or namespace within an assembly, .NET project file, .NET solution file, or NUnit project.

/include

Specifies the test categories to include in testing:

```
nunit-console.exe NUnitPocketReference.dll
    /include=MyCategory1
```

Separate multiple categories using semicolons:

```
nunit-console.exe NUnitPocketReference.dll
    /include=MyCategory1;MyCategory2
```

Categories with the Explicit property set to false will be run without being specified unless you exclude them by using the /exclude switch.

/exclude

Specifies test categories to exclude from testing:

```
nunit-console.exe NUnitPocketReference.dll
    /exclude=MyCategory1
```

Separate multiple categories using semicolons:

```
nunit-console.exe NUnitPocketReference.dll
    /exclude=MyCategory1;MyCategory2
```

/output or /out

Specifies the file for the standard output from the tests.

/err

Specifies the file for the error output from the tests.

/labels

Outputs each test name in the XML output.

/xml

Lets you specify a name of the XML output file instead of the default *TestResult.xml*:

```
nunit-console.exe NUnitPocketReference.dll
    /xml=NUnitPocketReference.xml
```

/xmlConsole

Redirects the XML output to the console:

```
nunit-console.exe
    NUnitPocketReference.dll /xmlConsole
```

The XML output follows any console output from your tests.

/transform

The console interface's output is generated by applying an XML transformation to the XML test results output. The /transform switch lets you specify a different XML transformation file:

```
nunit-console.exe NUnitPocketReference.dll
    /transform=MySummary.xslt
```

The default transformation file is *summary.xslt* located in the *src\core* subdirectory of the NUnit installation directory.

By default, NUnit looks for a custom transformation file in the same directory as the assembly being tested. You can specify an alternate location using an absolute path as shown:

```
nunit-console.exe NUnitPocketReference.dll
    /transform="c:\Alt Dir\MySummary.xslt"
```

/nologo

Suppresses the NUnit information that is prepended to the test results:

```
nunit-console.exe /nologo
```

/wait

The test runner console program does not end until you press Enter:

```
nunit-console.exe /wait
```

/? *or* /help

Displays brief help about all console switches:

```
nunit-gui.exe /help
```

```
nunit-gui.exe /?
```

Debugging with NUnit

The Visual Studio .NET debugger can attach to a program running in an external process. Use this feature to debug NUnit tests as follows:

1. Open the Visual Studio .NET project that you are testing with the Visual Studio .NET IDE.

2. Run NUnit and load the Visual Studio .NET project.

3. From the Visual Studio .NET menu, select Tools→Debug Processes... to launch the Processes dialog as shown in Figure 23.

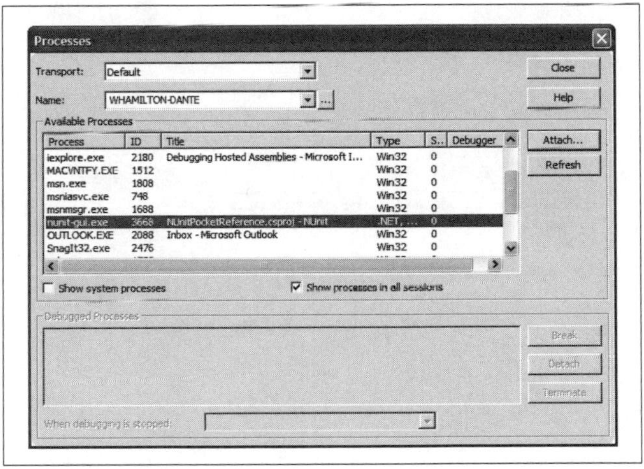

Figure 23. A Processes dialog

4. Select *nunit-gui.exe* from the list of processes and press the Attach... button to launch the Attach to Process dialog as shown in Figure 24.

5. Check Common Language Runtime in the Attach to Process dialog and click the OK button. The *nunit-gui.exe* process appears in the Debugged Process window of the Processes dialog as shown in Figure 25. Press the Close button to exit the Processes dialog (see Figure 23).

6. Run the tests in the NUnit GUI. You will now be able to debug the test assembly in Visual Studio .NET.

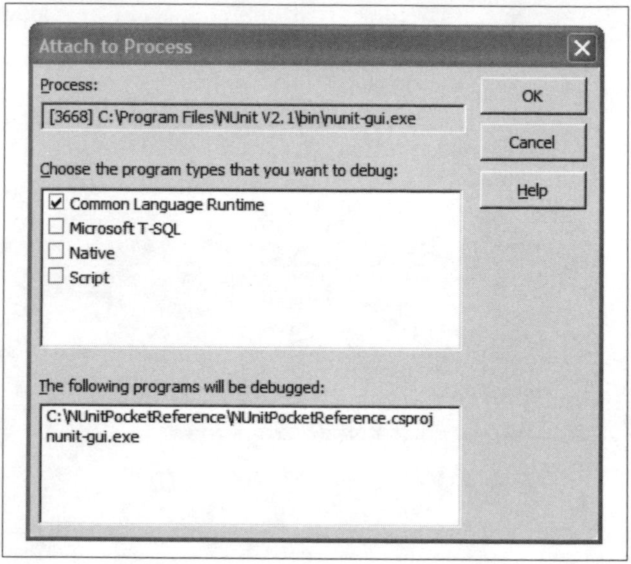

Figure 24. An Attach to Process dialog

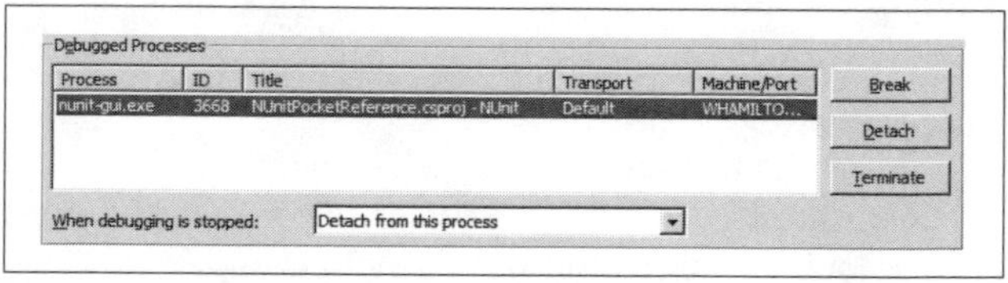

Figure 25. A Debugged Processes dialog

7. Once you have finished debugging, use one of the following techniques to detach debugging:

   a. Select Debug→Stop Debugging from the Visual Studio .NET IDE menu.

   b. Close the NUnit GUI.

   c. Select Debug→Processes from the Visual Studio .NET IDE menu. Select the *nunit-gui.exe process* from the Debug Processes window and click the Detach button.

Testing with Mock Objects

Mock objects simulate real-world objects that are external to your application. During development and testing, mock objects let you isolate your application from objects in the outside world with which your application would normally collaborate. Eliminating reliance on this external code leaves only the code that you need to test.

Mock objects:

- Offer better control when unit testing because you have complete control of the mock object.
- Improve test performance dramatically by replacing slow external dependencies.
- Simplify testing by letting you easily simulate states that are difficult or time-consuming to reproduce in the outside world.
- Raise any type of exception on demand, allowing you to test these conditions in a single test cycle.

The downside of mock objects is the effort required to identify and program their behavior to accurately simulate the behavior of the real-world object. Fortunately, as the use and popularity of mock objects increases, libraries of reusable mock objects are becoming available that might meet your requirements.

To use mock objects for testing, you must design an interface for the real-world object and implement that interface for both test and production code. Using an interface to represent the object allows you to use the mock object in debug code and the real object in production code.

NUnit 2.2 adds a lightweight mock object facility that allows you to:

- Dynamically create a mock implementation of any interface or marshal by reference class.
- Set the order in which methods are called and specify which methods are not to be called.

- Specify return values for specific or arbitrary sets of arguments.
- Verify that expected actions occurred.

The NUnit mock objects were developed primarily to support the testing of NUnit and are not meant to replace one of the full-featured mock object frameworks available for .NET such as NMock. For more information about mock objects and a list of available mock object frameworks, visit *http://mockobjects.com*.

Compatibility

This section describes how to run tests created in older versions of NUnit using NUnit 2.2 and highlights the most significant changes made in the last two releases of NUnit.

Using NUnit 2.1 Tests with NUnit 2.2

To run NUnit 2.1 tests with NUnit 2.2, recompile the tests using the NUnit 2.2 nunit.framework assembly. You might also need to add a reference to the nunit.core assembly if you are using core types.

Using NUnit 2.0 Tests with NUnit 2.2

There are two options for running NUnit 2.0 tests with NUnit 2.2. The first option is to upgrade the 2.0 tests and recompile the test assemblies using the new nunit.framework assembly.

TIP

The NUnit 2.2 documentation states that the Assertion class is deprecated and marked obsolete. Although not necessary, you might want to convert all assertions to use the new Assert class to ensure compatibility with future versions of NUnit.

The second option allows you to run NUnit 2.0 tests with NUnit 2.2 without changing the NUnit 2.0 tests. Create the appropriate binding redirect in the test runner configuration file (*nunit-gui.exe.config* or *nunit-console.exe.config*). The *nunit20under21.config* file in the *src* subdirectory of the NUnit 2.2 installation directory has the required redirect in the `bindingRedirect` element and can be used as is or as a template.

Upgrading from NUnit 1.x to 2.2

You cannot run NUnit 1.x tests using NUnit 2.2—the only option is to upgrade the Version 1.x tests. The following points outline the changes you must make to the NUnit 1.x test code:

- In the test source code, remove the constructor with the string argument that inherits from the `TestCase` class. The class must have a default constructor or no constructor (which implicitly generates the default constructor).

- In the test source code, update the reference to the NUnit 1.x framework with the NUnit 2.2 framework *nunit.framework.dll* assembly.

- The `Suite` property is no longer used. Replace any occurrences with the `[Suite]` attribute or use namespaces to automatically create test suites. If you use the `[Suite]` attribute, you must add the NUnit core types in the *nunit.core.dll* assembly.

- An `AssertionException` exception is now thrown when an assertion fails instead of an `AssertionFailedError` exception. If you have code that traps `AssertionFailedError`, replace the exception with `AssertionException`.

The *money-port* sample in the *src\samples\money-port* subdirectory shows the least amount of work needed to make NUnit 1.x tests run in NUnit 2.2. The *money* sample in the *src\samples\money* subdirectory contains the same tests written using the features of NUnit 2.2.

Changes from NUnit 2.1 to 2.2

The most significant changes in NUnit 2.2 are as follows:

- Separate configuration files to support .NET Framework Versions 1.0 and 1.1 are no longer required. The configuration file contains the binding redirects for Version 1.0 in addition to support for Version 1.1. The configuration file also allows you to select the .NET Framework version when multiple versions are installed.

- The NUnit framework and core types are in separate assemblies—*nunit.framework.dll* and *nunit.core.dll*. The framework contains all types normally referenced by tests. The core contains types used by the test runner console and GUI.

- `Assert.AreEqual` is extended to support comparing arrays with an equal number of elements of the same or compatible types.

- The `[Category]` attribute allows tests and test fixtures to be grouped using string identifiers. Categories can be used to select tests to run or to exclude tests from running.

- The number of assertions executed by each test is added to the XML output file.

- A built-in, lightweight mock object framework has been added.

The following changes are specific to the test runner GUI:

- Checkboxes can optionally be displayed in the tree view and used to select multiple tests to run.

- The name of each test can optionally be displayed in the standard output.

- Command-line switches allow you to load and run a test suite or a specific test fixture from an assembly.

- The number of asserts for each test and the test description have been added to the test properties dialog.

The following changes are specific to the test runner console:

- Command-line switches allow tests to be selected and excluded based on category.
- Command-line switches allow you to display the name of each test in standard output.
- Command-line switches allow you to redirect standard or error output from tests to files.
- A namespace can be specified for the /fixture switch to run all tests within the namespace (test suite).

Changes from NUnit 2.0 to 2.1

The most significant changes in NUnit 2.1 are as follows:

- NUnit can be run against .NET Framework 1.0 or 1.1. Configuration files are supplied for both versions. Installation detects the highest installed version of the .NET Framework and configures for that version.
- You can run tests across multiple assemblies.
- NUnit test projects (XML file with the extension .nunit) can be used to define and persist test configurations containing one or more assemblies.
- The [TestFixtureSetUp] and [TestFixtureTearDown] attributes define code that is run once before and after all tests defined in a test fixture.
- The Assert class replaces the Assertion class.
- Reporting of test failures and exceptions is enhanced.
- NUnit now runs under Windows 98 and Windows ME; changed assemblies cannot automatically be reloaded on these operating systems, however.

The following changes are specific to the test runner GUI:

- The tree view displays updates as tests run.
- A Stop button lets you cancel running tests.

- XML output of the test results can be saved. This format is the same as that generated by the console test runner.

- The complete stack trace is now available for an exception that is raised while trying to load, unload, or run a test.

- Automatic reloading of test assemblies can be turned off.

- You can create and load NUnit test projects from the File menu.

- Visual Studio solution and project files can be opened and can also be added to an NUnit test project.

- When a Visual Studio project or NUnit test project is loaded, you can switch between available build configurations—add, delete, and rename these configurations.

- Individual tests or groups of tests can now be run from the tree view.

- A Properties dialog is available to display information about any test, test fixture, or test suite in the tree view.

- Nested classes in the tree view are displayed using the format OuterClass+InnerClass.

- Tests in the tree view are sorted by name.

- Tests in the tree view execute in the order that they appear.

- You can collapse and expand the tree view from the View menu.

The following changes are specific to the test runner console:

- The command-line parameters have been changed to support loading multiple assemblies, Visual Studio solutions and projects, and NUnit projects. Several new switches are also available.

- In Debug Mode, the console output is sent to the Visual Studio Output window. Clicking a failed test in the Output window opens the test file at the assertion.

- The console output format is improved to facilitate viewing output that is redirected to a file.
- All errors are trapped and an error message is displayed.

Extending NUnit

A number of external tools are available to enhance NUnit or to overcome some of its limitations. Some of the most useful are discussed in the following sections.

Integrating NUnit with Visual Studio .NET

NUnit 2.2 is not fully integrated with Visual Studio .NET—it does not use the Visual Studio extensibility model. You must set up a custom tool entry to launch NUnit from Visual Studio. To do this, select Tools→External Tools from the Visual Studio menu. Click the Add button and complete the dialog as follows:

In this entry...	Type
Title:	NUnit
Command:	C:\Program Files\NUnit 2.2\bin\nunit-gui.exe
Arguments:	$(TargetPath)
Initial Directory:	$(TargetDir

Figure 26 shows the completed dialog.

NUnit will appear under the Tools menu and you can select it to launch NUnit.

NUnit AddIn for Visual Studio .NET

The NUnit AddIn is an open source project that simplifies using the NUnit framework from the Visual Studio .NET IDE by integrating NUnit functionality into the IDE.

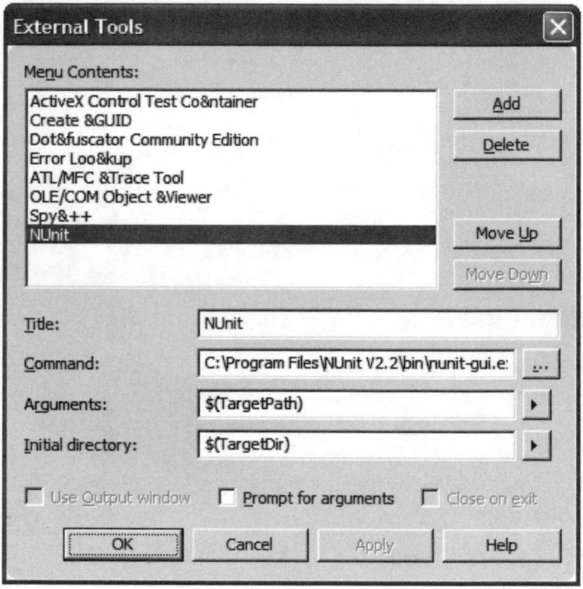

Figure 26. An External Tools dialog for NUnit

Download the latest version of the NUnit AddIn from *http://sourceforge.net/projects/nunitaddin/*. Once you have downloaded the NUnit AddIn Windows Installer File (*.msi* file), double click on it to install—the default installation options work well. The installation does not create any desktop icons or a program folder in the startup menu. The installer does not install any documentation or a *README* file and no documentation is available separately for download from SourceForge.

To run NUnit tests using the Nunit AddIn, open your test project, right-click on the solution or a project in the Solution Explorer window, and select Run Tests from the pop-up menu as shown in Figure 27. The add-in will rebuild the project if necessary.

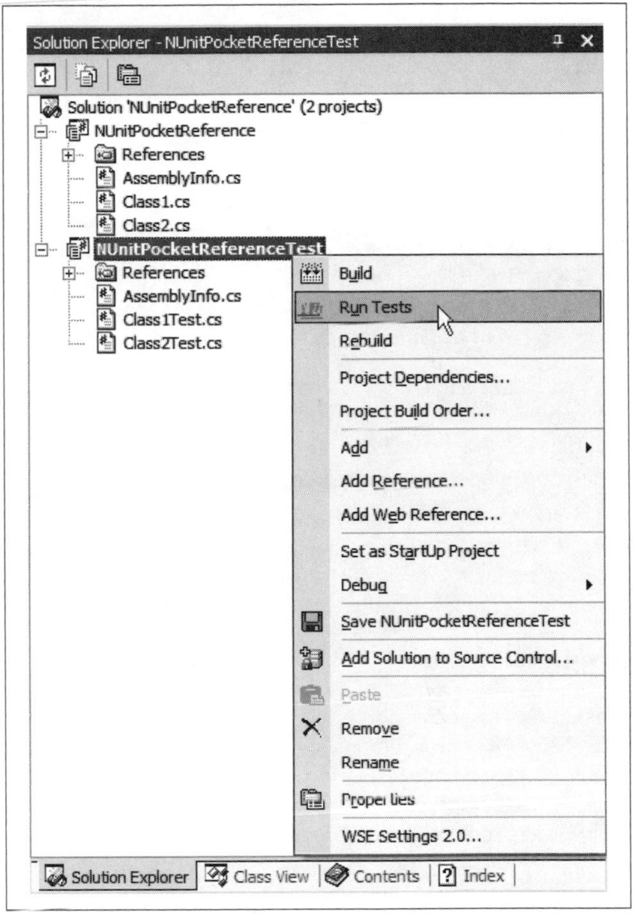

Figure 27. A Solution Explorer window with NUnit Addin

Test results are displayed in the Output window of the Visual Studio .NET IDE as shown in Figure 28.

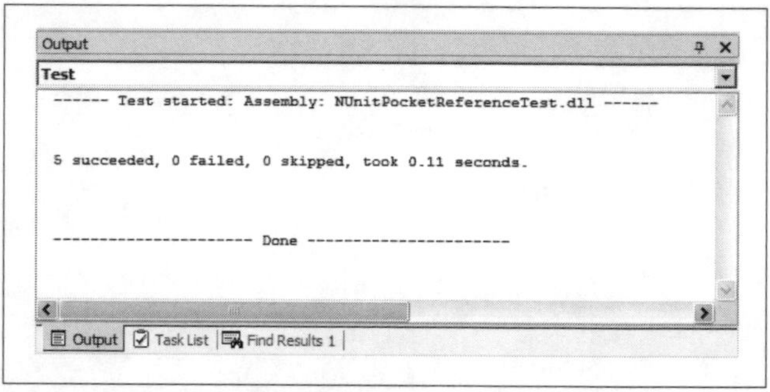

Figure 28. NUnit Addin test results

If a test fails, double-click on the line that failed in the Output window and the cursor will be positioned on the assertion that failed in the class.

The NUnit Addin does not provide all of the functionality of the NUnit GUI—for example, it is not possible to run a single test. However, it does provide a quick way to run tests without leaving the IDE; this is especially convenient for running tests repeatedly during test driven development.

VSNUnit

VSNUnit is an open source integration tool from Relevance LLC (*http://www.relevancellc.com/vsnunit.htm*) that allows you to execute NUnit tests from the Visual Studio .NET IDE. It provides a graphical tree view similar to the output from the GUI test runner within a dockable window.

Download the latest version from *http://sourceforge.net/ project/showfiles.php?group_id=94996*. The download is about 500 KB in size. After downloading the latest version, extract the zip file and run the Windows Installer File (*.msi* file) by double-clicking on it. The default installation options work well, and the installation does not create any desktop items or a program folder in the startup menu, and does not install any documentation except for a brief set of release notes. (There is also a user guide available at the download site under the Docs menu item.)

VSNunit installs a VSNUnit option under the Tools menu in the Visual Studio .NET IDE. Selecting the option in a test project opens a dockable window that controls VSNUnit.

NUnitAsp

NUnitAsp is an open source extension to NUnit that allows you to automatically test ASP.NET pages. NUnitAsp is a class library that lets you download, parse, and manipulate ASP.NET pages. It tests only server-side logic, ignoring client-side code.

The NUnitAsp library handles the details of rendering controls into HTML, simplifying your test code and allowing you to focus on testing functionality. NUnitAsp imitates the browser, letting you test the URL, cookies, and the static HTML output. NUnitAsp provides *tester objects* that imitate the most common ASP.NET controls, letting you manipulate and test the server-side behavior of *.aspx* pages as if you were actually receiving the page. It is easy to add support for other controls. You can use NUnitAsp to easily test complex web sites with pages containing nested controls.

Download the latest version of NUnitAsp from *http:// nunitasp.sourceforge.net/*.

NCover

NCover is a tool that helps measure how much of your code is covered by tests: the number of paths through the code that are actually tested compared to the total amount of code. Measuring code coverage helps identify untested code, improving the overall adequacy of existing tests.

There are two different test coverage tools named NCover. One is available in the GotDotNet Workspaces at *http://www.gotdotnet. com/Community/Workspaces/Workspace.aspx?id=3122ee1a-46e7-*

48a5-857e-aad6739ef6b9. You can download the second from *http://sourceforge.net/projects/ncover/*.

NAnt

NAnt is an open source build tool for .NET. The latest version of NAnt can be downloaded from *http://sourceforge.net/projects/nant/*. It allows you to integrate NUnit testing of your code into your build cycle.

Install NAnt by unzipping the download into a directory—*c:\Program Files\NAnt* is a good choice. Add the *bin* subdirectory to the system path: select Start→Control Panel→System, then the Advanced tab, and finally the Environment Variables button. Add the full path for the *bin* subfolder to the Path system variable, separated from the other entries with a semicolon.

Open a command prompt and type nant -h. If you have installed NAnt correctly, the version, copyright information, and some brief help should be displayed.

The NAnt build file is an XML file containing one project and one or more targets. A target can contain one or more tasks in the build process.

For more information about using NAnt, see the documentation in the *doc* subfolder of the installation directory.

Nantpad

Nantpad is an explorer-style editor for NAnt XML build scripts that makes it easy to both create and edit NAnt scripts. You can download Nantpad from *http://www.nantpad.com*.

Index

We'd like to hear your suggestions for improving our indexes. Send email to
index@oreilly.com.

Related Titles Available from O'Reilly

.NET

.NET and XML

.NET Framework Essentials,
3rd Edition

.NET Windows Forms
in a Nutshell

ADO.NET in a Nutshell

ADO.NET Cookbook

C# Essentials, *2nd Edition*

C# Cookbook

C# Language Pocket Guide

Learning C#

Learning Visual Basic.NET

Mastering Visual Studio.NET

Object Oriented Programming
with Visual Basic .NET

Programming
.NET Components

Programming .NET Security

Programming .NET
Web Services

Programming ASP.NET,
2nd Edition

Programming C#, *3rd Edition*

Programming
Visual Basic .NET, *2nd Edition*

VB.NET Core Classes
in a Nutshell

VB.NET Language
in a Nutshell,
2nd Edition

VB.NET Language
Pocket Reference

Keep in touch with O'Reilly

1. Download examples from our books

To find example files for a book, go to:
www.oreilly.com/catalog

select the book, and follow the "Examples" link.

2. Register your O'Reilly books

Register your book at *register.oreilly.com*

Why register your books? Once you've registered your O'Reilly books you can:

- Win O'Reilly books, T-shirts or discount coupons in our monthly drawing.
- Get special offers available only to registered O'Reilly customers.
- Get catalogs announcing new books (US and UK only).
- Get email notification of new editions of the O'Reilly books you own.

3. Join our email lists

Sign up to get topic-specific email announcements of new books and conferences, special offers, and O'Reilly Network technology newsletters at:
elists.oreilly.com

It's easy to customize your free elists subscription so you'll get exactly the O'Reilly news you want.

4. Get the latest news, tips, and tools
www.oreilly.com

- "Top 100 Sites on the Web"—PC Magazine
- CIO Magazine's Web Business 50 Awards

Our web site contains a library of comprehensive product information (including book excerpts and tables of contents), downloadable software, background articles, interviews with technology leaders, links to relevant sites, book cover art, and more.

5. Work for O'Reilly

Check out our web site for current employment opportunities:
jobs.oreilly.com

6. Contact us

O'Reilly & Associates
1005 Gravenstein Hwy North
Sebastopol, CA 95472 USA

TEL: 707-827-7000 or 800-998-9938
(6am to 5pm PST)

FAX: 707-829-0104

order@oreilly.com
For answers to problems regarding your order or our products.
To place a book order online, visit:
www.oreilly.com/order_new

catalog@oreilly.com
To request a copy of our latest catalog.

booktech@oreilly.com
For book content technical questions or corrections.

corporate@oreilly.com
For educational, library, government, and corporate sales.

proposals@oreilly.com
To submit new book proposals to our editors and product managers.

international@oreilly.com
For information about our international distributors or translation queries. For a list of our distributors outside of North America check out:
international.oreilly.com/distributors.html

adoption@oreilly.com
For information about academic use of O'Reilly books, visit:
academic.oreilly.com

O'REILLY®

Our books are available at most retail and online bookstores.
To order direct: 1-800-998-9938 • *order@oreilly.com* • *www.oreilly.com*
Online editions of most O'Reilly titles are available at *safari.oreilly.com*

A pink tinge flooded

"Having my father sho... to keep you here." She ti... ...um up in a gesture that reminded him of Catherine when she faced the consequences of some misdeed. "But I have to admit I'm grateful."

"Grateful." He felt an ominous calm settle over him. "Grateful that I've been turned into a useless cripple?"

"Better a cripple than a corpse," Hallie retorted.

Jacob stepped away from her. "What makes you so sure I would have gotten killed? I might have come back as an officer. At the very least, I'd know whether I could stand up to the sound of bullets whizzing past me without turning tail and running. I'd know that I'm a man." His tone grew rough. "And everyone else would know it, too."

Hallie spoke in a voice thick with emotion. "I said my prayers were answered, and I meant it, even though I never would have asked for you to be hurt. God really does know what's best, if you'll just let Him be in control instead of trying to figure it all out on your own.

"Why do men have to be so bullheaded and determined to do things their way?" She started to walk away, then looked back over her shoulder. "Don't you know God cares about you, Jacob? He loves you even more than I do." She strode away quickly, leaving Jacob standing alone in stunned silence.

CAROL COX is a native of Arizona whose time is devoted to being a pastor's wife, keeping up with her college-age son's schedule, home schooling her young daughter, and serving as a church pianist, youth worker, and 4-H leader. She loves any activity she can share with her family in addition to her own pursuits in reading, crafts, and local history. She also has had several novels and novellas published. Carol and her family make their home in northern Arizona.

Books by Carol Cox

HEARTSONG PRESENTS
HP264—Journey Toward Home
HP344—The Measure of a Man
HP452—Season of Hope
HP479—Cross My Heart
HP580—Land of Promise
HP592—Refining Fire

Don't miss out on any of our super romances. Write to us at the following address for information on our newest releases and club information.

Heartsong Presents Readers' Service
PO Box 719
Uhrichsville, OH 44683

Or visit www.heartsongpresents.com

Road to Forgiveness

Carol Cox

Heartsong Presents

Many thanks to Terry Schultz, Arizona State Livestock Officer, for answering my questions and giving me some good ideas.

A note from the Author:
I love to hear from my readers! You may correspond with me by writing:

Carol Cox
Author Relations
PO Box 719
Uhrichsville, OH 44683

ISBN 1-59310-542-8

ROAD TO FOREGIVENESS

Our mission is to publish and distribute inspirational products offering exceptional value and biblical encouragement to the masses.

All scripture quotations are taken from the King James Version of the Bible.

All of the characters and events in this book are fictitious. Any resemblance to actual persons, living or dead, or to actual events is purely coincidental.

PRINTED IN THE U.S.A.

Or check out our Web site at www.heartsongpresents.com

one

Tucson, Arizona Territory—March 1898

A cloud of dust mushroomed over the top of the rise ahead. Jacob Garrett spurred his horse up the low slope. Dust didn't billow up like that on its own on a windless day. A shrill whinny mingled with a man's frantic yells, heightening Jacob's sense of urgency.

ॐ

He topped the rise and took in the scene at a glance. A calf lay on its side in the sandy dirt. A rope stretched taut from the calf's neck to the saddle horn of a sweat-soaked dun who backpedaled, eyes wide and nostrils flaring, putting all his effort into breaking away from the dead weight that anchored him to the spot.

On the opposite side of the calf, a cow shook her horns and pawed another puff of powder-fine dust into the air. A man crouched behind the calf, using it as a living shield between himself and the cow. She made a quick sidestep to the right, then the left, as if sizing up her intended target.

Jacob jerked his rope from his saddle and began to build a loop while he circled behind the threatening animal. With a quick flip of his wrist, he pitched the loop and turned his horse as the rope caught the cow's right hind leg. He spurred his horse forward and jerked the cow off her feet.

The steel-dust gelding pulled back to keep tension on the rope, and Jacob sprang from the saddle and hurried over to

5

kneel on the cow's neck.

"Afternoon, Gus." He nodded to the gray-haired rancher, on his feet now and slapping the dust off his chaps. "If there's something you needed to do to that calf, you'd better do it quick, while I have his mama on the ground."

"I already finished doctoring him." Gus yanked the piggin' string loose. The little calf staggered to his feet and trotted over to his mother. "All I needed to do was smear some salve on a cut to keep the flies off. I was ready to let him up when she pitched her fit. No patience at all. Ain't that just like a woman?"

"If you wouldn't mind pulling my rope off her leg, I'd like to get up pretty soon. She's getting a mite testy."

Gus hobbled over to the cow and loosened the rope. "Give me a minute to get back on my horse, will you? I'm not as spry as I used to be."

Jacob held the struggling animal's head while Gus mounted the dun, then jumped back and raced for his own saddle.

The cow scrambled to her feet and gave them a belligerent glare before checking her calf for signs of ill-treatment.

"Whew!" The grizzled rancher pulled a dark blue bandanna from his hip pocket and swiped his forehead. "That was closer than I care to come to eternity anytime soon. Glad you happened along when you did."

"Glad I could save you from being stomped into the dirt. I was just out riding; I didn't expect to get a chance to play hero."

Gus grinned and settled his hat on his brow. "Want to come back to the house for supper? Martha's fixing your favorite tonight."

"I wish I could, but I need to talk something over with my folks."

Gus raised a white tuft of an eyebrow. "It must be something pretty important to lure you away from Martha's pot roast."

"You could say that." Jacob stared off toward the Rincon Mountains. He might as well confide in Gus, after all the man had done for him. He slid an envelope from his vest pocket. The letter felt unaccountably heavy in his hands. "I got this today."

Gus studied him but said nothing.

"It's from Dan O'Roarke. Remember him?"

"O'Roarke? Isn't that the fellow from up Prescott way? The one you brought by my place last year?"

"That's him. The one with the ranch up near Coyote Springs. I've known him all my life. His parents and mine have been friends for years." Jacob tapped the envelope on his saddle horn. "He's asked me to come up and work for him."

Gus's pale blue eyes gleamed. "That'll be a fine opportunity for you. Even if it means I'll be losing your help. I have to admit I've gotten kinda used to you coming around every now and then."

"If you hadn't taken me under your wing when I was a green kid, I wouldn't have known a heifer from a steer. You taught me everything I know about livestock." Jacob's voice thickened. "As a matter of fact, knowing I learned from you is what made Dan decide I knew enough about working stock to be a help instead of a hindrance."

"I'd have made you the same kind of offer if I thought you'd take me up on it." Gus leveled a knowing look at Jacob. "But I have a feeling your heart isn't set on staying around Tucson."

Jacob grunted assent. "You're right about that. My folks don't know it yet, though." He slid his thumb along the edge of the envelope. "I guess it's time I told them."

Jacob listened to the saddle leather creak in time with his horse's footsteps as the steel-dust ambled along. He resisted the impulse to touch his heels to the gelding's flanks and urge him into a lope. Instead, he settled back in his saddle and took note of the desert that stretched out for miles around him.

Some might describe the balmy Tucson weather as paradise on this early spring day. But this was March. In another couple of months, the temperatures would soar up to a hundred degrees and more, making it seem less like paradise and more like living next to the blast furnaces at one of his father's mines.

"I have learned, in whatsoever state I am, therewith to be content." The verse from the fourth chapter of Philippians sprang into his mind without warning. The apostle Paul had found contentment, even in the midst of persecution and imprisonment. Why couldn't he do the same? His parents could certainly make the same statement.

How had they managed to adjust to the searing heat after spending their early years in the cool forestlands of Colorado and northern Arizona? Jacob never could figure that out. But adapt they had. They both loved it here. He rocked along, taking note of the different types of cactus within his view: the saguaro, the deceptively fuzzy-looking cholla, the spindly ocotillo. *Everything around here has thorns.* But his mother would find beauty in each one, and because she did, his father would see the beauty, too.

Jacob appreciated the majesty of his surroundings when his mother pointed them out to him, but in his eyes the landscape rolled out as a vast barrenness, something like the wasteland his soul had become of late. For twenty-five years, he'd tried to live the life his parents had built up and loved. But that was their life, not his. More and more, he knew he needed a change. Now he just had to convince them of that.

The house and barn came into view all too soon. On any other day, the sight would have calmed his spirit. Today, though, he carried news that made him feel like a traitor.

Jacob took his time unsaddling his gelding, brushing him down, and tossing him some hay. Cap munched greedily at the brittle green stems. Long before Jacob was ready, he heard the call for supper.

"Better get this over with," he told Cap. The steel-dust pulled at another mouthful of hay. Jacob slapped him gently on the withers and turned toward the house with a twinge of envy. At least one of them would enjoy their supper tonight.

❧

"Seconds, dear?" Jacob's mother held out the steaming platter of roast chicken.

Jacob served himself, then passed the dish to his father at the head of the table. Truth be told, he had no interest in a second helping of chicken. Or string beans or even some of his mother's fluffy rolls. But the longer he dragged out the meal, the longer he could put off springing his news.

His father helped himself and set the platter on the table. "Everyone in town seemed to be talking about the situation in Cuba today. If you can believe what's in the newspaper, those people down there are being grievously mistreated by the Spanish."

His mother's fork clinked against her plate. "Is there more talk of war with Spain? President Cleveland always insisted that would never happen."

"True enough," his father agreed. "But McKinley is being pressured to take a different stance. I'd say it's only a matter of time."

Jacob chewed slowly, grateful for the diversion. He dawdled as long as he could before lifting the last bite to his mouth.

His father took a swallow of water and leaned back in his chair. "So what's on your mind, Son?"

Jacob nearly choked on his chicken. He reached for his water tumbler and took a hearty swig to help the bite go down, then coughed into his napkin until he recaptured his breath.

He shot a rueful smile toward his father. "I guess there's no point in asking what you mean, is there?"

Jenny Garrett looked at her son and gave a soft chuckle. "We've raised two children, Jacob. We know the signs. And I once owned a restaurant, remember? Of all the meals I served, I never once saw anyone trying to sop up gravy with his green beans until tonight. I'd second your father's guess that your mind is somewhere else."

Jacob held up his hands. "All right, I give up. Guilty as charged. I have something to say, and I've been trying to figure out how to break it to you. I thought I was keeping a pretty good poker face. Evidently, I didn't do such a good job of it."

He drew a deep breath and removed the envelope from his pocket. Pulling a sheet of paper from the envelope, he spread the letter out on the table. "I got this today. From Dan O'Roarke."

His mother clapped her hands. "How nice. Did he say anything about his parents? We haven't heard from Elizabeth and Michael in ages."

Jacob cleared his throat. "Actually it's more than just a friendly letter. Dan asked if I wanted to come work for him."

His mother beamed. "I think that's a fine idea. Don't you, Andrew? You'll enjoy spending the summer up there. I know how you hate the Tucson heat."

"Actually, Mother, it would be more than just this summer."

She studied him more closely and seemed to read something in his expression. "You mean you're thinking of leaving here for good?"

Here it comes. Jacob took a deep breath and plunged ahead. "I've done my best with every job Dad's given me to do in the mines, and I've tried to make a go of it."

A puzzled look shadowed his father's face. "You've done far more than try. You've learned the business well. As a matter of fact, I've been gearing up to put you in as manager of the new copper mine we'll be opening down by Bisbee. I hope you don't think I haven't been pleased with your work."

"No, Dad. That isn't it at all." He clenched his fists under the table. They weren't going to like what he had to say, not one bit. "I don't want to spend the rest of my life looking for ore in the desert. That isn't where my heart lies. I grew up hearing the stories about how you and Mother and Red Dwyer started the Silver Crown and built it up into the mining company you have today. How finding a strike is one of the most exciting things in the world for you." He shook his head, feeling like the worst kind of deserter. "But that isn't the way I'm made. I get that same feeling spending my days outside on horseback, not on the business end of a pick."

His father nodded slowly. "I can understand that, Son. If ranching is what you want to do, your mother and I would be happy to set you up with your own place down here."

"I'm sorry, Dad. If I thought it would work, I'd jump at the chance. But there's something in my soul that needs trees instead of cactus, green hills instead of brown desert. And I really want the opportunity to get out on my own and find out what I'm made of."

His mother and father exchanged a glance full of meaning. After a long silence, his mother sighed. "We went our own way; we can't very well ask him not to, can we?"

"That's what I love about you, Jenny. You always seem to know what I'm thinking." Jacob's father turned to him. "We know you'll do your best, Son. I believe God has some mighty plans for you. You need to go out and discover what they are." He gripped Jacob's hand in a firm clasp. "You have our blessing. And you know there will always be a place for you if you ever decide to come back here."

Jacob returned his father's grip, grateful beyond measure for their support. "Thank you. Both of you. I'll have to hurry to pull everything together in time. Dan wants me up there next week."

two

Lonesome Valley, Arizona Territory

"Hallie! Where are you, girl?" Burke Evans's bellow broke the stillness of the spring afternoon.

Hallie Evans scrambled down from her perch on the water tank catwalk and hurried toward the weathered ranch house. When her father roared like that, he expected immediate response.

Inside, she paused a moment to smooth her skirt and give her eyes time to adjust to the relative dimness. "I'm here, Pa."

Her father's heavy footsteps clumped across the plank floor. "Edgar Wilson stopped by on his way home from Prescott. Get us some coffee, would you?"

"I'll be right there." A glance out the front window showed her Mr. Wilson's sorrel mount tethered to the rail. *How did I miss hearing him ride up?* She ducked into the kitchen, where she checked the contents of the coffeepot on the back of the stove. Her father insisted on having a steady supply of coffee at the ready throughout the day. If he hadn't gotten into too much of it since lunch. . . Good, the pot was still nearly full.

Hallie set the coffeepot and two mugs on a tray, glad she wouldn't have to keep the men waiting. Edgar Wilson had even less patience than her father. Two short-tempered men in need of coffee would not make for a pleasant afternoon. For good measure, she opened the pie safe and added two servings of dried apple pie to the tray. From the ominous tone

13

of the voices rumbling from the front room, those two could use all the sweetening up she could give them.

"Where have they gone, and who's taking them? That's what I want to know." Wilson's harsh words rolled over Hallie when she pushed through the swinging door. The neighboring rancher stood before the empty fireplace, every line of his bearing shouting outrage.

"Here's your coffee." Hallie set the tray down on a low table and slipped back through the swinging door, then through the kitchen, and back outside. It wasn't wise to be around when Wilson and her father got started. She propped the back door open so she could hear if he should call her again. A week ago, they would have had the house shut tight against the late winter chill, but the past few days brought warmer, almost balmy weather. The fresh air would help chase away the stuffiness after being closed up for months.

How far could she go and still be within earshot? The catwalk beckoned, her favorite spot from which she could view the length of Lonesome Valley like a princess from her high tower. But if her father called, it would just mean rushing down the ladder again. She settled for dragging a sturdy chair across the packed earth and setting it beneath the raised platform the tank sat on. That would still provide a degree of privacy and relief from the sun's glare, but she could jump and run as soon as her father summoned her.

Despite his brusque, heavy-handed ways, she loved him dearly. Since her mother's death eight years before, it had just been the two of them. Some fathers might have lamented being saddled with a lone daughter, but not hers. The lack of a son never seemed to bother Burke Evans. If anything, he seemed to treasure their relationship as much as she did.

Hallie drew her feet up onto the wooden seat and folded her

arms atop her knees. Resting her chin on her arms, she stared out across the rolling valley. Fawn-colored hills stretched out in a broad sweep to the mountains in the near distance, Mingus Mountain to the east, the Bradshaws to the south. Their solid bulk surrounded her valley like a pair of mighty arms, shielding the range her father had claimed as his own— the Broken Box Ranch, the only home she had ever known.

This land was a part of her, its texture intimately woven into the very fiber of her being. For as long as she could remember, she had watched its many moods unfold. And for as long as she could remember, its familiarity never failed to calm her, to fill her with a sense of peace and satisfaction.

Her land. Her home. And yet. . .

A vague longing surfaced, one that filled her consciousness more and more often of late. Why didn't the majestic panorama provide the same satisfaction as before? What had changed? It couldn't be her beloved mountains. Their solid bulk stood just as imposingly as it had for untold centuries. The foothills, the valley—they remained the same as they had always been. No, if there was a difference, it must be within her.

A soft sigh escaped her lips. "What's the matter with me?"

A shadow fell across her lap and a voice grated near her ear. "Not a thing that I can see."

Hallie started and whipped her head around to see who had invaded her private moment. All her peaceful feelings scattered to the winds like dandelion fluff at the sight of Pete Edwards, her father's top hand, standing behind her. She fought to untangle her legs from her skirt and struggled to her feet.

Pete watched her with a slow smile that made her bring her hand to her neckline to make sure the buttons of her bodice were fastened. He spread his legs wide apart in a bold stance and folded his beefy arms, obviously enjoying her discomfort. "Need a hand?"

"No, thank you." Hallie looked at Pete with distaste. With his stocky build and self-assured air, he could almost pass for a younger version of her father. Their demeanor, though, could not have been more different. Her father's expression often looked as if it had been carved from a block of granite, but Hallie never doubted the depth of his love for her. Pete, on the other hand, generally sported a smile, but it held all the warmth of a coyote's grin when eyeing a cottontail.

Right now his smile set warning bells off inside her head. "Excuse me. I need to go inside now." She angled to her left, intending to give Pete a wide berth.

He took a step to his right and blocked her way. "You don't have to be coy, Hallie. I know you like me."

Hallie caught herself in midstride and shifted to the right. Pete followed suit. "Darlin', if you want to dance with me, just say the word."

Hallie flushed, and he let out a low rumble of a laugh. She felt the sting of tears.

Pete's broad face split in one of his coyote smiles. "Face it, Hallie. You can't get away from me unless I let you. You might as well give up and admit how you feel about me."

I can't tell you what I think of you, Pete Edwards. My mother raised me to be a lady. Hallie's glance darted from Pete to the kitchen door. Even listening to her father and Edgar Wilson haranguing would be better than this. "Leave me alone, Pete."

In answer, he spread his arms wide and took a step toward her. Hallie darted toward the left, then scurried to the right. The abrupt change in direction caught Pete off guard, and she slipped past him.

Her moccasins churned up puffs of dust as she raced toward the house. Behind her, Pete's taunting voice rang clear: "You can run away this time, but there'll be another. I know where to find you when I want you."

Hallie slammed the kitchen door shut and bolted it behind her. Wrapping her arms around her waist, she slumped to the floor and bent her head to her knees. "Thank You, Jesus."

With no thought but seeking the safety of her father's presence, she jumped to her feet and hurried to the front room, only then remembering they had a visitor. To her relief, Edgar Wilson stood on the porch, taking his leave.

"I'm telling you, Burke, this is a bad business." The lean rancher's eyes flashed. "We can't take it lying down."

Her father pounded his fist into his palm. "I don't intend to. If these fellows keep messing with me, they're in big trouble. Count on it." He stepped back into the doorway. A grim expression hardened his features.

Hallie held herself in check until he closed the door, then ran to him. "I need to talk to you."

Her father turned away from the door and looked at her. "It's a good thing Wilson stopped by."

"Pa, please. I don't know what to do."

Her father rubbed the back of his neck with a calloused hand. "I don't, either. It turns out I'm not alone. Wilson's been losing cattle, too."

"This is getting out of hand—"

"I know. I kept trying to convince myself it was due to natural causes—a mountain lion, maybe. But it doesn't look like that anymore. We never came across any carcasses, for one thing. And with stock going missing from both our places. . ." He shook his head slowly.

"It's getting so I'm afraid to go outside the house anymore."

Her father set his mouth in a grim line. "If someone's steal-ing cattle, I can tell you one thing: They're going to pay for it." He raised a meaty fist and slammed it against the wall. The window glass rattled in its frame. "I haven't spent twenty years building up this ranch to hand the profits over to some no-account too lazy to do an honest day's work."

Hallie grabbed his arm and hung on tight. "Dad, it's about Pete."

Her father's head jerked around. "Pete? What are you talk-ing about?"

She finally had his attention. The relief made her weak. "He keeps waylaying me whenever he catches me outside. I've asked him to leave me alone—more than once—but he won't. Could you talk to him, maybe tell him to keep his distance? I know he'll listen to you."

Her father bristled. His eyes took on a glint that made Hallie take a quick step back. "What do you mean, keep his distance? Has he touched you?"

"No, nothing like that. He just. . .comes up on me and talks to me. No matter what I tell him, he won't stay away. I really need your help, Pa."

Her father's bark of laughter grated on her ears. "So you've finally come out of your dream world long enough to realize you're a grown woman now." His tone softened, and he patted her arm awkwardly. "You're a fine-looking girl, Hallie. You take after your mother that way. You can't blame Pete. He'd be less than a man if he didn't notice. Don't take on about it. It's nothing serious."

The forbidding expression returned to his face, and he pointed a meaty finger at her. "Don't you go getting all uppity and running off my best hand, do you hear me? Pete knows nearly as much about raising cattle as I do, and with the problems I'm facing now, I need his help more than ever."

Hallie's jaw sagged. "But Pa—"

"Maybe I've made a mistake, letting you have the run of the range. I don't need you being out there causing problems and getting my men all stirred up."

"Pa!"

Burke strode off. "I'll be in my office. Call me when supper's ready."

Hallie stared after him, a feeling of helplessness spreading through her. A leaden weight settled in her chest. Choking back the tears that threatened to flood her eyes, she went to the kitchen to start the evening meal.

She pulled a slab of meat from the cooling box and began to cut it into chunks for stew. Her earlier discontent stirred within her again, a longing for something she couldn't define.

One thing she knew beyond a doubt: Whatever she was longing for, it had nothing to do with Pete Edwards.

three

Jacob squinted and tipped his hat brim farther down over his eyes. After nearly a week on the trail, he felt more than ready for the trip to end. Time to get down to business and put some of his dreams into action.

He checked the sun's position. If he hurried, he ought to be stepping up onto Dan's front porch just in time for supper. And if Amy was still as good a cook as he remembered, that would be a goal worth shooting for. He grinned and tapped the horse's flanks with his heels to push him into a trot down the length of Lonesome Valley toward Coyote Springs.

Lonesome Valley. The name suited the place, he'd always thought. A wide, rolling plain flanked by mountains on three sides. Lush grass waved in the light breeze, in stark contrast to the desert terrain he'd climbed out of the day before. Buckbrush and manzanita scattered across the valley floor, giving way to the cedars that covered the foothills and the pines crowning Mingus Mountain. This land promised a host of surprises, enough that it would take years to discover them all. Spending years—or the rest of his life—in this spot would suit him just fine.

Clouds hung low in the sky, forming a backdrop for the mountains. Where the clouds broke, golden light splashed over the ground below, as if an artist had dabbed it with a paint-laden brush.

Jacob reined his mount to the right, veering off the main road and heading toward Dan's ranch. The steel-dust pricked up his ears, seeming to sense his rider's eagerness to reach their destination. "We're almost there, boy." Jacob patted the horse's neck. "Just a few more miles and it's a rubdown and some oats for you." *And a new life for me.*

An hour later, he spotted a herd of cows dotting the hillside. He stopped to give his horse a rest under the only tree in the area while he looked them over. *A fine-looking bunch*, he thought. They'd wintered well, with a full contingent of wobbly-legged newborn calves at their sides. Off to the right, a massive white-faced bull pawed the earth, showering his red coat with dust.

Jacob pursed his lips in a soft whistle. Dan's letter said he intended to improve the quality of his stock. If he'd gone to the expense of bringing in a registered Hereford bull to build up the strain, he meant business.

Excitement flickered through him. Big things were happening here, and he would be a part of bringing them to life. He leaned forward and stroked his horse's neck. "Rested up, boy? Let's go get some dinner."

"Uncle Jacob?"

The voice seemed to come out of thin air. Jacob twisted from side to side in his saddle, looking for its source.

"Up here," the voice called.

He craned his neck to look up into the branches of the alligator juniper. Dusty boots, spindly legs, and a flounce of skirt dangled six feet above his head. Atop the calico dress, he spotted a crown of coppery-gold curls. Jacob felt his eyes bulge. "Catherine?"

"Uh-huh." Dan O'Roarke's eight-year-old daughter began to pick her way down from limb to limb. When she reached his level, she crouched on a branch and looked him in the eye. "Will you give me a ride home?"

"Why, sure." Jacob reached out and pulled the little girl into his arms, then scooted back onto the cantle to make room for her in front of him.

Catherine snuggled back against him as though they were getting ready to set out on a pleasure ride. "Thanks, Uncle Jacob. I was getting tired of sitting up there. My legs were starting to get stiff."

Jacob shook his head. "How did you get up there in the first place?"

"I climbed."

"I meant, what were you doing up there?"

"Oh, that. I got off my horse to. . .well, you know." She giggled and pointed off toward a clump of nearby bushes. "And then that ol' bull started pawing the ground and my horse spooked and took off and I had to climb the tree to get away from the bull."

"He didn't come after you, did he?"

"Not until I hit him with a rock. I thought it would make him go away. It didn't. That's when I decided I'd be better off up in the tree."

Jacob's blood ran cold at the thought of what a two-thousand-pound bull could do to a little girl. He touched Cap's flanks with his spurs and urged him into an easy canter. Another thought came to mind. "How far are we from the house, anyway? It's at least half a mile, isn't it?"

"I guess so." Catherine's casual air would have done credit to an actress on stage.

"You guess so? What's a little thing like you doing so far away from home by herself?"

Catherine adopted a haughty tone. "I was fine until that bull came along. I can go wherever I want."

Jacob kept his opinions to himself as they rode on. When

they neared the house, a small figure bounded off the porch and ran to meet them. Jacob recognized Catherine's brother, Benjamin.

"Where have you been?" the boy demanded. Then he added, "Hi, Uncle Jacob."

"Out riding." Catherine slid down off Cap's back and rearranged her clothing, then strolled off toward the back of the house.

Benjamin hurried to catch up to her. "Your horse came back an hour ago."

"I found her out where the cows are grazing," Jacob called. "About half a mile down the road."

Ben's eyes rounded. "Half a mile! Boy, are you going to catch it when Ma and Pa find out."

"Am not."

"Are, too."

"Am not!"

"Are, too!"

Their voices trailed off as they rounded the corner of the house. A few moments later, a smiling woman rushed out onto the porch, her hands outstretched in welcome. "Jacob! Catherine told me you just arrived. Welcome to the T Bar."

Jacob dismounted and stretched. "It's good to be here. Is Dan around?"

"I'm expecting him any minute. Supper is almost ready, so why don't you take care of your horse and wash the trail dust off? He ought to be here by the time you're finished." She clasped her hands together. "I can't tell you how excited we are to have you here. Dan's been talking about nothing else all week."

A weight lifted off Jacob's shoulders. He was home. He hurried to the barn and pulled Cap's saddle off, then brushed him down and settled him in a stall with a manger full of hay. After sluicing water from the rain barrel over his arms, face, and neck, he headed for the house.

Dan opened the door before Jacob reached the top of the porch steps and welcomed him with a bear hug. "Good to see you. Come on in. Amy has supper on the table."

The scent of steak and fresh-baked bread drew him toward the dining room where Amy sat, flanked by Benjamin and Catherine. "Have a seat and make yourself at home. I hope you enjoy the meal."

After Dan said grace, Jacob made quick work of his dinner. Amy's cooking was every bit as good as he remembered.

"Are you ready to start work in the morning?" Dan asked.

"You bet. What do you want me to do first? I'm ready to tackle whatever you want."

"I thought I'd take you around and show you the water holes and lay out the plans I have for this place." Dan's face took on a look of pride. "Wait until you see Imbroglio."

"Imbrolly-who?"

Everyone at the table laughed. "Alistair's Crimson Imbroglio. My new bull. He's a papered Hereford. I had him shipped in from back East."

Jacob chewed slowly, avoiding Catherine's pleading gaze. "I ran across him on the way in. He's a fine specimen, all right. He ought to do a good job for you."

Dan tilted his head. "Why do I get the feeling you're trying not to tell me something?"

Catherine pushed back her chair. "May I be excused, Mama?"

Amy frowned. "Yes, you may. But please don't interrupt. Go on, Jacob."

Both the children sidled toward the door. Jacob tried to

shake off the feeling he was being marked as an informant.

"I'm not the only one who encountered Imbroglio this afternoon. I found your daughter perched up in a tree about fifty yards away from him on my way in."

"Catherine?" Dan's face darkened. "Catherine Elizabeth O'Roarke, what were you doing out around those cows?"

The only answer was the sound of feet scuttling across the floor and Benjamin's voice: "Told you! You really will catch it."

"Will not."

"Will, too."

"Will not!"

Amy pressed her hands against her cheeks and gave Jacob an apologetic smile. "I'm sorry. This is no way to welcome you on your first night here."

Jacob chuckled. "Don't give it a second thought. They sound just like Emma and I did at that age. It makes me feel right at home. I'm just sorry for getting Catherine in trouble. I hate to be a tattletale."

"That child!" Amy spread her hands wide. "I don't know what we're going to do with her. She's always into something."

"She needs a strong hand, that's for sure." Dan arched his eyebrows at his wife.

Jacob decided it was time to change the subject. "She's sure growing up to be a cute one, though. Where did she get all that red-gold hair?"

"That came from my aunt Carrie," Dan replied. "According to my mother, Catherine looks exactly like her younger sister."

"But that mind of her own comes straight from your mother," Amy noted.

"True enough," Dan agreed. "But Mother isn't quite so quick to point that out." He and Amy both sputtered with laughter.

Jacob joined them, feeling more relaxed than he had in

months. A yawn stretched his lips wide, and he clapped his hand over his mouth. "I guess I'm farther gone than I thought." He pushed his chair back. "Where do you want me to stow my gear?"

"You're sleeping in the guest room tonight," Dan told him. He held up his hand when Jacob started to protest. "You can move out to the bunkhouse tomorrow, if you've a mind to, but tonight you're our guest, not an employee."

Jacob hesitated. Special privileges like sleeping in the boss's house wouldn't win him any points with the other hands. But after nights of lying on the hard ground, his weary body craved the thought of sleeping on a real mattress. He nodded and followed Dan down the hallway. He could get down to business tomorrow.

❧

"Look out! She's going under."

"Get a rope on her, Jacob."

Jacob pushed Cap as close as he dared to the edge of the mud around the water hole. He picked his way carefully, not wanting to get bogged down in the same clinging mire that held the cow captive.

He swung the loop around his head. Cap sidestepped to pull loose from the muck at the same instant Jacob released the rope. The loop fell short of the cow by a yard.

Jacob felt himself redden. Some asset he'd be to the T Bar, if he couldn't do a simple thing like roping a cow when her life was in danger. No telling how long she'd been struggling there. Long enough, at any rate, to get herself bogged down clear up to her belly with no means of getting out on her own. Long enough to wear herself out to the point she could barely hold her head above water level. Off to the side, her calf bawled plaintively.

If they didn't get her out soon, she would drown. Jacob backed his horse out to come in at a better angle. He looked up in time to see Eb Landrum's rope snake out in a graceful arc and settle over the exhausted cow's horns. Eb's horse dug in and leaned back on its haunches, holding the rope taut.

I should have been able to catch her. Jacob shook off his disgust and sprang from his saddle to wade across the mud. The bog pulled at his boots, sucking them deeper into the muck with every labored step. *Next thing you know, they'll have to lasso me to pull me out.*

The cow bellowed, a high-pitched sound that ended on a wheezing note. If they didn't get her out fast, she'd be a goner. Her calf bawled back at her and dashed back and forth. The cow's eyes rolled back until only the whites showed. Despite Eb's efforts, her nose hovered perilously near the water. *If I don't get to her soon. . .*

Jacob gave a lunge that placed him near the animal's head. "Hang on, girl. We're going to get you out of here." He reached for the trailing loop end of his rope and used both arms to shove it down into the miry clay and work it around the cow's belly. By the time he brought the loop up on the far side of the cow, he felt like his shoulders were on fire.

He dragged the free end of the rope over to him and threaded it through the loop, then tossed the end back to Buster, the other cowhand working with them. With two horses pulling and Jacob pushing, they managed to haul the cow back to solid ground.

Jacob staggered out of the mess and pulled both ropes off while she lay on the ground, panting. Her baby trotted over to her and nosed her face. The tired cow lifted her head and nuzzled back.

"Think she's going to be okay?" Jacob asked.

"She should be," Eb replied. "We'll give her a few minutes to catch her second wind, then we'll haze her over to another water hole so she won't get stuck here again."

Buster cackled. "Have you taken a look at yourself? I've seen hogs that looked cleaner than you."

Jacob looked down at his clothes. His denim pants were totally covered with the slimy goo; his shirt hadn't fared any better. He pulled off his hat and raked his fingers through his hair. From the feel of it, there wasn't an inch of him that wasn't coated with mud.

"Look on the bright side," Buster chortled. "With all that mud on you, you won't have to worry about the flies."

Jacob chuckled and scooped a handful of sludge off his rope. "The things we go through for these knot-headed bovines."

Eb coiled his own muddy rope and hung it over his saddle horn. "Don't let it get to you. You did a fine job out there. I wish Dan had been here to see it. He did a smart thing when he hired you on."

Jacob trudged over to Cap, feeling some of his chagrin roll away. He started to put his foot in the stirrup, then realized he was going to get his saddle caked with mud. But his only option would be to walk. He swung his sore body into the saddle. At least it wasn't as bad as the caliche clay they had around Tucson. This stuff just might powder off when it dried instead of turning to cement.

Eb rode up beside him. "Roundup starts next week. It'll give you a chance to meet some more of the folks around here." He winked. "Dan better hope the other ranchers don't try to lure you away when they see how good you are."

Jacob ducked his head to hide his pleasure. "I couldn't do any of this if it hadn't been for an old rancher in Tucson who took me under his wing." His mind trailed back to Gus's spread. He knew the place so well, he could picture every detail. Right about now the cactus would be blooming and the days would be warm and pleasant.

A spring breeze kissed his mud-smeared cheek. Jacob drew in a breath of pine-scented air. But down in Tucson the heat would just be beginning to build up. He remembered all too many summer days when a man couldn't go outside without feeling like the sun was going to cook his brains.

He grinned and felt the drying mud on his face crack. Oh, yes. He'd made the right choice when he decided to take Dan up on his offer.

four

Hallie leaned against the porch rail and watched her father ride up. Her hands gripped the rigid wood. "Please let him agree to this," she whispered.

"I hope you're packed and ready to go." He swung his leg over the cantle and dismounted.

"Roundup starts tomorrow."

Hallie squeezed the rail until the edges bit into her palms. "I'm not going this year." *Please don't ask me to explain why.* She didn't know how to make him understand that the memory of Pete's constant pestering the year before had soured her on ever going again, as long as Pete was around.

Her father's look of astonishment would have seemed humorous at a less serious moment. "What do you mean, you're not going? Clive Jensen packed up and moved his family back to Kansas, remember? You can't keep his wife company again this year. Where do you think you're going to stay?"

"I'm staying right here." She forged ahead to cut off his protest. "I'm twenty years old, Pa. I can manage on my own."

"This is foolishness, Hallie. You can ride as well as any hand. And if you don't want to work on horseback, you can help with the food. Your cooking beats anything we're likely to get out there. What would you do around here by yourself for a week?"

Hallie strived to keep her tone light. "For one thing, I can get my spring cleaning done. It'll be lots easier to scrub cupboards and air bedding if I don't have to stop to fix meals. And I can clean out the bunkhouse without coming across a pair of Homer's long johns draped across the door and embarrassing the poor man half to death."

Her father's laughter gave her hope. "It wasn't so much knowing you'd seen them as finding them mended, washed, and folded on top of his bunk." He patted her hand. "All right, Hallie. You're a woman grown. I guess you can handle yourself like one. Just remember, if you run into any trouble, the shotgun's in the corner."

"I'll remember." But with Pete gone along with the rest of the hands, she probably wouldn't need it for protection.

ঽ

A puff of acrid smoke rose from the T Bar branding iron as it burned into the calf's flank.

"Okay, let 'im up." Dan stepped back from the bawling calf. The two other cowboys from his fire crew released the steer calf and watched it scramble up to rejoin its frantic mother.

Jacob wiped his brow with his shirtsleeve and watched Eb drive the cow and calf over to the herd of branded animals. Looking around at the numerous teams at work, he felt thrilled at the efficiency of their labor. He shook out his loop and headed back into the gather for another unbranded calf.

He saw Buster dab a loop over the head of a brindle calf with white legs and face, then drag it to the closest fire.

"This one's a T Bar," Buster called. The ground man reached over to pull that iron from the fire and applied it quickly, while the other team members clipped the ear and applied salve to the wounds.

Jacob frowned. He could have sworn that little heifer belonged to a Seven X cow. He continued working, but vowed to stay aware of Buster's activity.

Within minutes, Buster pulled a small black calf with a white spot over its left eye out of the herd. "Here's another T Bar."

"Are you sure?" Jacob called. "I think that calf belongs to a Lazy EW cow."

Buster shook his head. "I'm sure. This is one of Dan's, no question about it."

"What's the problem?" asked the cowboy at the fire. "Do we know whose calf this is or not?"

Jacob shrugged. "I'm not trying to cause trouble, but I'm positive that calf was mothered up to a black Lazy EW cow. Buster, why don't you turn it loose and see where it goes?"

With an angry shake of his rope, Buster released the calf. It trotted back into the herd and immediately paired up with a black cow wearing the Lazy EW brand.

"Looks like you were right, Garrett." Buster stared at the calf, his mouth a grim slash. He nodded an apology to Edgar Wilson. "My mistake. I'll be more careful."

Jacob waited until the next time he and Buster were changing horses to talk to him alone. "How many calves are wearing the T Bar brand that don't have a right to?"

Buster glared. "What's that supposed to mean? In a roundup, those things happen all the time. It was just an honest mistake."

"Was it?"

The corner of Buster's mouth twitched. "What are you getting so worked up about? So Dan's got a few extra head. I thought he was your friend."

"He is, and I wouldn't count myself any kind of friend if I let his reputation get tarnished."

Buster gave a snide laugh. "You don't know how many T Bar calves are going to wind up wearing somebody else's brand by the time this week is over. If we don't get some back, we end up getting cheated. And if the scales tip in our direction, so much the better. Nobody gets hurt."

"Everybody gets hurt," Jacob shot back. He felt his features harden. "It isn't honest, and that's all there is to it. I wouldn't stand for someone taking Dan's calves 'by mistake' like that. Neither would you. And I won't stand for the T Bar growing its herd by dishonest means."

Buster glared at him in disgust. "You just keep living in your dream world. See how fast you get ahead." He mounted his horse and spurred back toward the herd.

Jacob slapped his gloves against his chaps. If Buster had anything to say about it, his stay at the T Bar wouldn't last long. It didn't matter, he told himself. Right was right, and he couldn't go along with anything less. He picked up his reins and turned to go back to roping.

"Hold it a minute, son."

Jacob pivoted on his heel. A lean man with a complexion like old leather stepped out from behind a tree holding the picket rope.

The older man studied Jacob with keen blue eyes. "I'm Fred Davenport, owner of the Diamond D. I heard what you said to Buster." The weather-beaten rancher stuck out a calloused hand. "I can't say I've seen that kind of integrity before, but I like your style, Garrett. We need more of your kind around these parts."

Jacob shrugged. "I just can't see fudging on things. It isn't the way I was raised. My parents tried to bring me up according to the Bible, and it seems to me God takes a mighty dim view of appropriating someone else's property."

Fred Davenport nodded appreciatively. "Sounds like you come from good stock, son. Dan better watch out."

Jacob shot him a questioning glance.

The rancher's leathery cheeks creased when he grinned. "If he isn't careful, half the ranchers in this area are going to be trying to steal his new hand." He laughed at Jacob's look of surprise, then turned to rejoin the men around the branding fire.

ِ⁂

"Garrett?"

Jacob looked up from braiding the hondo on a new lariat to see three men standing in the open barn door.

"I'm Lucas Rawlins, head of the Cattlemen's Association. This is Morris Atwater." He gestured to the man next to him. "I believe you already know Fred Davenport."

Jacob nodded a greeting and hooked his thumbs in his pockets. "What's on your mind?"

"Fred here wasn't the only one impressed by your honesty at the roundup," Rawlins told him. "I'd say word of what you did has pretty much spread through the area." He cleared his throat. "On behalf of the Yavapai Cattlemen's Association, I'd like to offer you the job of range detective."

Jacob stared at each of the men in turn.

"You'd be responsible for checking brands on cattle being bought and sold and investigating claims of rustling," Fred Davenport explained. "Since you'll be doing a lot of riding, you need to keep your eyes open for outbreaks of noxious weeds or anything else that might harm the stock. But the most important thing is to stop this thieving that's been going on. We need someone we can trust, and we think you're just the man for the job. What do you say?"

Jacob turned the idea over in his mind. With that kind of work, he'd be on the trail most of the time. He couldn't think of a better way to get to know every corner of this new area he had claimed for his own. He would still be dealing with livestock. And he'd have the satisfaction of knowing he would be contributing to the growth of the territory.

It sounded like the opportunity of a lifetime, a job tailor-made for him.

But he couldn't accept. The realization hit him with a sickening thud.

"I appreciate your asking me," he began. "But I just hired on with Dan. I can't see leaving him shorthanded." He pulled his hat off and ran his hand over his hair, then settled the Stetson back on his head. "Much as I hate to, I'm going to have to turn the job down."

Rawlins looked at his companions, then back at Jacob. "We were afraid you might feel that way. I guess that's what we could expect from a man of integrity. Thanks for giving us a listen."

Jacob stood in the barn doorway and watched them ride away. He flexed the rope between his hands. "I think I'd like extra credit for turning that job down, Lord. That was one hard choice to make."

Dan came trotting up on a long-legged buckskin. He reached over and patted the snorting horse's neck. "A few more miles on this young fellow, and he'll be ready for everyday use." He nodded toward the south. "Was that Rawlins I saw riding off? What did he want?"

Jacob forced a crooked grin. Not for the world would he let his friend see how deep his disappointment ran. "Oh, they had some crazy notion about wanting me to be their range detective."

Dan's face lit up. "It's nice to know they have some sense. When do you start?"

"You don't need to worry about that. I told them no."

"You turned them down? Sounds like you're the one who's crazy."

"Come on, Dan. You know I'm not going to come up here, then go haring off and leave you high and dry."

"Listen. What we need more than anything else in this county is someone we can depend on. All joking aside, Rawlins is no fool; neither is Atwater or Fred Davenport. They know a good thing when they see it, and that means you, Jacob. You've got the kind of honesty that will keep things straight around here. The last range detective around here was more interested in lining his own pockets than cracking down on shady branding practices. I know you won't do that, and so do those men. In the long run, having you in that position will benefit me as much as anyone else in the county, even though you won't be working directly for me. It's for the good of everyone, you included."

Jacob couldn't stop a hopeful smile from spreading across his face. "You mean that?"

Dan laughed at the eagerness in his voice. "Absolutely. Now, you'd better throw a saddle on Cap and catch up to them. You need to tell those men you've changed your mind."

five

Cap's hooves clattered over the rocky trail from the Verde Valley. Jacob pulled up to let the steel-dust catch his breath when they topped out on the ridgeline overlooking the broad expanse of grassland. Over the last week, he had been to half a dozen ranches, getting to know the local stockmen. More than one rancher brought up his concern about missing stock. His last stop had been Stuart Brannon's ranch.

Jacob thought back over his visit with the famed lawman turned rancher and chuckled when he remembered Brannon's calm reply that he hadn't lost any cattle and didn't expect to. Jacob had a feeling if anyone were foolish enough to mess with Brannon's stock, they'd be the ones hollering for help.

He slackened the reins and let Cap grab a few mouthfuls of grass while he got his bearings. If he remembered Dan's directions correctly, he ought to be at the east edge of Lonesome Valley. He would cut over to the Broken Box and make that his last stop before heading up the valley to Coyote Springs and the T Bar. Dan had been good enough to offer his guest room for Jacob's use as long as he needed it. Jacob couldn't complain about the central location—or continued access to Amy's cooking.

He held Cap down to a walk so he could take a good look around as he neared Broken Box headquarters. No one appeared in the yard when he approached.

He leaned on his saddle horn. "Hello, the house! Anybody home?"

A stocky, barrel-chested man appeared in the barn doorway. "Who wants to know?"

"It's Jacob Garrett. We met during roundup." Jacob swung out of the saddle and went to shake hands with Burke Evans.

Burke's quick grip went along with his no-nonsense bearing. "I remember. You're that young pup from O'Roarke's spread who got Fred Davenport so stirred up when you lit into Buster. I hear he talked Rawlins into hiring you to find our missing stock." Burke spat and wiped his mouth with the back of his hand. "Well, you've got plenty of them to look for. They've been disappearing by twos and threes for several months now. What do you think you're going to be able to do about it?"

"I've been out getting acquainted with the ranchers and the territory—"

"I don't know why they called in an outsider in the first place. What earthly good do they think you'll do?"

Jacob bit back a hot retort. "Why don't you give me a chance to show you what I can do before you pass judgment?" From the corner of his eye, he saw a flash of movement. A young girl darted from the edge of the barn toward the house, obviously trying not to be seen.

"Hallie! Come over here." Burke's voice sounded like gravel pouring over a sheet of tin.

The girl stopped abruptly and stood poised in the manner of a deer ready to take flight. Seeming to realize she couldn't pretend she hadn't heard, she crossed the yard and stopped ten feet away with her gaze focused on the ground. On closer inspection, Jacob realized she wasn't a girl after all but a young woman, probably only a few years his junior.

"This is—what'd you say your name was again?"

It took a moment before Jacob realized Burke was talking

to him. "Garrett," he replied without shifting his gaze. "Jacob Garrett."

"That's right, Garrett. My daughter, Hallie."

Jacob couldn't make out the words of her murmured greeting.

"I'm pleased to meet you." Well trained by his mother, he had said those words a hundred times before, but never had he meant them as much as at this moment. What was it about this girl—this woman—that made his heart race and his palms grow moist?

Hallie lifted her gaze to meet his. Her shy demeanor reminded Jacob of a watchful fawn. Her dark hair, held back at the sides by two combs, tumbled down her back in loose waves. A tinge of pink crept into her cheeks under Jacob's intense scrutiny. She looked down again and began tracing patterns in the dust with the toe of her moccasin. Without raising her head, she said, "Please excuse me. I need to go start supper."

Jacob watched her walk swiftly toward the house and kept on staring after the door closed behind her.

"So what are you going to do about it?" Burke's rough voice called him back to attention.

"Would you mind repeating that last part?" Jacob asked, uncomfortably aware he'd missed everything Burke just said. He shot a quick look at the rancher but saw nothing in his square face to indicate he'd caught anything passing between Jacob and his daughter.

Burke planted his hands on his hips and let his breath out in an impatient huff. "I said I'm not the only one around here who's been missing cattle. Wilson's lost nearly as many as I have. So have Miller and Ladd. I want to know what you intend to do about it." His stony gray eyes narrowed to slits, and his lower jaw thrust forward. He gave every indication of being a man used to getting his own way or knowing the reason why.

Jacob realized his first major test had come and hoped he would be up to the challenge. "I've been hearing the same thing from the ranchers I've visited. My first thought is to check the most obvious avenues—shipments that may have gone out on the railroad without proper paperwork, evidence of herds moving out of the area without any connection to a legitimate sale. If that doesn't turn anything up, I'll have to start trying to work out the trails and discover where they've gone."

"Sounds like a lot of wasted time to me. We need results and we need them soon."

Burke pivoted on his heel and headed back to the barn.

And a good day to you, too.

Jacob mounted and swung Cap back toward the road, casting one last look at the ranch house where Hallie Evans had disappeared.

&

Hallie hurried toward the house, her moccasined feet making whispers of sound against the hard-packed dirt. Inside, she leaned back against the door and pressed her palms against her flaming cheeks.

What a fool she'd made of herself, staring like that! *What came over me? I don't ever remember behaving like that. Mama would have been mortified if she'd been here to see.*

She squeezed her eyes shut and tried to stop the feeling that her whole world had just tilted off its axis. What had happened? Everything seemed normal up until the moment the stranger rode up while she was out in the chicken coop checking on the brood hen. Dressed in her most faded work clothes and with her hair hanging loose like a little girl's, the best course of action seemed to be to remain in the shadows of the barn.

But if she didn't get those potatoes on to boil, supper would be late. After a second glance, she'd decided the newcomer and her pa were engrossed in conversation deep enough to give her the opportunity to get across the yard unseen.

She'd almost made it, too. She would have, if her father hadn't called her over. *Of all the times for him to decide to observe the social graces.*

Sheer embarrassment fastened her gaze to the ground while she walked over to them. And if only she'd *kept* it focused there, she might not have humiliated herself. Her mother's training in deportment held true, though, and she forced herself to look up at the stranger when her father introduced him.

But he wasn't a stranger. Not since the instant their gazes locked and every thought left her mind except the desire to lose herself in the depths of his sky blue eyes. Some part of her felt like she had known him forever. His tanned face and wavy, dark blond hair seemed as familiar to her as her own features. Then came the awful moment when she realized she was staring at him, gaping like a fish.

Her cheeks burned against her fingertips. *What must he have thought?*

Not many visitors came to the Broken Box, and her trips to town were few and far between, giving her little opportunity to practice social skills. Would she have reacted as strongly to just anyone who happened to drop in unexpectedly? Hallie felt tempted to use that excuse to explain away her feelings, but she knew there was more to it than that. A current of recognition had passed between them, a sense of connection she couldn't begin to fathom.

She moved to the window and pulled back the edge of the curtain. Peering through the crack, she watched Jacob Garrett mount up and ride away. At the edge of the yard, he glanced over his shoulder and looked back at the house. His eyes appeared to focus right on her.

Hallie gasped and dropped the curtain as though she had singed her fingers on a hot stove. Had he seen her standing there, mooning after him? She tried to console herself with the knowledge she probably would never see the man again.

It wasn't much consolation.

She waited until he was a fair distance away, then stepped out onto the porch and wrapped one arm around a post, staring at his retreating figure. Long after he and his horse dwindled into mere specks on the horizon, she watched, fixing that significant moment in her heart.

Could it be possible the hunger for something more that stirred her soul of late was for some*one* instead?

Hallie leaned her head against the post and let her thoughts take wing until the sun's rays glared directly into her eyes, reminding her how much time she'd spent dreaming.

Catching her breath in dismay, she hurried to the kitchen and started peeling the potatoes. It looked like supper would be late, after all.

six

Jacob trotted up the steps of the red brick courthouse and walked down the hallway to an open door. A bespectacled young man sat working at a small desk. Jacob cleared his throat.

The young man started and peered up over the tops of his spectacles. "May I help you?"

"Is this the mayor's office?"

"You've got the right place." The clerk gestured to the open door behind him. "Go on back. He'll be glad to see you."

Jacob tapped on the door frame, then poked his head inside. "Mr. Mayor?"

The handsome, dark-haired man behind the desk rose. "I don't hold with formality. My friends call me Buckey."

His genial smile immediately put Jacob at ease. He reached out to shake the hand Buckey offered. The mayor had a strong, honest grip and a direct gaze that inspired in Jacob an immediate liking for the man.

"Glad to meet you, sir. My name's Jacob Garrett."

Buckey's trim mustache twitched upward. "So you're the one Lucas Rawlins and Morris Atwater tell me is the answer to their prayers."

"I'm not sure I'd go that far, but I hope to live up to the expectations they have of me."

"Sit down." Buckey waved Jacob to a straight-backed chair. "Lucas wore my ear out singing your praises, but he didn't tell me anything about your background. How long have you been in the area?"

"Just a few weeks. I was born and raised in Tucson, but I've known Dan O'Roarke and his family all my life. Prescott always seemed like a second home to me. My parents first met here, as a matter of fact."

Buckey stroked his mustache with his thumb. "Tucson, eh? Any relation to Andrew Garrett?"

The question startled Jacob. "He's my father. Do you know him?"

"Not personally, but I know of him. I have some mining interests of my own. His name is well known around the territory." He leaned back in his desk chair and his eyes gleamed with a friendly light. "If you have half the integrity your father is known for, I have no doubt you're the right man for the job."

"Thank you. He's given me a fine example to follow and some mighty big shoes to fill."

"You say your parents once lived here?"

"My mother did. My father was just passing through when they first met. They met again down in Tucson." No point in bringing up the stories he'd heard about that dark time in his mother's life before she discovered the love of both his father and Christ. Her years in Prescott did not hold happy memories for her.

"How long ago would that have been?"

Jacob pursed his lips. "She left in '69, two years after the capital moved from Prescott to Tucson. So that would have been. . .what? Twenty-nine years ago?"

"Before my time," Buckey said. "I didn't get up to these parts until the spring of '82, after the capital moved back up here again. Then we got into that squabble with Tucson and the powers that be decided to put both cities in their place and send the capital to Phoenix." He chuckled. "Maybe they'll keep it there, maybe not. But what the people of this territory need to do is forget our petty differences and move forward together. Seeing statehood come to Arizona, that's where my heart lies. It seems to me that thirty-five years as a territory is long enough."

"I couldn't agree more." The subject of achieving statehood was dear to the hearts of all Arizonans. "I understand you used to be sheriff?"

"That's right." Buckey placed his right ankle on his left knee. "I've worn a lot of different hats since I came here: sheriff, court reporter, probate judge. I lost a bid for Congress in both '94 and '96, but I managed to be elected as mayor last year." He uncrossed his legs and leaned forward on his desk. "This territory holds tremendous potential. I'm willing to do whatever I can to add a new star to our nation's flag." A mischievous light danced in his eyes. "That was a long answer to your question about my being sheriff. Was there a particular reason you asked?"

"Some of the ranchers have been missing cattle," Jacob said. "I intend to find the thieves and bring them to justice. But I'm new here. I don't know the lay of the land. I thought you might have some ideas on the best place to start looking. That is, if you don't think I'm out of line for asking."

Buckey smiled. "It's an intelligent man who knows when to ask for help. And don't think for a moment I feel like you're asking me to do your job for you. . .you'll have plenty to do on your own." He walked to one side of his office, where a large map hung on the wall. He traced a circle with his finger. "This is the area you're responsible for, all the way north to south from Ash Fork to Bumblebee Ranch, and east to west from the Verde Valley almost to Wickenburg. These dots mark the different ranches under your jurisdiction. My advice would be to pay a visit to each of the ranchers and get to know them. See who's missing cattle and who might know something. I'm sure we've got some in the area who wouldn't hesitate to buy cheap cows and not ask questions, but for the most part there are a lot of good solid citizens around here."

"I've already started along those lines." Jacob pointed out the ranches he had already visited. "This map gives me a better perspective on the whole layout, though."

Buckey clapped him on the shoulder. "I knew you were the right man for the job. Come back anytime you want to take another look at the map or to ask me any questions. I'm glad to help. If I'm not in my office or at home, you can generally find me down at the Palace. Speaking of which. . ." He pulled out his pocket watch and snapped the cover open.

"How would you like to meet some more of our local citizenry? I'm rather partial to a few hands of faro, and there's usually a good game starting up right about now."

"I'm not a gambling man, but I'd welcome the opportunity to get to know more of the folks around here."

"Fair enough." Buckey pulled his hat from a hook on the wall and settled it on his head. "Let's head to the Palace."

જ

It took a moment for Jacob's eyes to adjust to the dim interior. While saloons would never be his natural haunt, the Palace was well appointed, a comfortable place for local men to gather.

"Hello, boys!" Buckey wended his way toward a group of men clustered around a table in the back room.

"About time you got here," one called back. "We were about ready to send out a search party." A chuckle rippled around the table at his sally.

"Meet Jacob Garrett, formerly of Tucson, currently Yavapai County's new range detective."

"Pleased to meet you." The men shook hands with Jacob in turn.

"Any relation to Andrew of the same name?" quizzed a black-haired man on the opposite side of the table.

"My father." Jacob felt a glow of pride at the admiring response his father's name evoked. He truly did have big shoes to fill.

"Jacob here jumped right into a tough situation," Buckey announced. "Rustling has gotten beyond the two-bit stage and he's charged with finding out who's to blame. Sounds like he's already made a good start."

One of the faro players snorted. "That's more than Clive Jensen would have done."

Jacob shot a questioning look at the group. The black-haired man twisted his mouth in disgust and leaned closer to be heard over the noise of the crowd near the bar. "Your predecessor would have been more likely to turn a blind eye to such goings-on than try to do anything to stop them."

Jacob drew his brows together. "But why?"

A craggy-faced man shrugged. "Hard to tell. Some say he was getting a payoff from the rustlers; some say he just didn't care. All I know is, he never seemed to take loss of stock very seriously."

"That's going to change," Jacob promised.

"You fellows can help get the word out," Buckey said. "Let people know we have a range detective who means business. Sometimes just knowing someone is willing to act is enough to put a stop to that kind of thing."

A general murmur of approval ran around the table. The topic of conversation turned to Spain and the political situation in Cuba, but Buckey's comment sent Jacob's mind back to his talk with Burke Evans at the Broken Box. And from that to a mental picture of Hallie Evans. The voices from the table faded out as he daydreamed of that moment their eyes met.

Jacob wondered what it would be like to spend time in the company of Burke Evans's quiet daughter. Were her gentleness and sweet spirit as real as they seemed in that brief encounter? Her large brown eyes seemed to have looked into his soul. He hoped she had seen something worthwhile.

"What are your views on the subject, Garrett?"

The question pulled Jacob back to the present with a start. He stared at the men around the table. "Sorry," he muttered. "I'm afraid my mind was somewhere else."

The man beside him guffawed and dug his elbow into Jacob's ribs. "I've seen that look on a man's face before. You had some female on your mind, if I don't miss my guess."

The rest of the group joined him in ribald laughter.

Jacob forced a tight smile. "If you'll excuse me, gentlemen, I have to get back to business." He stepped outside and left the clamor of the saloon behind with a sense of relief.

seven

Half-dozing in the saddle, Jacob gave Cap his head and let him choose his own way down the slope from Harvey Fletcher's place to the valley floor. A newcomer to the area, Fletcher hadn't met many of his neighbors. He'd been glad to see Jacob, hungry for information about the local happenings, but hadn't added anything to Jacob's store of information about the rustling.

Jacob angled across the plain. If memory served him, this route ought to cut off a good two miles and get him back to the T Bar well before sunset.

Cap whickered and pricked up his ears at the top of the next rise. Jacob straightened in his saddle and peered in the direction Cap was looking. Up ahead stood a saddled mount. On the far side of the gray horse, a figure crouched next to a struggling animal in the tawny grass.

Jacob came fully alert. Keeping the gray between himself and the kneeling figure, he urged Cap closer. He let his right hand move down to his holster, and he slipped the loop off the hammer, never taking his gaze from the person in the grass.

When he had narrowed the distance, he circled out past the gray for a better look at the person on the ground. Long dark hair streamed down the back of the slender figure.

Hallie? He slowed when he drew near so as not to spook her horse. "What are you doing out here by yourself?"

Hallie swung around, eyes wide. She relaxed visibly and put

a comforting hand on the calf stretched out on the ground before her.

"I just needed to get outdoors for a while, so I took Gypsy for a ride. Then I came across this little fellow. Could you give me a hand? He has a broken leg, and I can't set it alone."

Jacob swung out of the saddle and hurried to her side. The calf's left hind leg lay twisted at an unnatural angle. The little animal's eyes were ringed with white, and it bleated pitifully.

"Shhh," Hallie murmured in a soothing tone. "It'll be all right. We're going to take care of you."

Jacob eyed the calf. "He looks pretty well done in already, and there's no telling whether it will heal straight or not. Do you think it's worth it?"

"I don't know," Hallie replied simply. "I only know I have to try. Will you help me?" She looked up at him, and he knew in that instant he'd do anything she asked of him.

"I found that cedar branch to use as a splint." She nodded toward a short length of wood on the ground. "But I can't hold him down and work on him at the same time."

Jacob knelt beside her. "You hold his head. I'll see what I can do to get this leg straight." He ran his hand along the calf's leg and winced at the thought of the additional pain he was about to cause. He glanced at Hallie's delicate features, wondering whether she was really up to the task at hand. "Ready?"

She wrapped her arms around the calf's chest and nodded. Jacob took hold of the leg below the break and pulled. The calf let out an anguished bawl and strained to get away.

Jacob glanced at Hallie. Her arms were still locked around the calf, her feet braced against the ground. She pulled back with all her might. Her lips trembled and tears pooled in her eyes, but her face bore an expression of firm resolve. She dug her heels into the ground and held on tight.

"Just a little bit longer," she told the frightened animal.

Jacob increased the pressure and felt the ends of the bone shift into place. He broke the cedar branch in half and applied the pieces to either side of the calf's leg, then bound them in place with a bandanna Hallie had torn into strips. "You can let go now. We're finished." He leaned back on one arm and wiped beads of sweat from his upper lip with his sleeve.

Hallie released her grip and bent over her charge. "There you go, little guy. The worst is over."

Watching her fingers move in gentle strokes along the calf's neck, Jacob marveled. What a combination of gentleness and strength. What would it be like to have a woman like that stand behind him? No, *beside* him. A prize like Hallie Evans should never be pushed into the background.

❧

"That's a sweet boy." A surge of relief swept through Hallie when she felt the calf's tense muscles begin to relax. "I'll fix up a nice place for you in the barn and you can rest and take it easy until you're better.

"Poor little thing, he must wonder what he did to hurt himself so badly. And where his mother is." She pointed up a nearby draw. "I saw tracks up that way, where the earth was all churned up. It looked like somebody was pushing some cows pretty hard. I wonder if the rustlers were herding them up somewhere, but this baby got hurt and they left him behind."

She stopped talking abruptly. "Oh, dear." She clamped her lips together.

Jacob glanced from side to side. "What's the matter?"

"I'm chattering. I never chatter."

His smile warmed her more than the spring sunshine. "I wish you'd do more of it. I like hearing your voice."

Hallie felt her cheeks redden. She pushed herself to her feet and glanced down at her riding skirt. The once clean fabric now sported a coating of fine dust and bits of grass.

She dusted her skirt with her hands. *He's going to think I'm some kind of ragamuffin.* She pressed her hand to her mouth. Jacob grinned.

"What?" she demanded.

"That dirt you just brushed off your skirt? It's all over your hands now. At least, it was until you wiped most of it off on your cheek."

Hallie scrubbed frantically at her face.

Jacob stifled a chuckle.

"I'm only making it worse, aren't I?"

"Here." He pulled a bandanna from his back pocket. "On you, even dirt looks cute as a bug's ear. But use this if it will make you feel better."

❧

"How is he doing?" Hallie twisted in her saddle to look at the calf riding across Jacob's lap.

"Not bad, but he'll be mighty happy to get down once we get him home."

"Not much farther," she promised.

The house and barn came into view quickly—too quickly, in Hallie's estimation. She wished she could stretch these last remaining moments out for hours. Being with Jacob was like a refreshing spring rain on parched earth. He hadn't minded her chatter; in fact, he'd encouraged her to talk. And with him, she found it easy to do.

"Here we are," she said when they rode into the yard. "Let me help you get him down."

Her father strode out of the barn with an expression like a thundercloud. "What's going on?"

"I found this little fellow hurt out on the trail," Hallie explained. "Jacob—Mr. Garrett—came along and helped me set his leg."

"And he had to trail you all the way home, I see." Her father gave Jacob a hard look.

"Just long enough to drop this little guy off." Jacob slid from his saddle and lifted the calf down in one easy motion.

"Hallie could have brought him home herself. She's a good worker. You'd best be on your way now."

Hallie felt her cheeks flame. "Pa!"

Her father leveled a warning glance at her, then turned back to Jacob. "I lost another half dozen head this past week. You'd do better to spend your time looking for whoever has been stealing my stock instead of making calf eyes at my daughter."

"*Pa!*"

Burke rounded on her. "You just settle down, young lady. You've hardly set foot off the ranch these past few years, and you don't know the first thing about the way a man's mind works. You're easy pickings for the first young buck who comes along."

"Pa, stop!" Hallie held up her hands as though she could ward off the harsh words that fell like lashes from a whip. "How can you say such things? Don't you know me better than that? And what about Jacob? How can you cast aspersions on someone you barely know?

"You're right about one thing," she continued. "I haven't spent much time off the ranch. But anyone with half an eye could see that he's a decent, upright man." Tears clogged her throat and she subsided, wrapping her arms around her middle.

Her father's eyes bulged and his face took on a ruddy hue.

"What's gotten into you, sassing back like that? You get yourself inside the house, girl. And you stay there, you hear?"

Unable to hold back her sobs a moment longer, Hallie sprinted for the front door.

Inside, she collapsed against the closed door, then slid down until she huddled on the floor in a heap. She hugged her knees and pulled her body into a tight knot.

"Why, God? Why can't he see? He's completely blind to Pete's advances, but he's ready to tear Jacob apart without even getting to know him."

Tears blurred her vision, and she pressed her forehead against her knees. With all her heart, she hoped her father's insinuations wouldn't keep Jacob from coming around again. But she couldn't blame him if they did.

❧

Burke turned from watching Hallie's dash to the house and fixed Jacob with a malevolent glare. He took a threatening step forward, meaty hands balled into fists. "I don't know what you did to make her spout off like that. She's never done a thing like that before."

Jacob felt the hairs on the back of his neck stand on end like the hackles of a dog facing a growling bear. "Your daughter is a fine woman, one you can be proud of. You'd do well to appreciate what you have."

"You'd better not have been appreciatin' anything you aren't supposed to, or I'll send you home draped over your saddle."

Jacob had to force his clenched jaw open before he could speak. "Mr. Evans, I resent your implications. Things happened out there just as Hallie said. I came upon her while she was trying to doctor that calf. She needed help; I gave it to her. We brought the calf back so she could tend to him while his leg heals. That's the whole story. Period." He jabbed his finger toward Burke, who maintained a stony silence.

Jacob swung up onto Cap's back. "And now I'm heading out to do some more searching for your rustlers." He dug his heels into Cap's sides and left Burke Evans standing in a cloud of dust.

All the way back to the T Bar, Burke's accusation churned his stomach. *How can such a hard man have such a sweet daughter?*

"He's a decent, upright man." Hallie's words floated through his mind, the memory of her passionate defense overshadowing her father's words.

He relaxed a fraction, finally able to loosen his jaw and work it from side to side. It was almost worth listening to that diatribe just to hear Hallie champion him like that.

"How could she know what kind of man I am? We've only spoken twice." Whatever the reason, he was glad. The memory of her support would bolster him for quite a while.

❧

The shadows stretched long through the windows and inched their way across the floor. Time to light the lamps. Past time to fix supper.

Hallie remained curled in her tight ball. Muscles cramping, head throbbing, she sat alone in her misery in the gathering dark.

The back door opened, then slammed shut. Boots tromped across the plank floor. "Hallie!" Her father's rough voice echoed through the house. "Where's my supper? I'm hungry."

He stopped in the doorway that separated the kitchen from the front room. He stood a long moment without speaking, then said in a quieter tone, "What is it? Are you sick?"

Hallie spoke without raising her head. "I'm fine."

"Then why are you just sitting there in the dark? Why

aren't the lamps lit? Where's supper?" He struck a match and touched it to the wick of the lamp on the mantel. "With everything else on my mind right now, I can't be worrying about going hungry."

"You're right." Hallie planted her palms on the floor and pushed herself up. "It wouldn't do for you to have any more worries. I'll make some sandwiches out of that beef we had for lunch."

Her father hung his hat on its hook and headed for his favorite chair. Halfway there, he turned back, a worried frown creasing his forehead. "You sure you're all right? It isn't like you to slack off like this."

He walked over and put his arms around her. "Tell your old dad what's going on. All we've had is each other ever since your mother died." He ran his work-hardened hand over her hair. "I know I've been short with you lately, and I'm sorry. It's the loss of all that stock. It just burns me to no end to think someone is strolling in here and trying to ruin everything I've worked so hard to build up."

Hallie leaned against him, remembering how it felt to be a little girl and know her daddy would take on the whole world to keep her safe. She let herself relax in his embrace and wiped her eyes on the front of his shirt.

She stretched her arms around his stocky frame. "Give me a few minutes, and I'll come up with something more substantial than sandwiches. You just sit in your chair and relax until then."

His strong arms squeezed her in a bear hug. "That's my girl. I knew you couldn't stay in a pout for long. You're a sensible girl, Hallie. At least when you're not all dewy-eyed over some footloose yahoo."

Hallie stiffened and pulled away. "I'll go make your supper."

"You gettin' all fussed up again? What did I do this time? I don't understand."

Hallie stormed into the kitchen and leaned her head against the doorframe. "That's just the trouble, Pa," she whispered. "You don't understand at all."

eight

Even though it was just after ten in the morning, the heat reminded Jacob of Tucson. His horse pushed through the milling cattle as he checked the final brands of this herd. He rode over to where the buyer and seller sat their horses beneath the shade of a large walnut tree.

"Everything looks good here. Every one of them a Heart Cross brand. I'll sign off on that bill of sale, Mr. Potter, and you can be on your way." He scribbled his name at the bottom of the paper. "How long will it take you to push them up to Ash Fork?"

"Four or five days should get us there, if we don't have any trouble." Potter folded the bill and placed it in his pocket. He shook hands and rode toward his cowboys to start the hundred head of breeding stock.

Jacob mopped his forehead with his bandanna, then used it to wipe the sweat band of his hat. "You've got some good-looking stock there, Bradley. From the looks of them, I'm guessing the range is in good shape over on this side of Granite Mountain."

"This year looks good. And I'll be able to upgrade my stock after selling these heifers." Will Bradley gave a satisfied nod and reached over to pat the gangly boy on the horse next to him. "By the time this button gets big enough to take over, we ought to have quite a spread built up."

Jacob studied the ten-year-old wearing a hat nearly as big as he was and held back a grin. By the looks of him, that boy wouldn't be ready to boss an outfit for a good long time.

The boy flashed a grin at his father, then pulled a book from his saddlebag. Propping it against his saddle horn, he settled back to read.

Jacob turned a puzzled glance at Will Bradley, who merely shrugged and grinned. "He gets that from his mother. You'll never find either one of them far from a book. He got his dark hair and those bright eyes from her, too. This territory has brought me a good family, a good life. Pulling up stakes and moving out here was the best thing I ever did."

Jacob could understand his desire to strike out on his own. "Where did you come from?"

"New Mexico, up in the northeast corner of the territory. My father and uncle have a good-size spread. My sister and her family are up there, too. It was hard leaving them all, but I wouldn't trade what I have here for anything." He turned to his son. "Alexander, show Mr. Garrett what you're reading."

"It's *A Connecticut Yankee in King Arthur's Court.*" Alexander's deep blue eyes lit up when he grinned. "It's all about knights and jousting and stuff like that."

Jacob chuckled at the boy's enthusiasm. "It sounds like quite a tale. That Mark Twain really knows how to spin a yarn."

"Have you found a place in Prescott?" Will asked.

Jacob shook his head. "I'm staying on at the T Bar for the time being. There's a fair amount of stock missing over that way, and I figure being on the spot might help me get a line on what's going on."

"Dan's a good man," Will said. "I'm glad he brought you up here. We've been needing someone like you."

Alexander looked up from his story. "You're staying with Mr. O'Roarke?" A mischievous grin crept across his face.

"Would you tell Catherine something for me, please? Tell her I got a new pet frog, and I'll let her play with him anytime she wants."

Jacob blinked at the odd request. "Sure. I'll be happy to pass that along."

Will Bradley eyed his son. "And just why would Catherine be interested in a frog, pet or otherwise?"

"Hey, look." Alexander stood in his stirrups and pointed toward the east. "Someone's coming. I'll just ride out and see who it is." He kicked his horse into a lively trot.

"We'll discuss this later," Will called to his retreating back. He shoved his Stetson back and scratched his head. "I have a feeling I'd better check into that. Those two have been feuding since they were babies."

"You never know," Jacob replied. "They may turn out to be the best of friends someday." The two men waited in companionable silence, watching the rider approach.

"That's a Broken Box rider," Will observed. "Bernie Harrelson, if I don't miss my guess."

Jacob nodded, recognizing the thin-faced man at the same moment. *What's one of Evans's riders doing way over here?* A knot twisted in his gut.

Harrelson pulled his horse up about ten feet away. "Afternoon, Mr. Bradley." He looked toward Jacob but didn't meet his gaze, focusing instead on a point just beyond his left ear. "Sheriff Ruffner said you might be out here today, Garrett, so I rode on over. Mr. Evans sent me."

"What can I do for you?" Jacob asked, afraid he already knew the answer.

"We discovered more stock missing over the last couple of days, nearly a dozen head this time. The boss is pretty upset."

Jacob watched the cowboy swallow repeatedly, like a cow

working her cud. "Is that all he wanted you to tell me?"

Harrelson's Adam's apple bobbed up and down. "He said he hoped you weren't going to just sit back and look the other way like the last fellow who had this job." He risked a quick glance at Jacob. "Those are his words, Garrett, not mine. Me and the boys know you're doing your best."

Jacob ducked his head in a curt nod. "Anything else?"

Harrelson's gaze shot back toward the horizon. "Just that you'd better find out who's stealing his cattle, and soon, if you know what's good for you." He wheeled his horse back toward the east. "I have to be getting back. The boss is going to have my hide for being gone so long. He figured you'd be sticking a lot closer to the Broken Box these days, with all the trouble that's been going on." Harrelson dug his heels into his horse's sides and rode back the way he came.

A muscle twitched in Jacob's cheek. He forced his clenched teeth apart. "That was a lovely bit of news."

"Don't let Burke get to you," Will said. "He wasn't like this years ago, back before his wife died. Most of it's just bluster, trying to cover up the hurt he's carrying around inside. He isn't really a bad fellow. He sure dotes on that daughter of his."

"I've seen them together," Jacob said shortly. "I haven't noticed much doting."

Will turned toward him, a speculative gleam in his eye. "From your tone of voice, it sounds like you might be a bit interested in his daughter."

"I'd better go see what I can do about those cattle." Jacob touched the brim of his Stetson. "Tell Alexander I'll deliver his message."

ঌ

In the days that followed, Jacob found—and lost—more trails

than he wanted to count. If a spring shower didn't come down at just the right time to wash fresh signs away, the tracks would lead him on a chase up into a stretch of rocky ground, then disappear. Like the ones he had just followed.

He swept his Stetson from his head and ran his fingers through his damp, tangled hair. *So much for getting into Evans's good graces by my dazzling tracking skills.* Bernie Harrelson's announcement that larger numbers of cattle were being taken at a time indicated that the rustlers were becoming bold, almost arrogant in their approach. Obviously, they didn't consider Jacob's presence on the range a threat.

He settled his hat back on his head and surveyed the slope below the rocky ledge where his most recent foray had led him. How could cattle disappear into thin air? The answer had to be out there somewhere, if only he could find it. Jacob slapped his rope against his chaps, sending a cloud of dust floating skyward. They had to know he was out here looking for them. Were they watching from some hidden spot right now, having a good laugh at his expense?

He scanned the slope and felt his heart quicken when he spotted something that caught his notice. "Let's try over there, Cap. It looks like that ground's churned up a bit."

Not just a bit, he discovered when he reached the spot, but crisscrossed by the mingled tracks of horses and at least a dozen head of cattle. "This is it, Cap, I can feel it. Let's just meander on and follow the trail and see where this one takes us."

The steel-dust seemed to catch his sense of excitement. The horse's steps quickened as he stepped out briskly, ears alert. They followed the tracks for nearly a mile. Twice, smaller numbers of tracks joined the main group from the sides. "They were pushing a pretty good-sized group here,"

Jacob mused. "Looks like they weren't afraid of being noticed. They're either feeling pretty confident of their ability, or they don't have a very high regard for mine."

But this time they'd overplayed their hand. The case was about to break; he could feel it in his bones. He half-expected to run across the stolen cattle every time he rounded a hill or topped a rise. A half mile farther, the trail made a sharp turn to the right, then dipped down into a dry wash.

Jacob felt the blood pound in his temples as he followed, then reined Cap to a halt. He stared helplessly at the bottom of the wash, where those clear-cut tracks became mere dimples in the sand, giving no indication of the direction they had taken. The familiar taste of defeat burned the back of Jacob's throat.

He slammed his fist against the saddle horn. Another dead end! With the number of failures he had racked up lately, he couldn't blame Burke for thinking he was on the side of the rustlers.

The man had every right to expect tangible results from Jacob and every reason to feel betrayed when he didn't receive them. Moreover, he was Hallie's father. That didn't make matters any easier. Bad enough to look like an inept fool in front of any one of the people he had promised to serve; even worse to do so in full view of the man he hoped would be his father-in-law one day.

"I can't afford to stay on his bad side," Jacob told Cap. "I have a feeling I'm going to be seeing a lot of the man." The one bright spot he could see in all this mess was the likelihood he would be making frequent visits to the Broken Box. The opportunity to spend time with Hallie was enough to sweeten any disappointment.

Jacob rode on, turning the situation over in his mind in the hope he might come up with a new angle he hadn't considered before. Other ranches had lost stock, but none had been hit as hard as the Broken Box. What made Burke Evans such a tempting target? Jacob tried to reason out an answer, but he couldn't see any major difference between the man and his neighbors. It wasn't like he had a shortage of riders or any other lack that would make him easy pickings. It was almost as though there were some personal reason for him to suffer the most loss.

Could someone hold a grudge against Burke? Now, that he could believe. Maybe it would pay to learn more about any enemies Burke might have made, someone who wouldn't quibble about stealing his cattle.

His mind went wheeling along possible lines of investigation. Had Burke ever done someone dirt? Shorted someone in a deal? The possibilities mounted, along with Jacob's excitement. Despite Will Bradley's assurances of Burke's goodhearted nature, Jacob had already witnessed a much darker side of the man, and he'd only known him a short time. He had tried his hardest to overlook as much as possible for Hallie's sake. Anyone else getting that kind of treatment might feel inclined to get some of his own back by whatever means necessary.

He felt a stirring of excitement at this first bit of encouragement he'd had in weeks. The next thing he'd do would be to delve into Burke Evans's background.

nine

Hallie swirled a piece of soft flannel in small circles over the surface of her saddle, spreading a coating of glistening oil across the polished leather. She breathed deeply and felt the tension of the past days slip away. The mingled scents of leather, hay, and neatsfoot oil never failed to relax her and fill her with a sense of well-being. She set the oil-soaked rag aside and wiped her hands on a scrap of burlap, careful not to get any oil stains on her skirt. She lifted the saddle and prepared to hoist it onto its stand.

A warm breath tickled the back of her neck. "Hello, you pretty thing."

Hallie whirled and clutched the saddle against her chest. Pete Edwards jumped back to avoid being slapped by the swinging stirrup leathers. "Whoa, there. You nearly hit me."

"What do you want, Pete?" After the scare he'd given her, Hallie felt in no mood to soften her tone.

His lips parted in a leer, and he leaned toward her. "Why don't you set that saddle down and let me show you?"

Hallie tightened her grip on the saddle's gullet and skirt. "Get out of here and leave me alone. I have things to do, and I'm sure you do, too."

Pete snickered. "I've got something in mind, all right. Let's start with a little kiss. You've been holding me off long enough." He moved nearer, forcing her back into the corner.

Her irritation gave way to a faint prickle of fear. "I said, leave me alone." She shoved the saddle at him and sprang to one side.

Pete knocked the saddle away, and it landed in a heap on the dusty floor. He jumped over it and moved quickly to put himself between her and the doorway. They stood in a frozen tableau, with only the sound of Pete's rough, uneven breathing invading the heavy silence. He flexed his fingers, and a slow smile worked its way across his face. "You got away from me the last time, but not today. I'm tired of playing games with you, Hallie. This time, things go my way."

Terror flowed through her veins like icy water. She did her best to inject a note of scorn into her voice, knowing if she showed her fear, she would be lost. "I'm not playing, and this is no game. Move out of my way." She started toward the door, hoping sheer bravado would carry her through.

Pete spread his arms wide and moved toward her, giving her no choice but to retreat into the corner near the stalls.

Her bluff wasn't working. Hallie fought to gain control over the panic that threatened to overcome her reason. She was no match for Pete in physical strength. She could scream, but was anyone near enough to hear her? And if no one did, what then? She rejected the idea. A scream would only let Pete know how vulnerable she felt. She couldn't afford to do anything to strengthen his position.

She inched backward, frantic at the knowledge that every step she retreated put her that much farther from escape.

Pete advanced, matching her step for step. His look of anticipation sent slivers of fear plunging through her. His voice softened and took on a cajoling tone. "You know you're going to give in one of these days, Hallie. Why not now? We could have a lot of fun, you and me."

A sense of unreality enveloped her. This couldn't be

happening, not in her own barn. Dread wrapped its steely talons around her heart. Hallie looked around, her mind scrambling to find some means of escape. The only exit lay through the wide barn doorway, and Pete stood square in her path.

If not escape, then defense. What could she use? Her gaze lit on a coil of rope, a pair of bridles. *Lord, help me!*

Pete made a grab for her, and she countered by ducking behind the center post. The sudden change in direction tangled her feet in her skirt, and she sprawled backward into a deep pile of hay. She lay motionless, the wind knocked out of her.

A satisfied chuckle rumbled from deep in Pete's throat. "There now. If that don't look inviting." He lunged toward her, a gleam of victory in his eyes.

"No!" Hallie's shriek reverberated from the rafters. With a burst of strength born of desperation, she dug her heels into the floor and pushed herself away.

Pete cursed and made a grab for her. His hand closed on the hem of her skirt. Hallie lashed out with her foot and saw his head snap back when her boot made contact with his chin. Pete cursed again. His lips drew back over his teeth in a feral snarl.

Hallie scrambled backward through the hay, knowing her only hope lay in breaking Pete's hold on her skirt. *Help me, Jesus.* Her hands clawed in the dust beneath the hay, and her fingers wrapped around a wooden handle. *Pa's sickle! Thank You!*

She yanked at her skirt with her free hand and heard the fabric rip. She scrambled to her feet and faced Pete, swinging the sharp sickle blade back and forth.

"Get away from me." The sickle blade flashed in a broad arc from right to left. "Do you understand? Leave me alone!"

She slashed the sickle in the opposite direction. "I don't want anything to do with you." *Slash.* "Now or ever." The blade flashed again.

Pete shuffled on his hands and knees, backing another step across the floor with every swing of the blade. At the doorway, he staggered to his feet and held his hands in front of him. "All right, Hallie, you win. For now, anyway." He caught his breath in ragged gasps and watched her warily.

Never taking her eyes off Pete, Hallie held the sickle before her like a sword and circled past him. When she reached the door, she turned and fled headlong toward the shelter of the house. Anguished sobs rose in her throat, but she fought to hold them back. She wouldn't give him the satisfaction of hearing her cry.

"I can be patient," he yelled from the barn. "Get it through your head, Hallie, you're mine. Next time there won't be a sickle around."

The air tore in and out of Hallie's lungs as she ran. *Oh, Lord, don't let there be a next time!*

&

The latch rattled under Hallie's fumbling fingers. She wrenched at it again and it finally shot home. Hallie sagged against the door, hardly daring to believe she had managed to escape. She bowed her head and clutched at her hair with both hands.

"I can't go through that again, Lord! I've got to make Pa understand."

But he wouldn't. The knowledge plunged a shaft of despair into her heart. In her father's eyes, Pete could do no wrong, and with his word against hers, today's encounter would be explained away as mere high-strung behavior.

If only the rustling situation hadn't claimed all Pa's attention!

With him so wrought over the missing stock, his dependence on Pete outweighed his usual good sense. Hallie racked her brain. There had to be a way to get him to listen to her long enough to be convinced of Pete's true character.

And then what? A chill crept up her spine at the thought of what would happen next if he ever fully understood the extent of Pete's unwanted advances.

She knew it as sure as she knew the sun would rise over Mingus Mountain in the morning: He would go after Pete. And in his present agitated state of mind, he wouldn't hesitate to shoot him.

Hallie sank to her knees at the sobering thought of what she could set in motion with only a few words. If her father killed Pete, he would be tried for murder. He might not hang, but he would suffer the indignity of arrest and trial, a fate almost as bad as death for someone with her father's brand of pride.

Worse yet, from all accounts, Pete was fast on the draw. What if he killed her father? He could tell the law anything he wanted. Knowing Pete, he would be sure to make it look like a case of self-defense. And given Burke's outbursts of temper lately, most people would have no problem believing he had finally snapped and gone into a murderous rage.

And Hallie would be left alone, at Pete's mercy—a possibility too horrible to contemplate.

"I can't do it," she whispered to the empty room. Setting her father against Pete could ruin their lives, and the responsibility for that would lie at her own feet. She could not—would not—jeopardize her father's well-being, maybe even his very life.

She had no choice. She would keep her troubles to herself and do her best to stay away from Pete.

ten

Jacob tapped on Buckey's office door. "Do you have a few minutes, or are you busy?"

"Never too busy for a good round of talk." The mayor of Prescott set down his pen and slid the paper he'd been writing on to one side of his desk. "How goes the rustler hunt?"

"I hoped talking to you might give me some new insight. I'm fresh out of ideas."

Buckey's dark eyes held a gleam of sympathy. "It's that bad, eh?"

"Worse." Jacob slumped into the nearest chair. "I've covered more miles than I can count, looking for some clue to what's been happening. Every time I find sign of someone moving stock, I lose it again. It seems like I can only get so far on a trail, then it just peters out."

He leaned his head against the back of the chair and stared at the map on the wall. "I've checked at the railheads in Ash Fork and Jerome, but neither place has any record of stock going out without the proper paperwork, duly signed by me."

"That would seem to eliminate that angle as a possibility."

Jacob jumped up and paced the office. "It beats me how they're moving these animals. Where are they taking them? How are they getting rid of them? They just seem to vanish into thin air."

Buckey leaned back and tented his fingers. "I heard a while back about a fellow up in Holbrook who was making a tidy profit butchering stolen cattle, then selling the beef. You might ask around and see if anything like that might be going on around here."

He pursed his lips. "If not, they almost have to be connecting with the railroad at some point in order to get that many head out of the area. Otherwise, somebody would have spotted them."

Jacob halted in midstep. "Unless. . ." He crossed to the map in three quick strides. "Have you heard of any new ranchers who have come into the area recently? Anyone who might have an interest in building up a herd without paying for it?"

Buckey nodded slowly. "We've had an influx of new people over the past year or so. There's a family near Walnut Creek, up past Williamson Valley. Then there are a couple of fellows over toward Clarkdale, on the other side of Mingus Mountain, who registered two or three new brands. And I heard about another outfit over at the base of the Bradshaws."

He stroked his mustache with the back of his forefinger. "I haven't heard anything to make me think any of those folks would be involved in something like that, but it wouldn't hurt to check them out."

"Thanks. I'll do that." Jacob resumed his seat with a lighter spirit. It felt good to have Buckey as a friend. At least one person didn't think of him as an incompetent loafer. He rolled his shoulders, easing away the tension that had been a part of him for so long. "I've been so busy running around like a headless chicken that I haven't kept up on the latest news. What's the word on Cuba?"

"Spain is trying to placate Washington, but it may be a case of too little, too late."

"You think we're looking at a war, then?"

Buckey's face took on a somber expression. "At this juncture, I'd say it's inevitable."

❧

Jacob walked down the courthouse steps with a handful of scribbled notes. Acting on Buckey's tip, he had checked on new brand registrations. He stopped under a tree near the edge of the plaza and studied the sketches he'd made: the C Bar J, the Ladder M, the 2 Lazy 2.

Jacob chuckled at the last one. *Too lazy to what?* The clever ways some of the ranchers found to incorporate a sense of humor into their chosen brands had long proved a source of amusement.

His gaze shifted back to the Ladder M, and he bent to study it more closely. The Broken Box brand was made up of two facing brackets. Jacob stooped to pick up a fallen twig and used it to sketch the brand in the dust.

And the Ladder M. . . He connected the top and bottom lines of the brackets and extended them outward, then added another vertical line in the center. As a final touch, he wrote an M next to the figure, then rocked back on his heels to study the result.

His pulse throbbed in his temple. The Broken Box brand could be overwritten into a Ladder M with very little effort. *This could be it.* He looked again at his notes. The Ladder M brand had recently been registered by one of the newcomers Buckey had mentioned over Clarkdale way.

Jacob tucked the paper into his shirt pocket and glanced at the sun's position. Too late to get all the way out there that afternoon. He walked to the hitching rail and loosened Cap's reins. He would go home to the T Bar for the night, then head over Mingus to visit the Ladder M at first light.

❧

Jacob reined Cap in a southeasterly direction. "I know, boy," he said when the steel-dust tossed his head. "We're supposed to be heading for Clarkdale. But this is right on the way. Well, almost on the way," he amended.

Truth to tell, the detour took him a good bit out of his way, but he needed to check in on the latest state of affairs at the beleaguered Broken Box. It would remind Burke he was staying on top of the situation.

And if things went the way he hoped, he might get a glimpse of Hallie.

He felt a grin crease his cheeks at the thought of seeing her again. Cap whickered and flicked his ears back and forth.

"You're right," Jacob said. "Seeing Hallie is a powerful draw for going there, but I'm just as interested in focusing on my job."

Cap shook his head and snorted. Jacob tugged his hat brim down lower over his forehead. If he couldn't convince his horse, he sure wasn't going to convince Burke Evans.

He rode into the yard at a trot, anxious to put his best foot forward. Before he could swing his leg over the cantle, the front door burst open. Burke stormed outside and planted himself squarely in Jacob's path.

"I hope you've come to tell me you've got those thieves locked up and facing a trial."

"Not yet." Jacob pulled off his hat and rolled the brim in his hands, waiting for an invitation to go inside the house. After a second look at Burke's grim expression, he knew he might as well give up on that notion.

He sent a quick glance at the front windows, hoping to see Hallie peering out at him. The curtains hung neatly across the glass. It looked like this detour was going to turn out to be strictly business after all.

Jacob turned his attention back to Burke. "I just wanted to

stop by and see if anything more had happened since the last time we talked."

Burked tipped his head back and spread his arms wide as if appealing to the heavens. When he looked back at Jacob, the expression on his face could have curdled milk. "Seems to me like you spend a powerful amount of time looking for answers in all the wrong places. For the life of me, I don't understand why you keep looking around here instead of trying to track down whoever's been stealing my stock."

He went on, his voice weighted with exaggerated patience. "If I had my cattle tucked safely away close to home, I wouldn't need your help. But they aren't here, are they?" He scooped up a pebble from the ground and threw it across the yard. "How hard is it to find some cowboy who's spending more money than he should? I could do it myself with one eye shut."

Be my guest, Jacob thought. *Let's see how far you get.* Aloud, he said, "If you have all the answers, maybe you don't need me on the case at all."

Burke fixed him with a glare. "I can't run a ranch and chase after thieves at the same time. Tracking these crooks down is what we're paying you for, and I say you're showing a pretty poor return on the wages you've been drawing."

Easy. Don't let him get to you. Jacob paused to draw a long breath and took his time forming a response. "Then instead of criticizing, why not help me do my job? Do you have any more ideas who may be behind this?" He watched Burke closely. "Anyone who might hold a grudge from the past? Someone who wants to get back at you, for whatever reason?" *The list must be a mile long.*

"I've never done anything to anybody, nothing that would be worth this, anyway." Burke set his lips in a thin line. "You seem to be mighty interested in what I may or may not have done. Suppose you tell me what you've been doing to earn your pay?"

Jacob drew himself up. "I'm on my way over to check out a new rancher in the Clarkdale area, see if he can account for all his stock."

"Don't waste your time harassing the other ranchers. They're a hard-working lot, all of them. If you're set on checking out newcomers, you ought to take a look at that batch of nesters back up in the foothills. All this started since they came here a few months back."

Burke spat on the ground and continued. "It wouldn't surprise me if the reason you can't find traces of any stock being moved is because they've been hiding them all back in the hills, trying to build a herd without having to buy foundation stock. Go see what you can find up their way, if you want to do something worthwhile. It's what I'd do. . .and what you'd be doing if you had a lick of sense."

Jacob felt his body go rigid. "I'll check into it. It would sure be hard for them to explain having cattle, though, if they didn't bring any with them when they came."

Burke scrubbed his hand through his wiry thatch of salt-and-pepper hair. "It's not your job to second-guess what will happen before you even go out there. You're supposed to get out and get to work and find these no-goods who are robbing me blind. Now get out there and do your job before I decide to find a rope and take care of things myself."

"Animals can be replaced," Jacob said. "You can't say the same for a man's life."

Burke tucked his head down between his shoulders, looking like a bull about to charge. "Someone has decided to help themselves to what I've worked for all my life. I wouldn't lose a bit of sleep over stringing up anyone who'd stoop that low.

Those are my animals, my livelihood. I'm the one who worked night and day all these years. You have no right to tell me how I ought to feel."

"You may be right about that," Jacob admitted. "I won't try to tell you I know how you feel. But I do know what the Bible says about forgiveness. 'If ye forgive men their trespasses, your heavenly Father will also forgive you.' I know that if you harbor unforgiveness in your heart, it will do you more harm than the person you're holding a grudge against.

"Forgiveness is God's way," Jacob went on. "Maybe you ought to try it. You'll sleep better at night than you would if you went out and lynched a man."

Burke's face turned as red as a brick. "The Bible also says God owns the cattle on a thousand hills. I don't have nearly that many, and it's getting less all the time. That kind of talk is fine for someone who hasn't gone through what I have, but I'm the one who's about to lose my livelihood. If you want to do something to spare a few miserable lives, you better get out there and catch those thieves before I do. Now I suggest you quit wagging your jaw and go get busy." With a low grunt, he turned and strode off toward the barn.

Jacob took his time tightening his cinch and scanned the front windows again. Still no sign of Hallie. He contemplated walking right up those porch steps and knocking on the front door like any normal suitor, but thought better of that plan. Burke's demeanor left Jacob in no doubt of the man's probable response to making a social call on his daughter.

He cast one last look at the house. His heart doubled its pace when he saw the edge of the curtain inch back.

Hallie peered out of the narrow opening and fluttered her fingers in a tiny wave. She mouthed something, but Jacob couldn't understand what she was trying to say.

He shot a glance toward the barn and saw Burke watching him from the doorway. As casually as he could, he made a show of checking his cinch and nudging Cap around so he blocked him from Burke's view.

He looked back at the window, where Hallie waved again, then pointed toward the southeast. Jacob dipped his head in a casual nod, then mounted Cap and rode off.

❧

Hallie ducked down into the wash that ran behind the house. Her moccasins sent tiny showers of sand up behind her with every step.

Had Jacob understood her signal? And if he had, what would his reaction be? Her bold action in setting up a clandestine meeting and slipping away from the house like this shocked her. She could just imagine what her father would say if he found out. The thought put wings to her feet. The farther away she got, the less likely he would be to spot her.

She rounded a bend in the wash and caught sight of Jacob, standing next to his horse twenty yards ahead. His presence both thrilled and terrified her. Bad enough to think about her father's reaction; what did Jacob think of her impetuous behavior?

His warm smile melted her fears. She slowed to a more decorous walk but was still panting for breath by the time she reached him.

"I was hoping I'd get to see you," he said, as though meeting her like this were the most natural thing in the world. "How's the calf?"

Hallie adopted a tone as casual as his. "He's fine. His leg is healing nice and straight. I even caught him trying to kick up his heels yesterday. He's going to be as good as new."

"That's good." Jacob shifted his weight from one foot to

the other, looking suddenly ill at ease. "I guess you heard me talking to your father."

"Half the county probably heard him." Hallie grinned and tried to pull off a laugh, but her smile wobbled. "To be honest, I heard him bellowing, but I couldn't make out what he said. I got the feeling he wasn't any too happy with you, though."

"You could say that." Jacob shot her a rueful grin. "He probably thought I was way out of line when I quoted scripture to him. I told him he needed to forgive whoever is behind the rustling and let the law deal with them. He didn't take it too well."

"I can imagine." Hallie plucked a blue flax blossom from the edge of the wash and twirled the delicate stem between her fingers. "He's always had a temper, but it didn't used to be so close to the surface. Looking back, I think it's been getting worse ever since Mama died, but losing so much stock has pushed him right over the edge. It seems like he's angry all the time anymore. It's like a poison eating away at him." Unbidden tears stung her eyes. She dashed them away with the back of her hand, but more welled up and spilled over to trace slow trails down her cheeks.

Jacob closed the short distance between them. His eyes, normally sky blue, took on the gray hue of a cloudy day. "I'm sorry. This can't be easy for you." He cupped her chin in his hand and wiped away her tears with his thumb.

Hallie leaned her cheek ever so slightly into the comforting warmth of his palm. "The Bible also says I ought to honor my father. How can I do that when the Bible itself doesn't condone his behavior or his attitude?" She blinked back another round of tears and stared up at Jacob.

His expression darkened. "He doesn't take his anger out on you, does he?"

"No." *Not unless you count being so preoccupied with his missing cows that he can't see his daughter's virtue is being threatened by his favorite hand.* She forced a laugh and tried to shrug away her concerns.

Though her tears had dried, Jacob still cradled her cheek in his hand. "That's a tough proposition when his actions run counter to God's Word. But I don't believe honoring your father means you necessarily agree with everything he does. Just remember that your highest responsibility is to the Lord. Love your father. . .but serve God first."

Hallie had a feeling that with her father being the one in question, that suggestion would be easier said than done.

eleven

Lucas Rawlins and Morris Atwater smiled when Jacob approached them in the back room of the Palace.

"You have news for us?" A look of anticipation lit Rawlins's face.

"Only to give the two of you a report on my progress. . .or, rather, my lack of it." Jacob outlined his investigation and its resulting dead ends. "I feel like I'm at the end of my rope," he confessed. "I've tried everything I can think of, but I keep coming up dry. I'll go on as I've begun and keep looking if you want me to. But if you feel I'm just wasting my time and your money, I'll understand." He waited stoically for their response.

The ensuing silence was shattered by the sound of the outer door banging against the wall, followed by a voice Jacob knew all too well.

"Where's Rawlins and Atwater? This whole mess has gone on too long, and I want to know what they're going to do about it." Burke Evans stomped into the room. Crimson splotches mottled his face. He stopped abruptly when he spotted Jacob, and his mouth twisted in a sneer.

"I might have known I'd find you lollygagging around here instead of out doing your job. Did you ever get out to check on those nesters, or was that whole story a trumped-up excuse to stop by my ranch in the hopes of impressing my daughter?"

Lucas Rawlins stepped forward and gripped the angry

man's shoulder. "Hold on, Burke. Jacob was just telling us about the steps he's taken to find out what's happened to those cattle."

Burke shook off Rawlins's restraining hand. "I'm not surprised. He's good with words, does a powerful lot of talking. He seems to have Hallie eating right out of his hand. But what's he done? That's what I want to know. Tell me what's happened beyond just talk."

"I went out to see those folks just after I left your place," Jacob said. "There were no signs of cattle, yours or anyone else's. They aren't rustlers, just decent, hard-working people trying to build up farms, not raise stock."

"Well, if it isn't them, who is it?" Burke thrust his chin forward. "You'd better get out there and find out instead of wasting your time loitering around town or hanging around my ranch trying to catch a glimpse of my daughter."

Burke narrowed his eyes to mere slits. "Or maybe I've been looking at it all backwards. Maybe you're just using Hallie as an excuse to snoop around my ranch. What do we know about you, anyway? Only that you showed up on our doorstep one day and waltzed right into this position without any experience to back you up. Maybe you know a whole lot more about this rustling business than you're letting on."

Muscles knotted in Jacob's jaw. "If you're implying—"

"That's enough, Evans." Rawlins stepped between them, holding his arms out like a referee in the boxing ring. "Go home and cool off before you say something you'll regret."

Burke stood as though wanting to say more, then swung around and made for the door. At the threshold, he turned and jabbed a stubby finger at each of the men in turn. "Just remember, someone out there deserves to swing at the end of a rope, and I don't much care who it turns out to be."

❧

Hands clenched inside his pockets, Jacob finished his second lap around the perimeter of the plaza and began a third. The circular route wouldn't take him very far, but he had to do something to work off the head of steam that erupted inside him after Burke Evans's tirade.

He slowed to let a cluster of chattering women saunter past, chafing until he could pick up his pace again. It might be a mild April morning in Prescott, but his rising temper made him feel as blazing hot under the collar as a Tucson afternoon in July.

If it weren't for the fact he's Hallie's father...

He felt a hand grip his shoulder. Wheeling around, he spotted Buckey O'Neill's friendly grin. "What's eating you? You look like you're being chased by Coxey's army."

Jacob answered with a rueful smile. "Is it that obvious?"

Buckey hooked his thumbs behind his belt. "Let's just say I've been watching you from my office window for the past twenty minutes. By my count, this is the third time you've circled the plaza, looking like a man ready to throttle anyone who gets in his path. You want to talk about it?"

Jacob set off again, and Buckey fell in step beside him. His expression sobered when Jacob poured out the story of Burke's outburst.

"That description doesn't fit the person I met when I came here in '82," Buckey said. "Hallie was just a little thing, and her mother, Annabel, could light up a dark night with her smile. Burke struck me as one of the most contented men on the face of the earth back then. He had a temper, sure, but he knew how to keep it in check. Now it seems that temper rules him instead of the other way around."

Jacob considered his friend's words, then nodded. "That

pretty well sums it up." The two men walked in silence, completing another lap around the courthouse square before Jacob spoke again.

"He has reason enough to be angry about what's happening now, but I get the feeling it goes back to more than just the loss of his stock. It's almost like he's mad at God for something. Whatever the case, he needs to turn it loose and move on instead of letting it consume him like this."

"You could be right. Bitterness can eat at a man like a canker." Buckey shook his head, then his face brightened. "Have you heard the news about Cuba? Major Brodie is ready to recruit a whole regiment from the West." His face lit up with an eager fire. "I say we can recruit a thousand from Arizona Territory alone. Why, we have the best of the West right here. These men have been tested by fire already. They can ride, they can shoot, and they won't run at the sound of a bullet."

He clapped his hands. "We'll put together the finest cavalry unit the world has ever seen. If that doesn't show the nation we're ready for statehood, I don't know what will."

His words stirred something deep inside Jacob. Buckey's passion was born of a love for a land he had come to as a young man. But Arizona Territory was Jacob's own birthplace, the place he planned to call his home for all the rest of his days. Why not take a leaf from Buckey's book and pour himself into helping to shape Arizona's future? "Statehood does have a sweet sound to it."

A spark of enthusiasm flickered and grew into a flame. "As for going to war to do it, I guess nothing good is achieved without some risk, is it?"

Buckey stopped abruptly and faced him. "Just think of what the results could be." His face lit up. "Who wouldn't gamble for a star on the flag?"

Jacob felt his excitement grow to match Buckey's. Giving of himself for his territory—his country—might be the finest thing he'd ever be called to do. Not everyone was handed the opportunity to invest themselves in such a noble cause.

A more prosaic thought insinuated itself into his mind: Going off to war would also serve as an honorable means to get him out of the tangle he'd become enmeshed in here. Unless God worked a miracle, this might be his only chance to prove to himself and everyone else that he wasn't an incompetent fool.

It's about time I show the folks around here I can do something right.

A broad smile spread across his face. "Let me know where to sign up. I'm going to Cuba with you."

twelve

"That's the best fried chicken I've had in a long time, Amy." Jacob leaned back and rubbed his full stomach. "I don't know why all these years of eating your Sunday dinners hasn't turned Dan into a round ball."

Amy blushed, and Jacob offered a silent apology to his mother. She would always be the finest cook he had ever known, but still, Amy's cooking came in at a close second.

Dan helped himself to a mound of mashed potatoes, then passed the serving bowl to Jacob. "Any more luck on finding those rustlers, or shouldn't I ask?"

"Nothing worth getting excited about," Jacob said. The change in subject dampened his contentment. Then he remembered his earlier conversation.

"I did hear something worthwhile, though. Buckey O'Neill told me they're getting ready to recruit troops for the war with Spain. I'm going to sign up the first chance I get."

Dan leaned forward eagerly. "It's getting that close, then?"

"It sure looks that way." Jacob took another bite of fried chicken and chewed with renewed enthusiasm. "At least that way I'll have something to show for my efforts. Not like—" A sharp clatter halted him in midsentence.

Amy stared at Dan, her face pale. "What does that look on your face mean? Do you have some notion of running off to join up, too?"

Dan shot an apologetic glance at Jacob before answering. "If I were a footloose young buck, I probably would. When I think about the way we tend to take our freedom for granted, then realize there's a country full of people not far away who have never tasted that kind of freedom. . .well, it makes me want to jump right on the bandwagon and go help drive the Spanish out.

"But then I remember that God has given me responsibilities right here at home. Who would take care of you and the children? Who would look after this place? I can't go haring off and leave all that in someone else's lap. It wouldn't be right." He reached across the table to take Amy's hand. "Don't worry, honey. I'm not planning to rush off anywhere."

He squeezed her fingers, then turned back to Jacob. "I almost forgot. I wanted to pass along something I heard yesterday. Tom Miller of the J Bar D said he saw George Dixon at the Prescott saddlery the other day. Tom figured he was taking an old saddle in for repairs, but it turns out Dixon was ordering a brand, spanking new one. Really fancy from the sounds of it—fully carved and with a passel of Mexican silver."

Jacob set his fork down and stared unwaveringly at Dan. "That had to cost a pretty penny."

Dan nodded. "Nearly three months' wages, from what Tom figured. Dixon has never been known for being much good at hanging on to his pay. Tom wondered where he got hold of that kind of money."

Excitement throbbed in Jacob's veins. "This could be the break I've needed. Who does Dixon work for?"

"He's with the Flying V."

"The one a few miles down the valley from the Broken Box?" At Dan's nod, Jacob's mind whirled, considering the implications of this news. He picked up his water tumbler and set it directly in front of his plate. "Let's say that's your place. This—" he positioned a spoon to the left "—is the Broken Box."

He lined up the salt cellar and a bowl of peas, completing the model. "That would put the Flying V and the Rafter Five here. . .and here." He leaned forward over the layout he had created and studied the relationships of the places. "Look at this, Dan. The Flying V land butts right up against Broken Box range. It just might be the connection I've been looking for."

"And all those ranchers said they've been missing stock?" Dan eyed the diagram and pursed his lips.

"You figurin' out how to catch those rustlers, Uncle Jacob?" Ben spoke around a mouthful of mashed potatoes, earning him a reproving look from his mother.

Thoughts wheeled through Jacob's mind faster than he could keep up with them. "Do you remember hearing about what happened up in Wyoming when that bunch of cowboys decided they weren't getting paid enough and figured they ought to do something about it?"

Dan's brow puckered, then he nodded slowly. "Weren't they the ones who decided to pick up some extra money by rustling some of their employers' stock?"

"They're the ones. That was the beginning of all the trouble that led up to the Johnson County range war. Maybe we have something similar happening right here."

"You've already visited Owen Ladd at the Flying V, haven't you?" Dan leaned over the diagram, ignoring Amy's repeated throat clearing.

"He was one of the first ones I met." Jacob felt his newfound excitement flicker. "But he said he hadn't lost that much stock."

"But that could make sense if his own cowboys were a little hesitant to steal too much from their own boss."

Jacob stared at his friend, sickened by the thought of that kind of betrayal. "I'd sure hate to be caught doing something like that. A man could get strung up mighty quick if—"

"Could we bring this conversation back to lighter topics?" Amy's honeyed tone softened the implied rebuke. "I'm afraid this kind of talk isn't good for our digestion. . .or for little pitchers with big ears." She tilted her head in the direction of Catherine and Ben, both listening avidly.

"Sorry, Amy." Jacob ducked his head and scooped up a bite of potatoes. Amy had every reason to be upset. Youngsters like Benjamin and Catherine shouldn't have to listen to him expound on topics like lynching and the threat of war.

He'd been the one to steer the conversation in the wrong direction. It was up to him to find a new subject. A memory stirred, and he brightened.

"Hey, Catherine, I almost forgot. I have a message for you."

"For me?" The little girl looked up from gnawing a chicken leg, round-eyed. "From who?"

"Whom," Amy corrected.

"Whom from?"

Jacob grinned. "From Will Bradley's boy over at the Heart Cross. He said to tell you he has a new pet frog, and you can play with it anytime you want."

Catherine jerked upright so hard her red-gold curls quivered. "That Alexander Bradley! He'd better watch out."

Dan eyed his daughter. "What's all this about? Sounds to me like he's just trying to be friendly."

"Not him." Catherine shook her head emphatically. "That wasn't what he meant at all. Last fall at the church picnic, he put a slimy ol' frog down the back of my dress, then he just hooted when I screamed and couldn't get it to drop out."

Ben snickered, and she rounded on him with a vengeance. "You hush! It wasn't a bit funny. I had to go down to the creek where there were some bushes to hide behind, then I had to peel clear down to my—"

"Catherine." Amy's voice held a warning note.

"Sorry, Mama." Catherine's lower jaw jutted out mutinously. "But it wasn't funny. And now he thinks he's warning me he'll get me again. If he tries anything else like that, he's really going to catch it."

"Catherine Elizabeth!" Amy's stern tone left no room for argument.

"Yes, ma'am." She dropped down to a whisper. "But he'd better watch his own back, that's all I have to say."

Jacob caught the muttered threat and smothered a grin.

"Are you two finished?" Dan asked. "I think it's about time you were excused."

The children scraped their chairs back with alacrity and scooted out the door.

Benjamin's voice floated in from the front porch. "They're just being nice because Uncle Jacob is here. I bet you're really going to get it later."

"Am not."

"Are, too."

"Am not."

Their bickering tones faded into the distance, and Amy sighed. "If it isn't rustlers, it's wild children." She rose and picked up a dish from the sideboard. "Apple pie, anyone?"

❧

Jacob lay under his blankets that night, staring into the darkness and going over the information Dan had shared. Dixon had more money than anyone would expect him to. Dixon worked for the Flying V, which adjoined the Broken Box. . . and several other hard-hit ranches.

Could Dixon be responsible for the thefts plaguing the valley over the past few months?

The thought turned his stomach, but it had to be considered. What would make a man ignore his loyalty to his own brand?

Jacob punched the pillow into a wad and folded his arms under his head, pondering his next move. If Dixon was brazen enough to flaunt ill-gotten money around town like that, it would line up with the attitude he had observed recently in the rustlers' behavior. *That's one cowboy who's going to bear watching,* he decided just before he faded into sleep.

A sudden noise brought him bolt upright. Jacob sat motionless, every sense focused on the sound that had jolted him back to wakefulness. Had he imagined it or. . .

There it came again, a soft tap on the window glass. Jacob swung his feet over the edge of his bed, lifted his pistol from the holster slung over the bedpost, and padded across the plank floor. He had opened the window partway before retiring to let in the fresh spring breezes. Jacob caught one edge of the fluttering curtain and eased it back.

Only the darkness met his gaze, but he sensed the presence of someone just outside.

"Who's there?" he whispered.

A boot scraped against the dirt. "It don't matter," came the hoarse reply.

Jacob pushed the window open farther and started to lean out.

"Hold it," said the disembodied voice. "I've got some information to pass on, but I don't want to give myself away. Don't strike a match; don't try to see who I am. Agreed?"

"Okay." Jacob drew back inside. "I'm listening." He heard a whisper of sound, as though the other man shifted his position closer to the window.

"Those rustlers you've been after? They've got the makings of a herd bunched up in a box canyon back in the foothills at the north end of Broken Box range. They're getting ready to move them out soon. They're talking about calling it quits after selling this herd. They know they're pushing their luck, running the operation this long, and they're ready to move on."

Jacob clutched the windowsill with his free hand. "Where? When?"

"Late Friday night. There's going to be a full moon. They plan to push them over the mountain, then sell them to the mines and some of the army posts over in New Mexico. If you want to catch them, that's the time to do it."

"How do you know all this, and why should I believe you?"

"I've been a part of it almost from the beginning, but I can't do it anymore. Some good people are getting hurt, and it's been eating at me. I'm pulling out tonight."

"You know who they are. Give me some names."

"No." The emphatic tone told Jacob there would be no point in arguing. "I'm not that much of a traitor. You want to catch them, you get out there and do it. That's all I'm going to tell you."

Jacob fought back the urge to reach out through the window and choke the information out of the man. "Just one name then. Who's the leader?"

Gravel crunched and footsteps faded away into the night.

Jacob stuck his head outside and peered into the darkness. He saw the faint outline of a shadow melding into the deeper gloom, then nothing.

He stared up at the three-quarter moon. By Friday, it would be full, giving the rustlers plenty of light to move the stolen cattle.

And giving him plenty of light to put a crimp in their plans.

Jacob smiled and stretched out on his bed again, too wide-awake to think of sleep. He had plans of his own to make.

thirteen

Monday morning, Jacob rose with the sun, surprised he'd gone back to sleep at all after his midnight visitor. He made a quick breakfast of biscuits and coffee, then saddled his mount and rode south from the T Bar in the direction of the Broken Box.

He took his time, studying the terrain with a new appreciation for the rustlers' choice of location. It would be easy to drive stock from the other ranches in the area to this place. After a short push over Mingus Mountain, they would be able to hit well-traveled routes to the mines, army posts, or even Mexico. Whoever was in charge of this outfit either laid his plans well or managed to stumble onto the perfect setup.

Cap seemed to pick up on his mounting excitement and moved into a brisk trot. Jacob held him back to a more relaxed pace. No telling who might be watching from behind rocks in these hills or from just inside the line of cedars. It wouldn't do to show undue interest in the area and take a chance on spooking his quarry.

Up ahead, a lone rider appeared over the top of a rise. An honest cowboy just out doing his job or one of the rustlers? Jacob slouched back in his saddle and adopted a bored expression, grateful the oncoming rider wouldn't be able to see his heart hammering against his ribs. The rider waved, and Jacob returned the salute.

By the time they were thirty yards apart, Jacob recognized one of Edgar Wilson's riders. He pulled up and waited just west of a large rock formation.

"Morning," he greeted the lanky cowboy.

"Howdy. What are you doing over this way?"

"I'm supposed to see a fellow over in Camp Verde. Is there a quicker way over Mingus than just following the road to Jerome?"

The cowboy shook his head. "Nah, this is probably your best bet. If you wanted a way that isn't as steep, you could cut over to Cherry and go around that way, but that'll be farther and take longer to get there."

Jacob nodded his thanks, then touched his heels to Cap's flanks and set off again. At the rock formation, he twisted around to see if the other rider was watching before moving to put the stack of broken boulders between himself and the cowboy. To his relief, the other man seemed to be riding away with a total lack of concern.

Jacob eased Cap toward the right side of the trail, then slipped in among some brush and faded into the tree line.

From his earlier studies of Buckey's map, he had a fair idea of where to look for those box canyons, but he needed to determine their exact locations. He picked his way through the rough terrain until he found a rocky promontory. Tethering Cap at its base, he climbed to the top and sat cross-legged at the summit.

Perfect. The higher elevation gave him a bird's-eye view of the whole area. He took out his field glasses and proceeded to sweep the area. He took it in small sections, examining a bit at a time, checking for movement of cattle or horsemen. When he headed back down and started investigating, he would need to know just how to get to the box canyons. And he wanted to make sure he'd be alone.

He spent the better part of an hour checking things out and getting a feel for the lay of the land. From his vantage point, he spotted three likely looking canyons. The hint of a trail appeared to lead toward the farthest one.

Jacob lowered the glasses and studied the approach to that area. If he wanted to hide a bunch of cows, that spot would be a prime choice. He would check all three canyons, though, just to be thorough. Anticipation at the thought of finally getting the goods on his quarry made his pulse pound.

He clambered back down the steep slope and mounted Cap. He took his time and chose what he thought would be the least visible route. He hadn't spotted a soul out there apart from Wilson's rider but couldn't be positive no one sat watching him. "Come on, boy," he whispered. "Let's go see what we can find."

Thirty minutes later, he had eliminated the first canyon as a possibility. A thorough examination showed only a few tracks heading into it. From the canyon rim, he spotted one lone cow grazing down in the bottom.

He made a mental note of her description: one horn pointed up and one pointed down. The tip of the upright horn had been broken off at some point. That cow would be easy to recognize if he ever saw her again. He pulled out his glasses and looked for the brand. A Rafter Five. He'd have to remember that.

The second canyon yielded even less: no tracks, no sign, no livestock. With a feeling of certainty welling up within him, Jacob pressed on toward the third.

Along the way, he spotted fresh tracks and cow flops. *This is it.* He guided Cap as close to the rim of the canyon as he dared to keep his own tracks from being noticeable to anyone who might ride that way. And he felt sure there would be someone. Every instinct told him this was the place.

Cap let out a soft whinny. "Easy, boy," he murmured. He

stroked his hand along the steel-dust's neck. He hadn't seen signs of any other riders about, but he didn't want to be surprised.

Spotting the glint of water on the canyon floor below, he pulled up and took a long look. A small pond shimmered in the sunlight. The earth around the pool had been churned into a patchwork of mud.

Beyond the pond, a brush fence stretched from one side of the canyon to the other. A trail led up to the line of brush, then reappeared on the other side. *Gotcha*. The tracks told the story. The cattle had been driven into the canyon, then fenced in where they had abundant feed and water. And they were still down there, he knew it, just waiting to be moved on Friday night.

He dismounted and hunkered down in a clump of cliff rose so he could study the layout and determine his next move.

From deeper in the canyon, he heard lowing, and a line of cattle ambled into view. Jacob swept the herd with his gaze and did a quick estimate. There must be upward of seventy-five head down there. If the rustlers got the going rate. . . He pursed his lips in a soundless whistle. That would add up to a nice chunk of money. Depending on the number of people involved in this scheme, it could add up to as much as several years' wages for each of them. Plenty of reason for some men to ignore their scruples.

His sense of justice pushed for going down there right now and returning those cattle to their rightful owners, but his better judgment held him back. Returning the stolen animals wouldn't bring the rustlers to justice. How often had his father advised him to take his time and do things right? Waiting went against his grain, but he knew it was the right thing to do.

All right. He'd wait for Friday night and the full moon,

then he would see it finished. He could have the whole matter resolved before he rode off for Cuba and glory.

Jacob stood up and worked the stiffness out of his knees. He remounted and rode along the rim, seeking the entrance to the canyon and looking out for the best place to set up his ambush Friday night. More than likely, they'd bring in the last batch of cattle and slap on a road brand. That would cost them precious time and give Jacob a chance to nab them.

Down there, he decided, where the canyon opened up to the valley beyond. The slope wasn't too steep and offered concealment in the form of scattered brush. He would lie in wait there and let them drive the cattle inside the canyon, then stop the herd when they came back out.

He eased Cap through the trees to the edge of the meadow. Several likely clumps of manzanita and buckbrush caught his notice. Any one of them would make an excellent watching place.

Should he let anyone else in on his plans? Form a posse of trustworthy riders, perhaps? He considered the possibility but decided against it. The more people who knew about this, the greater risk of having someone give away information. Even if that were done unwittingly, it would still prove disastrous to his plan.

What about Dan? He discarded the idea almost as soon as it sprang into his mind. His lifelong knowledge of Dan's character left him in no doubt as to his friend's trustworthiness. But Dan had a wife and children, and cornering a group of desperate men could prove dangerous. Jacob had a feeling Amy wouldn't be any crazier about Dan taking on a bunch of rustlers than she was about the idea of him going off to war. No, he'd just have to do it alone.

He would arrive early and take up his position late Friday

afternoon. Come full dark, he would be in a perfect spot to watch their every move.

In another four days, it would all be over. Jacob longed to get his hands on the miscreants who had been causing him such misery.

He glanced up at the sun's position. No point in continuing on the road to Jerome today. By the time he got to Camp Verde, it would be late.

But it didn't matter. A ripple of elation set his heart dancing. His sole purpose in talking to the rancher over there was to check with him about missing stock. With the lead his mysterious nighttime informant had given him, the trip over the mountain just might not be necessary after all.

Instead, he turned Cap in a wide loop and swung back by the Broken Box. It wouldn't hurt to put in an appearance and let Burke Evans know he'd been hard at work.

And there was always the chance he might see Hallie again—without having to sneak out to the wash this time.

❧

The clang of a hammer on an anvil echoed throughout the yard when Jacob rode up. He spotted Burke shoeing a horse in the shade of the barn. The door of the house flew open at his approach, and Hallie trotted down the steps to greet him with a bright smile.

Burke started in their direction, still carrying the heavy hammer. Hallie pulled up and halted a few yards from Jacob. She settled a more demure expression on her face, but the light in her eyes didn't dim. Jacob felt his heart do flip-flops.

"Something you wanted to see me about?" Burke's lowered brows formed a hard, straight line over the bridge of his nose.

Jacob gave Hallie a quick smile and turned to Burke.

"I wanted to let you know I've come up with some new information. There's a good chance I may be on their track at last."

The lines in Burke's face softened. "What have you found out?"

Jacob hesitated. Given Burke's hotheaded nature and tendency to shoot his mouth, did he want to trust him with the only decent lead that had come his way?

"I can't tell you anything definite right now," he hedged. "But I do have something pretty solid to go on this time." The answer sounded like a poor excuse, even to his ears.

Burke grunted and turned back toward the barn. "I've got to get back to that shoe while it's still hot. Not all of us can go lollygagging around, pretending we're working."

This isn't going well at all. If he ever wanted to make a connection with this man, he needed to start now. Jacob hesitated and glanced back and forth between Burke and Hallie. Tempting as it would be to stand visiting with Hallie, the better choice would be to start mending fences. He turned and followed Burke.

Hallie threw him a quizzical glance, then trailed after both of them. She dragged an empty crate over to the shade and sat on it not far from where her father worked.

Burke grabbed the red-hot horseshoe from the fire with a pair of tongs and held it on the anvil. He gave it a few more taps with the hammer, then held it up to check it against the old shoe.

After a minor adjustment or two, he dropped the shoe into a nearby bucket of water. Steam rose with a loud hiss. Burke slipped the tongs into a loop on the side of the anvil stand, then turned to Jacob and planted his meaty fists on his hips. "You got something else on your mind?"

"Not really." *This was really a stupid idea.* "I just thought we could visit a bit."

Burke snorted, then retrieved the tongs and fished in the bucket for the horseshoe. Water dripped off it to the ground, but no steam. Burke carried it to the tethered horse, where he checked the fit against the mare's hoof.

Still bent over beside the mare, he called over his shoulder, "So did you have anything to say, or were you just wanting to learn the right way to shoe a horse?"

Jacob felt his face grow warm. He'd come up with the bright idea of suggesting a visit; now he floundered for some topic of conversation. He glanced at Hallie, hoping for inspiration.

She shrugged, but gave him an encouraging nod and made hand gestures for him to continue.

"I guess you've heard the news about Cuba?" He flinched as soon as the words left his mouth. Of course Burke had heard the news. It was the topic on everyone's lips.

Burke picked up a rasp and leveled off the bottom of the horse's hoof. "Can't say I've paid much attention to it. I have enough problems of my own."

Jacob perked up. Finally, something he could sound knowledgeable about. "It looks like war is on the horizon. Mayor O'Neill is recruiting troops for a special Arizona regiment. I plan to sign up as soon as he's ready to accept volunteers."

Burke dropped the rasp and straightened slowly, his face growing redder by the second. He leveled a beefy forefinger at Jacob's chest and advanced toward him. "You mean to tell me you plan to take off and just leave this job hanging? Let me get this straight. You can tell me every last detail about what's going on, on some island nobody cares about, but you don't know the first thing about what's happening closer to home?"

He stepped nearer, so close that Jacob could smell the coal smoke that clung to him. "I want you to understand something, and understand it right now: I don't care about a bunch of foreign rebels three thousand miles away. I care about my cows!" A fresh wave of red crept up his face. "You don't seem to want to do your work, and I can't get mine done with you standing there jawing at me." He threw down the rasp and strode toward the house. "The mare can wait. I'll finish the job later."

Jacob stared after him, unable to look at Hallie. "I did a fine job of botching that, didn't I?"

Only silence met his question. He forced himself to meet her gaze.

She stared back at him, her face pale. "You're really planning to leave? Just like that?"

I'm doing a great job of breaking this news. "Riding gives a man plenty of time to think, and I've been doing a lot of that. We Americans have been blessed by God with the freedoms we have. It only seems right to help others who want to gain that same freedom. Don't you agree?"

Hallie looked down for a moment, then raised her head. Tears shimmered along her lower lashes. "In principle, yes. But I'm finding it's easy to agree with a principle when it doesn't cost you anything."

Jacob took her hands and drew her to her feet. Could her words mean what he hoped they did? She stared up at him, her eyes luminous pools of confusion. He pressed her hands against his chest. "This isn't a decision I've made lightly. I know we've barely had time to get to know each other, but leaving you is one of the hardest choices I've ever had to face. God brought us together, and I want to find out what He has in store for us."

Hallie's lips trembled. "I want that, too. But how is that going to happen if you go off to Cuba? You're willing to give your life for people you don't even know when there's so much here to live for."

He stared at the softness of her lips, longing to taste their sweetness. "Sometimes a man has to be willing to make a sacrifice."

"But it isn't just yours. You're asking your family. . .and me. . .to make that sacrifice, too. You want us to lay our happiness on the line, and we don't get to make that choice for ourselves."

Jacob lowered his head until he could feel the soft brush of her breath against his cheek. "Will you wait for me, Hallie? It shouldn't take long."

She pulled back slightly and stared at him as if fixing that moment in her mind for all eternity. "I feel like I've been waiting for you all my life. I'll still be waiting when you come back." Her voice quavered. "Just make sure you do come back."

Jacob pressed his lips against her eyelids, then crushed her against him in a tight embrace. "I'll come back to you, Hallie. I promise."

He felt her arms slide around his shoulders, and she pressed her face into the hollow of his neck. "I'll be praying," she whispered.

fourteen

The sun shone bright in a cloudless sky, and a light breeze filtered down through the cedars. A perfect spring afternoon, and all the more perfect because she could spend it outdoors. Hallie kicked Gypsy into a lope and reveled in the joy of being out on her own. She had plenty of time to herself at the house, but it wasn't the same as being outside where she could look across the rolling hills.

Somehow, prayer didn't come as easily at home when she found chores waiting for her everywhere she turned. Prayer was what she needed just now, and lots of it. In the four days since Jacob told her of his intention to march off to Cuba, she'd needed nothing more than time like this to pour out the cry of her heart to the Almighty.

"He's the one I've prayed for all my life, Lord. Am I going to lose him before we ever get the chance to discover this love You've given us?"

Her breath caught in her throat. *Did I say "love"?* "I do love him," she whispered. Then she threw her head back and said it right out loud. "I love Jacob Garrett!"

Her joy dimmed when she thought of their last conversation. "Please, God, isn't there any way You can keep him from going to war? I do want the Cuban people to have freedom. I think that's what You want, too. But I don't want to risk Jacob for them to have it."

She pulled Gypsy down to a walk and asked the question that had tormented her for the past four days: "Is it fair for

102

me to ask You to keep him home when so many other women will be sending their loved ones off?"

Desire for Jacob warred with the desire to honor her Lord. "But I don't have any 'right' to him, do I? Jacob belongs to You and You alone."

A sigh of surrender escaped her. "All right. You win. I'll try to accept Your will in this, whatever it may be. And I leave Jacob. . .and our love. . .in Your hands."

She swept her fingers across her cheeks to brush the tears away and tried to regain her joy in being out on her own. At one time, her afternoon rides had been her delight. How long had it been since she'd enjoyed the freedom to come up into the foothills alone like this?

Since Pete Edwards started trying to push himself on me? The words flashed through her mind like a bolt of lightning. She rolled her shoulders as if she could shrug off the sudden impulse to look behind her. Pete wasn't anywhere around today. He and the other hands had been checking the grass at the south end of the range since Wednesday.

What a contrast! On the one hand, there was Pete and his unwelcome overtures. On the other, Jacob, with his tender heart and caring ways. Two more opposite men would be hard to imagine.

Hallie closed her eyes and breathed in the cedar-scented air. The first moment she laid eyes on Jacob, she sensed someone special had entered her life. *I just didn't dream how special. Please, God, don't take him away just when I've found him.*

Gypsy slowed when she reached the bottom of the slope, as if waiting for direction. Hallie glanced over her shoulder at the house and barn in the distance and wondered whether she should turn back or proceed up through the trees.

Her sense of adventure won out. She hadn't been up in the

hills in months. She nudged Gypsy into a trot and rode uphill.

She smelled it before she saw it—the acrid stench of smoke. Hallie straightened in her saddle and peered around, probing the woods with her gaze. Where was it coming from? A brush fire could get out of hand more rapidly than anyone could imagine; the blackened area near the top of the hill attested to that. Hallie remembered watching from the safety of the ranch yard three years before, praying her father and the cowboys would get it under control before it could sweep across the plain, consuming everything in its path. She couldn't let that happen again.

She pushed deeper into the trees. *Where is it?* And could she put it out alone once she found it? Hallie's stomach clenched, and a dozen thoughts spun through her mind. Her father was moving one of the bulls to a different section, two miles or more away. How long would it take to track him down and bring back help?

Too long. She had no choice; she would have to take care of it alone.

Hallie tilted her head back and scanned the sky. *There.* Not far ahead, a thin gray thread of smoke snaked up through the trees.

She started to spur her horse forward, then frowned. That seemed an odd place for a fire to start. Could some drifter have gone off and left a campfire unattended?

He'd have to be an idiot to do something like that, as dry as it gets around here. But not everyone understood the possibilities of wildfire—or cared. However the fire started, Hallie had to check it out. She guided Gypsy uphill, weaving her way through the cedars.

The thick trees opened up onto a flat grassy area. Hallie

heard a calf bawl somewhere ahead of her. Then she spotted it: slate-colored smoke seeming to rise from the ground. She looked again and realized it was coming up over the edge of a small canyon.

Prickles of unease danced along her arms. She could think of only one reason a fire and bellowing cows would go together: branding. But all their cowboys were busy on the south range.

Fear squeezed her throat. She slid off Gypsy and dropped the reins to the ground. "Wait here," she whispered, sliding her hand along the mare's glossy neck.

Hallie crouched and crept across the ground, careful not to make a sound that would give away her presence. Ten feet from the lip of the canyon, she dropped down and covered the rest of the distance on all fours.

She approached the edge gingerly. Even before she reached it, the telltale smell of singed hair assailed her nostrils, and she knew her suspicions had been correct. Someone was branding cows in the canyon, and none of the Broken Box hands were in the area. It could mean only one thing: She had found the rustlers.

Now what? It would be absurd to even contemplate trying to capture them on her own. But she had to do something. *What?* She flattened out, pressing her chest against the dirt, and inched nearer to the edge. If she could actually witness them at work, get descriptions of them or their horses, she could pass that information to Jacob. Finally, he would have something solid to work with. Elated at the thought, she raised her head high enough to peer over the dirt ledge.

A hiss of disappointment escaped her lips. A clump of cedars grew along the bottom of the shallow canyon. Their tops rose up directly in front of her, blocking her view. She would have to find a better vantage point. Drawing back slightly, Hallie pushed herself along a course parallel to the canyon rim.

Muffled voices floated upward. "Two more to go, then we'll run these on back with the others."

Hallie's stomach knotted. If she didn't hurry, they would leave before she could get a look at them.

A small clump of sagebrush stood near her. She reached out to grasp a branch and pulled herself up to the rim. The trees thinned out at that point. If she pushed herself forward just a bit, she ought to have an unobstructed view.

She inched forward. The ground crumbled away under her hands, sending a thin stream of dirt trickling down the twenty feet to the canyon floor below. Hallie scrambled back, heart pounding at her near escape. She pressed her knee into the dirt for better purchase and felt the ground beneath her shift, then give way.

Hallie clawed at the dirt frantically, desperate to find a handhold. Her fingers grasped the branch and she hung on. The stout bush held firm for a few moments, then she watched as the roots pulled free of the soil.

She slithered down the slope, her fingers digging into the loose soil. *Jesus, help me!* It took all her willpower not to scream the prayer aloud. Maybe by some miracle the rustlers wouldn't hear her bumpy descent.

Her body slammed against a rock, knocking the wind out of her and loosening her tenuous hold on the canyon wall. With nothing to slow her fall, she began to roll downhill with increasing speed. Branches tore at her clothing as she crashed through a tangle of bushes and landed in a heap on the canyon floor.

They know I'm here. No one could have missed the racket

she had made on the way down. Hallie lay as she had landed, face down, hardly daring to breathe.

Heavy footsteps pounded across the dirt. Hallie lay motionless and prayed for God to intervene.

She glimpsed two pairs of denim-clad legs approaching. *Please, Lord, don't let them see me.* She squeezed her eyes shut.

fifteen

"Well, what do we have here?" A harsh voice spoke from a point in front of her, dashing her hopes.

"Looks like we've got us a visitor." The second speaker drew nearer, and his voice tightened. "Ain't that the Evans girl? What's she doing out this way?"

Hallie heard other footsteps behind her. A hand gripped the back of her head and shoved her face into the dirt. "Get a rope." She could barely make out the deep, gravelly voice over the thrum of blood pounding in her ears. "We'll hogtie her now and take care of her when we're finished here."

No! Hallie brought her hands up under her shoulders and pushed against the ground with all her might, but she couldn't raise herself an inch.

Her captor chuckled. "Won't do you a bit of good," he rasped. "Me and the boys are used to tying calves all day long, and calves are a lot bigger and stronger than a little thing like you."

As if to prove his point, the cowboy's rough hands seized her wrists from behind and bound them together with a few quick twists of rope. Hallie kicked and struggled, but she was no match for the men. She gasped for air and drew in a lungful of dust. She flailed wildly with her feet and felt her boot connect with something solid.

One of the men cursed. "That's enough. We'll see how much you can kick when I get through with you."

Hallie felt her ankles gripped and lashed together. Then her feet were yanked up toward her back and bound to the rope holding her wrists.

"There. That ought to take care of her."

"Just a minute." The deep-voiced man kept his hold on the back of her head. "It won't do a bit of good to tie her if she can still get a look at us." He pressed his knee into the middle of her back, holding her immobile while he wound a kerchief around her head and pulled it tight over her eyes.

"That's better." He stood, releasing the pressure on her back. "Let's get back to work."

Hallie rolled onto her side, spitting gobs of dust out of her mouth, fighting for air.

"Did you hear me?" the rough voice growled. "Get back to work!"

"Wait a minute." It was the first voice she had heard, now thin and tense. "What are we going to do with her?"

"We're going to finish what we've started, then you boys can get out of here. I'll see about letting her go. . .if she promises to behave herself."

The footsteps moved away, and Hallie heard a new set of noises: scuffles and thumps, the sound of something heavy being dragged across the earth, the sizzle of burned flesh, then a plaintive bawl.

They're altering brands. She heaved in great gulps of air, trying to calm herself. She had to think, to focus.

If they were going to kill her, they would have done it already. She was safe, at least for the moment.

But they can't just let me go. I know too much. Her chest tightened with the dull ache of fear.

"I knew things had gone too easy for us," the first speaker worried aloud. "Just when we're ready to wrap the operation up, look what happens. Maybe we oughta just pull out with what we've already got instead of waiting for tonight."

"Shut up! One more night means more money than any of us could make in three years of punching cows. I don't intend to quit before we've got all we can handle. Just leave it to me. I'll deal with her."

"You ain't going to kill her, are you?" Footsteps crunched on loose rock, and the voices grew softer.

Hallie strained to hear.

"And get the whole country out after us? Of course I ain't going to kill her." He chuckled. "Here's a thought: Maybe I'll take her along and send back word we've eloped."

His companions snickered.

A low moan escaped Hallie's throat. Maybe death wasn't the worst thing she had to fear.

She had to get away. If she could just reach one of the knots. . . No good. Her fingers had gone numb.

Hallie wriggled and strained against the knots. All she succeeded in doing was make the rope cut more deeply into her wrists. She rolled over to her other side, desperate for relief from the constant pull against her limbs. Her shoulders felt like they were being wrenched from their sockets.

"Let's get this bunch up the canyon with the rest. Then we'll call it good until tonight."

"What about the girl?"

Hallie froze.

"I told you, I'll take care of her when we get back. She ain't going nowhere." The creak of saddle leather was followed by horses snorting and the cowboys yipping as they moved the cows along.

Gritting her teeth against the raw pain in her shoulders, Hallie squirmed with all her might, but the knots held fast. Her desperation mounted. She had to get away. She *had* to!

Maybe she could find a sharp rock, something she could use to cut through the ropes. If she could only see! Hallie rubbed her face against the ground, trying to pull the blindfold loose.

She felt the vibration under her cheek before she heard the patter of feet running toward her. Determination gave way to despair, and the strength drained from her limbs. She had given it her best, but she had lost. She braced herself for what would come next.

Light fingers brushed against her hands and tugged at the ropes. "Hold still," a small voice ordered. "I had to make sure they were gone before I came down here. We've got to hurry before they come back."

"Wha— Who—"

"Oh, sorry." The knots on the kerchief loosened, and the blindfold fell free.

Hallie blinked and squinted at the sun's glare. *"Catherine?"*

The young girl squatted beside Hallie, the tip of her tongue peeking out from between her lips as she concentrated on picking the knots apart. "Roll over a little farther. Maybe I can get at the rope better that way."

Hallie complied. "What are you—never mind, we'll sort that out later. Can you get the knots undone?"

"I'm trying. Almost done. . . There!" She sat back on her heels with a look of triumph. "Good thing Dad taught me something about knot tying, huh?"

Hallie brought her hands around in front of her and massaged her tender wrists, wincing at the pins-and-needles sensation when the blood flowed back into her hands. When she regained some command over her fingers, she forced herself to sit up and reached for the rope still holding her ankles. She picked at the knots and pulled the rope free, then flung it aside.

"Where's your horse?"

Catherine pointed toward the rim of the canyon. "Up on top, next to yours." She helped Hallie to her feet. "I was out looking for the calf Dad gave me last summer, and I came across a fresh trail. Looked like three or four head being driven this way."

Hallie attempted a couple of steps on her tottery legs. The pain from her abused muscles nearly drove her to her knees. Catherine put her arm around Hallie's waist, and she accepted the little girl's help gratefully. "How are we going to get out of here?"

Catherine pointed up ahead. "There's a trail over on the other side of those trees. We can climb up to the top that way and get our horses."

She led Hallie a few more steps and picked up the thread of her story. "Uncle Jacob is always complaining about not finding any fresh sign, so I thought I'd trail these a ways and maybe catch the rustlers. Then I saw you riding over this way and decided I'd catch up to you, instead."

She pulled at Hallie, urging her up the slope.

"But then I saw the smoke and saw you get down off your horse and start crawling on the ground." She giggled, then sobered. "I got worried when you rolled off the edge into the canyon, so I thought I'd better come see if you were all right." A grin flashed across her tanned cheeks. "Good thing I checked, isn't it?"

They reached the top with Hallie blowing like a winded horse.

"Catherine O'Roarke, I ought to tan your hide, but I'm too happy to see you." The feeling was starting to come back into her legs. She tried to ignore the sharp ache by reminding herself it would help her keep her balance in the saddle, assuming she could lift her leg high enough to reach the stirrup.

After two unsuccessful attempts, Catherine planted her shoulder against Hallie's backside and braced herself. "Ready? One, two, three. . .up!"

Hallie flopped into her saddle with all the grace of a sack of potatoes. She clung to the saddle horn for a long moment, trying to control the tremor in her limbs. "Where did you learn that little trick?"

Catherine shrugged. "It just seemed like the thing to do."

Hallie collected herself. She couldn't give in to weakness now, not when the rustlers could return at any moment. She gathered her reins. "Come on. We've got to get out of here."

They ran their horses for half a mile before Hallie felt safe enough to slow down a bit. She looked over at Catherine. "Did you see them?"

"Just their hats and the backs of their shirts. They pulled bandannas over their faces, remember?"

"Oh." She hadn't seen much of anything except clods of dirt, two pairs of legs, then blackness when the blindfold was tied around her face. Why had they bothered to cover her eyes if they were already masked?

She checked her surroundings to assess their location, then gave Catherine a sharp glance. "How did you get this far on your own? You must be a good three miles from home. Your parents are going to be frantic."

Catherine's face folded into a frown, then brightened. "You'd better come back home with me and tell everybody how I saved you. Then I won't be in trouble." She scrunched her forehead. "Well, not as much, anyway."

sixteen

Hallie dug her heels into Gypsy's flanks and cast a worried glance at the late afternoon sky. If she hoped to make it home before dusk, she would have to sprout wings and fly. Bending low over the gray mare's neck, she urged the horse on to a reckless pace. She didn't have a moment to lose.

Taking Catherine home had cost her precious time, but she couldn't in good conscience let the child go back alone. Not when there were ruffians about. Dan and Amy hadn't been home when they clattered up into the yard, much to Catherine's relief. Hallie's, too, if she were being honest. It saved her from having to explain her disheveled appearance and dust-coated clothing.

Hallie left the little girl with Benjamin, with strict instructions that neither of them was to leave the house until their parents returned.

Jacob hadn't been there, either, and hearing that sent a fresh wave of misery washing over her. With all her heart, she wanted to give him the information that would let him make an arrest and put an end to the matter.

Be honest, Hallie. You wanted him to take you in his arms and make what happened back in the canyon seem like a bad dream. Well, yes, there was that, she admitted. But right now her main focus was set on seeing the rustlers apprehended so they could pay for their crime. If she couldn't let Jacob know, she had to get word to her father.

The canyon where the stolen cattle were hidden lay

southeast of the T Bar and northeast from the Broken Box. Hallie angled her horse behind a series of low hills on the west edge of the valley to keep from being seen. The wind rushed by her head, loosening her braid and setting her hair free to flow behind her like a dark ribbon.

Gypsy was laboring now, breathing hard with every step. "Hang on, girl," Hallie crooned. "It isn't much farther." The house and barn loomed up ahead.

Drawing nearer, she could see her father pulling the saddle from his favorite mount. "Pa!" she screamed.

Burke's mouth rounded in disbelief when Gypsy pounded up beside him. "What's gotten into you, girl? You know better than to lather a horse like that."

Hallie sagged over the mare's neck and struggled for breath. "The rustlers, Pa. I found them. They've got the cows penned up in the box canyon up near that old burn. They're going to move them out tonight."

Burke gaped as though staring at an apparition. "How do you know that?"

Here came the hard part. He'd be mad enough to shoot the rustlers on sight anyway. If she told him how she'd been man-handled, she didn't want to think what he might do. "I heard them talking," she said simply. *Please don't let him ask me how.*

"Did you get a good look at them?"

Hallie shook her head. "I couldn't see them clearly." That was true enough.

Burke settled the saddle on his horse's back again and tightened the cinch.

"You're not going out after them alone, are you?" Worry stretched her voice reed-thin.

"You see anyone around who's going to help me? I'm going to get my cows back and see some thievin' coyotes get their just desserts." He swung into the saddle and checked the rifle in its scabbard.

Sudden panic seized Hallie. *Of course he's going after them himself. What did you expect him to do?* "Please, Pa. Don't do anything foolish."

"They're the ones who've been the fools, not me." He kicked his horse into a gallop and rode off, grim determination written in every line of his bearing.

Hallie twisted her fingers through Gypsy's mane and watched him until the gathering dusk obscured him from view. "Keep him safe, Lord. Don't let him get hurt. . .or hurt anybody else."

ð

The sun hung low in the western sky when Jacob arrived at the box canyon. He rode along the rim until he found the spot where the canyon opened out onto the range. Below him he could see the smoldering remains of a fire.

Worry tightened his throat. Was he too late after all?

Faint lowing from deep within the canyon reassured him. They hadn't left yet. He tied Cap in a thick clump of cedars some distance from the canyon mouth, pulled his rifle from its scabbard, and unhooked his lariat from his saddle horn.

Dragging a huge fallen limb to the canyon's brink, he stood it on end and propped it up against a tree trunk. He tied a secure knot around the middle and looked for a likely place from which to watch.

Over there, by that low-hanging cedar. He ducked under the drooping branches and braced his back against the rough trunk. With his Winchester propped across his knees and the free end of the rope in one hand, he settled in to wait.

His chosen position put him at the edge of the rim with an unobstructed view of this end of the canyon without putting him in harm's way. No point in giving them the opportunity to push those cows right over him. There wouldn't be enough left of him to scrape up and send home. He scooted around to make himself more comfortable, then focused his gaze on the point where they would drive the cattle out around the bend.

For the dozenth time, he hoped he hadn't made the mistake of the century by not taking anyone into his confidence. It seemed the right thing to do, back when he made the decision without the pressure of this moment on him. In the here and now, though, the odds of one man against a group of unknown size seemed painfully evident.

It would work out all right, he reassured himself. It had to. He went over his plans again. He'd known from the first that what he lacked in strength of numbers he would have to make up for in cleverness.

Knowing that, he'd taken a leaf from one of his favorite Old Testament stories. When the lead cows reached that scrawny cedar in the middle of the canyon, he would yank the rope to send the log crashing down below and create enough noise to convince them they faced an entire posse. If it worked for Gideon against the Midianites, it ought to work here.

If they didn't stop, he would place a bullet close enough to one of their horses to make it rear. If he could get just one rider on the ground, he could at least work on that one to get the names of the others.

The sun finished its descent behind Granite Mountain and the shadows lengthened. Silence settled over the canyon. Jacob shifted again and stretched his legs. He couldn't afford to be stiff when it came time to move.

A silver disk inched its way over the top of Mingus Mountain. Jacob watched the glowing circle slide upward until the whole valley lay washed in moonlight. He flexed his fingers and rolled his shoulders. Any time now. There was plenty of light for the rustlers' purpose. . .and for his.

He waited in the stillness, wanting them to come and dreading it at the same time. Numbness threatened his legs and had already defeated his backside. As he sat alone in the dark, doubts beset him again. Should he have asked for help, after all? Was his not doing so motivated by wisdom—or pride?

He heard the click of hoof on stone and felt his heart race. Too late now for second-guessing. A horse whickered. Low voices murmured. Jacob stiffened, all his senses on full alert. He gripped the rope, rose to his feet, and cocked his Winchester.

And waited some more. Jacob fidgeted with the rope end. The sound of many hooves echoed around the bend. Suddenly he saw the moonlight glint off dozens of horns.

This is it. Be with me, Lord. Against the silver-washed canyon floor, he could make out a sizable herd and three mounted riders pushing them forward.

Jacob held back a shout of exultation. He tightened his grip on the rope and waited until the lead cow neared the scraggly cedar.

Closer. . .closer. . .now! Jacob jerked the rope. The limb teetered on the brink of the canyon, then tipped over the edge and tumbled downward, picking up speed and pulling a shower of gravel down with it as it went.

Jacob stepped as close to the rim as he dared and shouldered the Winchester. "Hold it right there! We've got you covered. Throw down your guns."

He watched the three riders freeze, their doubt a palpable thing. Without warning, hooves pounded on the far side of the canyon.

One of the rustlers threw a shot up toward Jacob; another

shot toward the opposite wall where the newcomer could be heard.

Who's over there? He couldn't take time to wonder. Jacob took aim, ready to snap a shot in front of the nearest horse. He aimed at a point five feet ahead of its front hooves and fired.

A gunshot cracked from the other side of the canyon. Jacob's leg went out from under him, and he teetered on the edge, then plummeted over the side.

છ

Jacob lay still in the darkness, listening to the sounds of hooves pounding and riders yelling, and tried to get his bearings. The cattle were stampeding. He could hear their frightened bellows and the mad scramble of hooves.

He lay on the canyon floor with a mouthful of dirt and enough bruises to make him sore for a week. And he'd lost his rifle on the way down.

Hoofbeats drummed across the ground and faded into the distance. *They're getting away!* Jacob jumped to his feet, but his leg gave way again, this time with a stabbing pain that made him cry out. He grabbed at his thigh and felt a sticky wetness under his palm.

A lone set of hoofbeats approached, making their way across the uneven ground. Jacob drew back against the canyon wall and scrabbled in the dirt for his rifle.

"Come on out of there, you lowlife. I know I got you; I saw you fall."

Jacob shifted his weight and let out a groan. He heard a scatter of rocks and the sound of boots pounding across the ground. Moonlight shone on the barrel of a Winchester much like his own, pointed straight at him. Jacob looked up into the triumphant face of Burke Evans.

seventeen

Clouds scudded across the leaden sky. Jacob pulled his coat tighter around his neck to ward off the blustery wind. He took two halting steps forward and looked down with distaste at the cane in his hand.

"It's only for a little while," Dr. Haskins had told him. "Just until those torn muscles heal." The doctor pulled at the ends of his white mustache. "It's a good thing that bullet didn't nick any bones, young man. You'd really be in bad shape then. You have a lot of deep bruising, and you won't be sitting a saddle anytime soon, but you're young and healthy. As long as infection doesn't set in, you'll be right as rain before long."

And what is the good doctor's definition of "before long"? Jacob tried to adopt a jaunty air, as though he carried the cane for show and not because he'd be sure to fall flat on his face without it. He swung his injured leg forward and staggered, putting an end to his attempt at nonchalance.

It had been nearly a week already. Jacob grimaced and forced himself to walk a few more steps. He'd never been laid up more than a day or two at a time before, certainly never faced the prospect of being out of commission for an extended period of time. The thought didn't set well with him, especially now.

Over on the plaza, people were beginning to gather. Jacob hobbled across the street to join them. He couldn't bear to miss this day; at the same time, he wished he could be almost anywhere else. The pressure of the bandage made the wound throb. He set his jaw and kept walking. If he could stand the jouncing wagon ride into town the night Burke shot him and the way Doc Haskins ran that rod through the wound to clean out any debris, he could endure this comparatively minor pain.

The doctor might be pleased about the location of the wound, away from any major blood vessels, but he didn't have to cope with the difficulty it caused Jacob. The bullet entered the side of his upper right thigh and exited just below his hip. Doc might be justified in his pleasure over it not nicking any bones, but Jacob could think of better places for it. Its placement made walking difficult and sitting in a saddle—or nearly anywhere else—impossible.

Jacob checked his pocket watch, then snapped it shut and replaced it in his vest. Three thirty. The crowd was growing larger by the minute. He wavered at the edge of the street. Maybe he should go to his room and forget the whole thing.

No. He had to see this through.

"Came to see us off, did you?"

Jacob used his cane to pivot around and saw Buckey O'Neill standing before him. The mayor's dark eyes shone with a sympathetic light.

"Wouldn't miss it." Jacob forced a smile, then dropped all pretense at pleasantries. "Go ahead and swear me in, Buckey. Let me go with you. This thing won't take long to heal. I'll be fit for duty before we get on the boat for Cuba."

Buckey's smile dimmed. "If I had my choice, I'd like nothing more than to take you with me, but I can't."

"But you know I intended to sign up the day after this happened." He gestured at his wounded leg. "I'm practically a part of the group already."

Buckey shook his head. "The requirements are that recruits be able-bodied and physically fit for duty, and right now. . ." He nodded at Jacob's cane. "Regulations. I'm sorry."

Jacob's shoulders sagged. "I know. I just had to try."

"You're right, though. You'll be back in the saddle in no time." Buckey's voice took on a more jovial tone. "I'll rest better in Cuba, knowing you're helping to take care of things here at home. You're a good man, Jacob. I'll be seeing you soon. It shouldn't take us more than three months to whip the Spaniards and be home again. One of these days, we'll be celebrating statehood together."

"Buckey!" shouted a man across the grounds. "We're ready to muster the troops. We need you with your men."

Buckey gave Jacob a quick wave and trotted across to where some men stood in a cluster along the north edge of the square.

Jacob watched the men try to form some semblance of order. All walks of life and manner of dress were represented in the group. They might not look like much of a military unit now, but he knew these men, knew their hearts. With a little training, they'd shape up to be as fine a company as ever served the country.

A lump swelled in Jacob's throat. Pride or longing? He couldn't tell which. He swallowed hard and pushed his way through the jubilant throng. Women stepped aside to let him pass, glancing at him, then his cane, then quickly away. Jacob gritted his teeth.

He took up a casual stance next to the bandstand, where the Fort Whipple band was in full swing. Might as well look like he was enjoying the music. Not a care in the world, not he. No one would have reason to think he attended the ceremony as anything but a well-wisher, nor suspect the fierce disappointment that burned within him.

The band music ceased, and the stirring tones of a cornet pierced the air. Jacob turned to look, along with everyone else. A young boy, no more than fourteen, held the instrument to his lips. The plaintive notes drifted over the plaza.

A man standing in front of Jacob turned to his companion. "Isn't that the band master's boy?"

His friend nodded. "LaGuardia's been a real boon to Fort Whipple. It's a shame he's leaving along with the rest. And this young fellow has his father's gift for music, that's for sure. If he keeps it up, he might make a real name for himself someday."

While the last notes still hung in the air, the young lad trotted down the bandstand steps. His father nodded at him with obvious pride. Jacob heard him whisper, "Good job, Fiorello," before taking up his baton and striking up the band again.

The boy's shoulders straightened proudly. Jacob watched him walk past, remembering when the prospects for his own future looked just as bright. His lips tightened. Not so long ago, he felt he was on the verge of capturing the rustlers and bringing them to justice; he had found the love of his life; and he planned to march off with the local troops and bring freedom to a captive people. *It just goes to show you how everything can change in a heartbeat.*

The men marched out of step to form ragged ranks across the plaza's north lawn. Jacob clenched his teeth together so hard he could hear them grate. *They're ready to go. And I should be with them.*

Bitterness choked him. They all stood on the same grounds on the same day, but he wasn't one of their number. And why? *Because some bullheaded rancher who didn't think I was man enough to do my job shot my leg out from under me.*

The crowd stirred and someone jostled his elbow. "Hello there."

Hallie Evans smiled up at him, her dark brown eyes shining with pleasure. The sight of her upturned face only added to his black mood. He tried to hold his feelings back. She had come, like the rest, to join in the patriotic fervor and send the able-bodied men on their way.

He gritted his teeth again. Not even to Hallie would he admit just how raw his feelings were. "So you came to see the troops off, did you?"

"No." She pressed closer to him. "I came to see you."

Came to see him, a cripple and a failure? Jacob stared at her intently. "Why?"

Her answer was drowned out by the swell of applause as the governor was introduced. Jacob worked his jaw and tried to focus his attention on the solemn proceedings going on just in front of them.

He had to settle for trying to look like his attention was focused there. Hallie's nearness drove all other thoughts from his mind. Jacob nodded and clapped along with the crowd during Governor McCord's address to the troops. He cheered when the governor presented Buckey with an American flag sewn by the ladies of the Women's Relief Corps of Phoenix.

He managed to applaud when Prescott's city attorney gave the departing mayor a tooled holster and engraved six-shooter and laughed along with the rest when the owner of the Palace Saloon presented the troops with a young mountain lion as a mascot.

And all the while, his whole being roiled in a tumult that rivaled the upheaval in Cuba. The speech-making droned on. The crowd grew restless, but Jacob felt he could stand there all night, injured leg or no, as long as Hallie stood beside him.

And yet he stood there as one who could not serve his country or fight alongside comrades he admired. Desolation at being left behind threatened to consume him. He choked back the bitter taste of gall.

At last the ceremony ended. The band struck up a lively

rendition of "Hot Time in the Old Town" and led the way north along Cortez Street to the depot, where a special Santa Fe, Prescott, and Phoenix Railway train awaited them. The new recruits straggled behind them in a ragtag version of a march. The cheering throng trailed along, shouting out exuberant words of encouragement.

Hallie moved as if to join the crowd, then hesitated. "Do you want to go or. . ."

He should have known. Jacob shook his head and bit back a hot retort. "Go ahead if you want to."

Hallie moved next to him and rested her hand on his arm. She seemed to be searching for words. "I know this is a big disappointment for you, having to see your friends go off together like that. But I look at them all." She took a deep breath and gestured in the direction the departing troops had taken. "I see how excited they are, but in my heart I know some of them won't be coming home."

She gave him a wobbly smile. "I guess God answers prayers in unusual ways sometimes."

In the distance, the band music faded away to be replaced by the sounds of the locomotive building up a head of steam. A chorus of voices took up the refrain "God Be with You Till We Meet Again." The solemn lyrics floated back to the plaza on the evening air.

Jacob stood without moving a muscle and stared at Hallie. Finally he lifted his cane and held it up between them. "You're saying you prayed for this to happen?"

A pink tinge flooded Hallie's face. "Having my father shoot you was hardly my idea of how to keep you here." She tilted her chin up in a gesture that reminded him of Catherine when she faced the consequences of some misdeed. "But I have to admit I'm grateful."

"Grateful." He felt an ominous calm settle over him. "Grateful that I've been turned into a useless cripple?"

"Better a cripple than a corpse," Hallie retorted.

Jacob stepped away from her. "What makes you so sure I would have gotten killed? I might have come back as an officer. At the very least, I'd know whether I could stand up to the sound of bullets whizzing past me without turning tail and running. I'd know that I'm a man." His tone grew rough. "And everyone else would know it, too."

Hallie spoke in a voice thick with emotion. "I said my prayers were answered, and I meant it, even though I never would have asked for you to be hurt. God really does know what's best, if you'll just let Him be in control instead of trying to figure it all out on your own.

"Why do men have to be so bullheaded and determined to do things their way?" She started to walk away, then looked back over her shoulder. "Don't you know God cares about you, Jacob? He loves you even more than I do." She strode away quickly, leaving Jacob standing alone in stunned silence.

≈

Jacob pushed open the door of the Ponderosa Café. "That's another fine meal," he called to the proprietor. "I'll see you again this evening."

Stepping outside into the morning sunlight, he ran his finger along the inside of his waistband. If he didn't get back to work pretty soon, he'd be looking like some portly city slicker before he knew it.

He strolled along Cortez, still favoring his right leg. He'd seen significant improvement, though. At least he could now walk unassisted. When he'd given up the cane five days ago, he felt like dancing.

"Jacob? Jacob Garrett!" Lucas Rawlins waved from across the street.

Jacob limped across to greet him, and the two men exchanged a warm handshake.

"Good to see you!" Rawlins beamed. "How are you getting along? About ready to pick up where you left off?"

Jacob shook his head. "Doc says it'll be at least a few more days."

Rawlins's mustache drooped. "I'm sorry to hear that. It's been three weeks since you got shot. We hoped you'd be back in the saddle by now."

Jacob gritted his teeth. Rawlins couldn't know how much he'd hoped the same thing. "So did I," he said mildly. "If that infection hadn't set in, I would have been back at work a week or so ago. As it is, Doc says I'm lucky it wasn't any worse."

"Mm." Rawlins chewed on his lower lip. "Things quieted down after that brush you had with the rustlers. We thought maybe you'd spooked them enough to drive them out of the territory, but some of us have started losing stock again." He gave Jacob a long, measuring look. "I hope you're up and around again real soon."

Jacob watched him stride away. The breakfast he had so recently enjoyed now lay in a congealed mass in his stomach. Did Rawlins think he'd considered his enforced time off some kind of vacation?

I'd like to tell him what it's like with nothing but time on your hands. To keep his legs from stiffening up on him, he walked the perimeter of the plaza several times a day. By now, he'd become a familiar figure to the people whose businesses faced the town square. Familiar enough to receive smiles and nods every time he made his circuit. But he hadn't missed the curious glances, the ones that asked why he wasn't off with the troops.

Life had taken on an unfamiliar emptiness. In fact, the town itself felt empty without Buckey. The widely respected mayor's absence left a rent in the fabric of community life, one that couldn't be filled by anyone else. Jacob sorely missed being able to drop by Buckey's office to pass the time of day or exchange the latest news.

And Buckey wasn't the only person he missed. Jacob hadn't seen Hallie since the day he growled at her over near the bandstand. The memory of his ill-tempered behavior made him squirm. He'd lain awake every night since then, remembering her parting words, then wondering if he had imagined them. What was she feeling now? Would she ever want to see him?

He couldn't blame her if she didn't. One brief moment on a moonlit night had turned his world upside down. And all because of the impulsive, shoot-before-you-think actions of her father. If Burke's ill-conceived attempt to apprehend the rustlers on his own led to the loss of Hallie's affection. . .

Jacob started another circuit around the plaza, more to work off his frustration than for the exercise. Speculation was going to drive him round the bend. He had to get out to the Broken Box and find out for himself how Hallie felt. But how was he going to manage that?

He limped across the square to a sturdy bench and lowered himself carefully, wincing only slightly when his injured leg made contact with the wooden seat. That was an improvement. A week ago, he wouldn't have thought of sitting on anything harder than a feather pillow, let alone considered trying a saddle.

A saddle? Where had that idea come from? The more he pondered it, the more his resolve grew. He needed to see Hallie, regardless of the cost.

He could do it. He pushed himself up off the bench. Painful or not, he had to get out there. He headed toward the livery across the street from the south end of the plaza.

He would rent a horse and ride out to the Broken Box today. He'd make it, no matter what he had to endure. At the moment, any discomfort he might suffer paled in comparison with his concern over what he would say to Hallie and what her response might be.

He crossed the street lost in thought. A buggy wheel missed him by bare inches, and a voice called, "Where do you think you're going?"

Jolted from his reverie, Jacob looked up to see Hallie perched on the buggy seat. The sight of her brought a wave of pleasure so intense it shocked him. That joy was almost immediately replaced by profound embarrassment when he remembered the churlish way he had behaved at their last meeting.

Hallie's lips parted in a wide smile, and light flooded back into Jacob's soul.

He spoke before he could lose his nerve, watching for her reaction. "I was planning to rent a horse and come out to pay you a visit."

"Oh no, you don't." Hallie's dark braid swung from side to side when she shook her head. "I checked with Dr. Haskins. He told me any riding in a saddle might tear that wound open again." Her mouth curved in an impish grin. "But he said a buggy ride—on a nice, cushioned seat—might do you a world of good."

The light spread into every part of his being. A buggy ride with Hallie? Things were definitely looking up.

As though taking his hesitation for a refusal, she reached in the back of the buggy and held up a covered basket. "Fried chicken, biscuits, and dried apple pie," she announced. "We can go for a picnic. If you're interested, of course."

A buggy ride *and* a picnic? Only his game leg stopped

Jacob from breaking into a jig. "I don't know," he teased. "I really ought to be trying to get some work done instead of going out for a pleasure ride."

Hallie grinned. "That's what my pa said. He offered to let you use our buggy while you're having trouble getting around."

"He *offered*?"

"Well, he did after I reminded him of the reason you couldn't be out riding." Hallie's lips twitched. "I thought maybe you'd want to drive around to some of the ranches after our picnic."

Jacob grinned and put his foot up on the buggy step. "Ma'am, you just made yourself a deal."

❧

Jacob popped the last crumb of Hallie's flaky piecrust into his mouth and leaned back on one elbow. The edges of the checkered tablecloth she spread out to hold their repast rose, then lowered with every warm puff of breeze. Jacob sighed and stretched, feeling a sense of utter contentment he'd thought he might never experience again.

Hallie sat with her back resting against the broad trunk of one of the cottonwoods that dotted the banks of Granite Creek. Above them loomed the massive rock formations of the Granite Dells.

"I need to apologize for snapping at you the other day," Jacob said. "It wasn't easy to watch Buckey and the rest go off without me, but I had no call to take it out on you like that."

Hallie's lips stretched in the gentle smile that never failed to warm his heart. "That's already part of the past. I'd rather look ahead to the future, wouldn't you?"

"I'm not sure." The words came out without conscious thought on his part. He saw Hallie's startled look and tried to find a way to explain. "Just about the time I thought I had my future all mapped out, everything fell apart. I was going to put an end to that rustling operation; I was going to serve my country and help set a captive people free." *I was going to ask you to marry me.* He held that comment back. How could he even think about a future with Hallie when he'd made such a dismal failure of his present?

He cleared his throat and went on. "I had all these grand plans built up, and what happened to them? They've all turned to dust. I've failed at every one."

"Failed? Don't speak to me of failure, Jacob Garrett." Hallie reached out to him and wrapped her fingers around his hand. "I know you've had some bitter disappointments, but don't lose heart. It isn't over yet. You're going to come through this all right, but you need to trust God."

Jacob drew his brows together. "Are you saying there's something wrong with the way I've been acting?"

"I'm saying you need to believe He has your best interests at heart, even if He doesn't have your life arranged the way you'd like it to be. He knows the direction He wants your life to take. You need to ask Him to show you what it is." She eyed him solemnly. "For both our sakes."

"All I want is to be able to finish the job I was hired to perform. Is that too much to ask?" Bitterness edged his voice.

Hallie stood her ground. "Have you prayed and asked for an answer on how to deal with this, or are you just trying to figure it out all on your own?"

"We'd best get going if we plan to get any work done today. I'll help you pack this up." Jacob scooped up the plates and stacked them beside the basket, then shook the crumbs out of the tablecloth.

Hallie loaded their dirty plates into the picnic basket without saying a word. But Jacob didn't miss the flash of disappointment that flitted across her face.

eighteen

"I can't figure it." Tom Miller swept his hat from his head with his left hand and ran his right palm over his thinning hair. "They're disappearing without a trace, just like before. Some of my riders checked back around that canyon where you found them penned up the last time, but it looks like the thieves have already pulled out and moved that part of their operation somewhere else. That would be the sensible thing to do, at any rate, and it doesn't look like we're dealing with a pack of fools."

Jacob felt the familiar sinking sensation in his belly. "Do you have any thoughts on who might be behind this? Any at all?"

Miller pulled at his earlobe. "I keep wondering about those nesters holed up back away from everybody. There are plenty of blind canyons up that way, lots of room for them to keep a bunch of cattle on the quiet."

"I suppose it's possible," Jacob said. *Even if it isn't very likely*.

"They drift in and out," Miller continued. "They could leave here taking our stolen stock with them. The next place they light, they'll just be people who came in with some money in their pockets, and no one will be the wiser."

"I'll keep it in mind," Jacob promised. He picked up the reins and slapped them lightly on the horse's rump, turning the buggy back toward Prescott.

Hallie tapped her fingers together. "That's the third time

today we've heard someone blame the nesters for this. What do you think?"

Jacob shook his head. "The ones I talked to didn't strike me as the type to do something like this." The sense of failure settled over him again like a pall. "But maybe they're just pulling the wool over my eyes. It wouldn't surprise me a bit."

Hallie fell silent and stared off in the direction of Thumb Butte.

Jacob winced when the buggy wheel jolted in and out of a rut in the road. He shifted on the cushion, trying to find a more comfortable position. As tender as his backside felt, the pain in his heart felt worse. He would give anything to be able to take back that last remark, or at least remove the surly tone from his voice. Hallie didn't deserve that, didn't deserve the sour attitude he'd been showing ever since the night his dreams of success ended with the crack of a Winchester.

What Hallie deserved. . .his heart swelled. She deserved more than he, or any man, could ever hope to give her. What an amazing combination of attributes: that sweet nature with a core of steel hidden underneath. *And she's stood by me, even when her father—and probably every other rancher around these parts—doesn't think I'm the man for this job.*

What would it be like to have a woman like that stand beside him for the rest of his life? No. Not just any woman. Hallie. His imagination took wings and soared.

The wagon wheel bounced over another rut, bringing him out of his happy daydream. Probably just as well, he decided, easing his weight off his tender leg. Thoughts of romance would have to be set aside for the time being. He needed to redeem himself in his own eyes and prove himself to Burke first, and that wouldn't happen until the mystery was solved.

That issue had to be settled once and for all before he could ever hope to ask for Hallie's hand.

☙

Hallie set the last of the breakfast dishes back on the shelf and glanced around to see if anything else in the kitchen needed her attention. Satisfied she had finished her indoor chores for the morning, she donned her work gloves and walked out to her vegetable garden.

Her father cut a length from a roll of wire and stretched it over a gap in the garden fence. He looked up when she approached. "You've been fussing about the chickens scratching around your plants. I figured I'd patch that hole while I had the chance."

Hallie smiled her thanks and picked up her hoe. "That last rain did the vegetables a world of good, but it sure set the weeds to growing, too." She worked the hoe between the rows of carrots. Dirt rose in even heaps on either side of the blade as it cut through the soil.

Look at that. A few quick strokes with the hoe, and the weeds are rooted out. Hallie heaved a small sigh. If only the "weeds" in her life could be dealt with so easily.

She glanced over where her father knelt beside a fence post. What had happened to them? Life seemed to have taken a ragged turn of late. It used to be that her days went along in a pleasant flow, with no problems more difficult than deciding what to fix for the next meal and staying out of Pete Edwards's way. Then Jacob came into her life, and the very thing that brought her joy became the cause of the greatest conflict she'd ever had with her father.

Why did it all have to be so complicated? She ran the hoe through another patch of weeds. Her father was a good man, despite his recent outbursts of temper. So was Jacob. She had adored her father all her life. She would always love him, but her heart had enough room for Jacob, too.

She loved them both, and yet that love didn't seem to be enough to bring the two men together and heal the hurts they had all suffered.

Something had to change. And neither Jacob nor her father seemed incline to take the first step toward making that happen. That left it up to her. She finished the row of carrots and stopped to stretch the muscles in her back. Across the pathway that bordered the garden, her father hammered a fencing staple into the post.

Hallie leaned on her hoe and watched him work. His strength and unwavering devotion had sheltered her all during her growing-up years. She studied the face she had loved from her childhood. Throughout her early life, it had reflected that loving strength. Lately, its features were set in harsh, unyielding lines more often than not, and she felt a stranger lurked behind its stony exterior.

Today, though, her father looked more relaxed than she had seen him in months. He tapped another staple into the post, humming snatches of one of her mother's favorite hymns. Maybe this would be as good a time as any to speak to him of what lay on her heart. Hallie summoned up her courage and stepped across the path.

"It sure is good to see you looking happy again."

Her father looked up, his expression softening further when their gazes met. "It's good to lose myself in a routine job. Takes my mind off my troubles." He wiped his brow on his sleeve and fixed his gaze on a point across the valley. "I guess I haven't been too easy to live with ever since those cattle started going missing."

Hallie managed a small smile and gave him an encouraging

nod. "I know it's been hard on you." She watched his shoulders relax and took heart. "At least we got most of them back when you and Jacob scared the rustlers off." She watched him out of the corner of her eye, trying to gauge his reaction.

Her father's jaw set, and he raised the hammer again. "But they got away. We still don't know who they are." He set the next staple in place and gave it a series of sharp whacks. "We had a chance to round them up and get rid of them for good. . . but it didn't work." He shook his head, suddenly looking years older. "After things went quiet, I thought they'd lit a shuck and left the country. Then we started losing steers again."

He straightened and flung the hammer to the ground. "We could have been rid of the whole mess by now if Garrett had shot right at them instead of spooking the herd and giving them the chance to get away."

"Or if you hadn't jumped into the middle of things without taking time to find out what was really going on?" Hallie kept her voice low, not wanting to provoke him. "He had a good idea; you know he did. It probably would have worked if things had gone the way he planned."

"If I hadn't shot him, you mean." Her father's face turned a dusky red. "How was I supposed to know it was him up there and not someone they'd posted as a lookout? Someone shot at me, and I fired at the only flash I saw. What was he doing up there, anyway?"

"His job," Hallie shot back, stung by the injustice of his attitude. "Just like you kept pushing him to do." She leaned the hoe against an undamaged section of the fence and stepped closer to her father. "You've acted all along like you thought he didn't care about our problems. But he does, Pa. He had it all worked out. He just doesn't do things the same way you do."

"So what you're saying is, it's all my fault? You're blaming me for letting those thieves ride away scot-free?" He drew himself to his full height and loomed over her. "Garrett's twisted your thinking so much you're willing to turn against your own father. I can't believe this is happening, Hallie. You can't see the truth when it stares you in the face."

"And you're so full of anger and hate, you can't give a good man credit for getting things done his own way or give him a chance to prove himself."

Her father's jaw worked. "Don't you talk to me like that. He's proven himself, all right. Proven he isn't half the man you think he is. Proven the only thing he's capable of doing is to stir up strife between the two of us. He managed to do that without even breaking a sweat."

Hallie saw the hurt in his eyes, and her own filled with tears. *Oh, Pa.* "Nothing is coming between you and me except that temper of yours." She rested her fingertips on his brawny forearm. "Can't you give Jacob another chance. . .for my sake?" She felt his muscles tense beneath her fingers.

"A chance for what? All I can see he's ever done is come sniffing around here trying to sweet-talk you. I just wish I'd shot straighter that night."

Hallie's knees buckled. She clutched at the fence post for support. "You don't mean that!"

"Don't I? Look at what he's done, trifling with your affections, getting you so stirred up you spend all your time mooning over a man who'll never amount to a hill of beans. Why, if I had my way—"

"But I love him, Pa." The whispered words stopped him cold.

Her father's face twisted and he raised his arm. Hallie ducked away, sure he was about to strike her. Instead, he hoisted the roll of wire above his head and pitched it halfway to the barn.

He turned back to face her, his chest heaving. "He'd better watch himself, or I will shoot straighter next time."

Hallie took a step back. "Pa, don't. You're frightening me."

"I mean it, Hallie. He's got your mind so full of pipe dreams you can't see straight, and I won't have it. You're not to go off the ranch again. Not as long as he's around."

"But, Pa—"

"Don't you sass me, girl! You stay up close, by the house and the barn. And if he ever shows his face around here again, you get inside the house and you stay there, you hear?"

Hallie clasped her hands under her chin. "You can't mean that!"

"Don't I?" His features contorted. "You just try to cross me and you'll find out."

Tears blurred Hallie's vision. She blinked them away, then wished she hadn't. In her father's face she saw no sign of the softness she had observed earlier; the hard-faced stranger had returned. With a low cry, she pressed her hands against her cheeks and ran for the house.

nineteen

"Maybe I ought to just quit."

Dan O'Roarke looked up from where he sat braiding a lariat and stared at Jacob. "And do what?"

"Come back to work for you, if you'll have me."

Dan went back to weaving the strands of sisal together. "And what would you accomplish by that? I've never thought of you as a quitter."

"I'm no quitter, just realistic." Jacob strode across the barn floor and kicked at the center post. "I've never been this stymied before, Dan. They hired me because they thought I had what it took to stop the thieving. It looks like they were wrong. It's still going on, as strong as ever."

Dan set the lariat aside and leaned forward with his elbows on his knees. "It's a big territory for one man to cover. You came close that one time, real close."

Jacob shifted his weight to his left leg. "I'm just glad Evans didn't get any closer."

Dan raised his hand to his mouth, but it didn't quite muffle his snort of laughter. "They're bound to make a mistake sooner or later. When they do, you'll be there to nab them. . . assuming you don't walk off the job and settle for punching cows."

"It's honest work. There's nothing wrong with that."

"I didn't say there was, but there isn't a lot of money in it for a fellow who might be wanting to start a family one of these days."

Jacob felt his neck grow warm. "When did I ever say anything about that?"

"When did you need to? I've known you all my life, remember? Long enough to recognize the signs every time a certain young lady's name is mentioned." He walked over to Jacob and clapped him on the shoulder. "You picked yourself a good one, my friend. Hallie Evans is as true as they come."

Jacob looked away. "Yeah, and her father hates me. And I can't say as I blame him. Who'd want to trust their daughter's future to a man who can't do something as simple as track down a few rustlers?"

"It's not for lack of trying. You've spent many a night camped out there on the trails trying to spot some movement."

"And with absolutely nothing to show for it." Jacob sent a hissing breath out through his clenched teeth. "It's been weeks, Dan! How long is it supposed to take before everyone gives up on me, myself included? If I'd gone off with Buckey's troops, at least I'd feel like I was doing something worthwhile."

"Sweltering in the heat and coming down with fever? I hear they're losing more men to illness than to bullets over there." Dan stepped directly in front of Jacob and locked gazes with him. "You know as well as I do that God doesn't make mistakes. Getting shot in the leg wasn't in your plans, but He knew all along it would happen."

"Why didn't He stop it, then?"

Dan spread his hands wide. "His plans are bigger than ours. He had His reasons. And apparently having you here instead of in Cuba is part of them."

"But why, Dan? What good am I doing here? I can't find the rustlers; I can't even see Hallie. Her father's forbidden her to have anything to do with me, did you know that?" Jacob paced the width of the barn and raked his fingers through his hair. "I haven't talked to her for a month. I don't even know whether she's all right. The way her father acts, I wouldn't put it past him to—"

Dan put himself in Jacob's path, bringing him up short. "I don't know the answers any better than you do. I just know who I can trust."

A horse bolted into the yard at a dead run. Eb Landrum leaped down from the saddle and dashed to the barn.

Dan crossed over toward him, his face creased with worry. "What's wrong, Eb?"

The cowboy stood rigid in the doorway, his pale face twisted in a look of pain. Jacob could see traces of moisture around his eyes. "I just came from town." His voice was stretched as tight as piano wire. "A telegram arrived while I was there. Everyone was talking about it."

"What is it?" Dan demanded. "What's happened?"

Eb drew in a ragged breath. "It's Buckey. Some Spaniard shot him."

Jacob closed the distance between them and gripped the cowboy's arm. "He's dead?"

Eb nodded. Jacob saw the muscles bunch in his jaw. "Right away, from the sounds of it. He didn't even have time to say a word before. . ."

His voice trailed off, but Jacob had heard enough. He bolted out the door without listening for more. He strode across to the far side of the yard and stood with his hands balled into fists, looking up into the sky.

"Why, God? He was a good and decent man. He had so many plans for himself, for this territory. Why Buckey?"

And why wasn't I there with him? Anguish tore at him. Would it have happened if he'd gone along? Could he have seen something, done something to warn his friend and prevent this awful thing from happening?

Despair wrenched his heart. He would never know. The fact of the matter was, he hadn't been there. And all because of Burke Evans.

⋅⋆⋅

Hallie swished a dinner plate through the rinse water and set it on the drain board. She clenched her hands around the dishcloth and squeezed. Warm trails of water slid past her wrists and dripped off her elbows. She squeezed harder. Squeezed again, until her hands trembled with the effort and the cloth yielded its final drop.

She forced her fingers to open, one by one. The cloth fell back into the sink with a splash, but her hands continued to tremble. Hallie spread them flat against the counter to hold them steady.

There, that was better. Only a faint tremor remained. She hated the feeling of being out of control like that, loathed the inability to make her body obey the simplest commands.

And that happened a lot lately. The simplest tasks rose up before her like insurmountable obstacles. Even a routine chore like washing the dishes sapped every bit of her energy.

More than once during the weeks of her enforced separation from Jacob, she found herself walking into a room without remembering what she planned to do once she got there. And just last week, she spent hours searching for the eggs she'd just gathered from the chicken coop, only to find them tucked away in the flour bin.

Maybe I'm going crazy. That might explain why she jumped like a frightened deer at every sound and her recent tendency to burst into tears with only the slightest provocation.

Her father chalked it all up to feminine stubbornness. "Don't think you're going to change my mind by any of your theatrics," he warned. "I've always done what I thought was best for you, and keeping you away from Garrett is the best thing I've done in years."

No amount of tears or pleading could sway him from his resolve. Hallie now made it a point to retreat to her room when she felt tears threaten. There, she could bury her face in her pillow to muffle her sobs and save herself from being subjected to more of her father's scathing comments.

The loose fit of her clothes told her she had lost weight over the past few weeks. If she needed confirmation, she had only to stand in front of the mirror to see her sunken cheeks and the hollow circles under her eyes.

What was Jacob doing? The question pounded in her mind every moment of every day. Had he overcome his bitterness and reconciled his anger at God for allowing him to be injured? Was he any closer to ferreting out the band of rustlers?

And did she invade his thoughts as often as he did hers?

Hallie might be denied Jacob's physical presence, but he was with her in her dreams, her thoughts, in every fiber of her being. Without him, her familiar world felt out of kilter, as though she moved through it as a stranger. What used to be reality now seemed like a dream world, one from which she wished she could wake up and find herself in Jacob's arms.

She drained the water from the sink and used the dishcloth to wipe down the counter. Her hands moved in practiced strokes, mechanically following the same routine they had so many times before. But her mind wheeled freely, sifting through a myriad of thoughts in search of a way to escape her anguish.

If she could only find a way to send a message to him and to get word in return. More than once, she had considered sending a note along with one of the hands. But her father had made it clear that all contact between Hallie and Jacob was to be cut off, and the hands' first loyalty was to her father. Any message she tried to send through them would surely wind up in his hands.

She wet the cloth again and started on the dining table. Her hands began to quiver again, and she crossed her arms, clamping them tight against her sides. If she never heard from Jacob again. . .

No. She pushed that grim thought out of her mind. There had to be a way. She just had to find it.

In her more daring moments, she made plans to sneak off the place without her father's knowledge and ride to the T Bar in the hope of finding Jacob there. The thought of what her father would do if he caught up with her was enough to put an end to those schemes before she worked up enough nerve to put them into practice.

Hallie pressed her fists against her temples. *There has to be a way. Think!*

The front door banged open. Hallie jumped and clutched the dishcloth to her chest, making a damp circle on the front of her dress. She heard the sound of several pairs of feet entering from the front porch. *Now what?*

She set the dishcloth down and pushed through the swinging door. "Pa?"

Her father stood near the fireplace, facing Edgar Wilson and Lee Moore. All three of the men turned stony faces toward her.

Despite the summer warmth, Hallie felt a chill run down her arms. She forced her dry throat to swallow. "Can I get you anything?"

"Just coffee, then leave us alone. We're talking business."

Stung by the curt reply, Hallie ducked back into the

kitchen without another word. She grabbed the nearly full coffeepot from the stove and set it on a tray along with three mugs. A sob rose up in her throat, and she choked it back down.

It's a good thing he didn't ask for more in the way of refreshments. She hadn't bothered to bake a cake or roll out a piecrust in weeks. These days, she could barely manage just getting through the basic routine from day to day.

She lifted the tray and backed through the swinging door just in time to hear Edgar Wilson ask, "What do you plan to do if they turn out to be the ones behind it?"

Her father snorted. "I plan to take a short rope and find me a tall tree, that's what."

Hallie gasped. The mugs rattled against the tray.

All three ranchers wheeled and looked her way. Avoiding their glances, she walked across the room with an air of calm she did not feel and set the tray down on a side table. She poured coffee into each mug, then walked back to the kitchen, schooling her features not to betray her.

As soon as the door swung shut behind her, she pushed it open again, just the barest crack. She pressed her ear against the tiny opening and listened.

"What about that so-called range detective?" Hallie recognized Edgar Wilson's irate tone. She clamped her lips together and held her breath, anxious not to miss a word they said about Jacob.

Her father made a sound of disgust. "You haven't seen him make any arrests, have you? The young fool wasn't any good before I shot him; he's worth even less now."

Grim chuckles followed his remark. Hallie had to restrain herself from bursting into the front room and flying to Jacob's defense. It would serve her purpose better to hear the rest of whatever the men had to say.

Lee Moore finally spoke, his nasal voice easy to distinguish from the others. "So we just ignore him? We don't let him know what we're doing?"

"It'll be easier that way," Hallie's father responded. "Easier and less likely to be botched up like the last time."

Hallie covered her mouth with both hands to hold back her cry of dismay. Tears welled up in her eyes. *What are they up to?* Whatever it might be, it boded ill for Jacob.

Edgar Wilson spoke again. "So what's the plan?" Hallie swiped the tears away with her fingertips and pressed closer to the door. She must not miss a syllable.

"You and Moore need to get back to your ranches and gather your riders," her father said. "Send the men you trust most to notify the other ranchers that we're going to settle this thing tonight."

A chair scraped on the wood floor, then her father's voice went on. "Wilson, your riders will cover the area to the north and east. Moore, yours will take in every place to the south and west. Tell them to round up as many men as they can and meet here this afternoon."

"What time?" Lee Moore asked.

"I say we make it four o'clock, no later than five. We'll catch those nesters napping and put an end to this foolishness."

A scream rose in Hallie's throat, and she clapped her hands over her mouth again. Ropes. Nesters. They couldn't be planning—

"That's a lot of territory to cover in just a few hours," Moore put in.

"He has a point," Edgar Wilson said. "Will we have time to reach everyone? What about O'Roarke? He's so tight with Garrett there doesn't seem to be much point in sending a man to his place. I can't see him agreeing to go with us, and he'd be more than likely to try to warn Garrett."

"Agreed. We don't want to give Garrett an inkling about what's going on and have him out there trying to save his precious nesters."

Hallie couldn't stand it another minute. She slammed the door open and rushed to stand before her father.

All three ranchers stared at her open-mouthed.

"What's the matter with you?" her father bellowed. "I told you we had to talk business."

"Is that what you call this? Business?" Hallie pivoted slowly to look at each of them in turn. "Are you all crazy? You're planning to murder innocent people."

"Innocent?" Wilson's lips drew back in a sneer. "Not very."

Hallie turned back to her father. He had a solid core of good sense, if only she could get through to him. "What proof do you have?"

"It's the only thing that makes sense," he said in a flat, emotionless tone that made the hairs on the back of her neck stand on end. "Look at them living up there the way they do, keeping out of sight of the rest of us. Pete thinks I'm right, too," he added with a note of triumph. "He said he's seen a couple of them in places they had no business being, and that happened right around the time some of our cattle went missing."

Hallie shook her head in disbelief. "You know that wouldn't stand up in court. If you have any real evidence, turn it over to the law. Sheriff Ruffner hates rustling as much as anyone. He'll see that justice is done." She didn't dare bring Jacob into it. No telling what the mere mention of his name might stir up, with the mood these men were in.

"What do you know about the law?" Her father waved his

hand in a dismissive gesture. "Go back to the kitchen and quit wasting our time. We've got plans to make."

Hallie grabbed his arms. "Plans for murder, Pa? Mama always said she could hold her head up high, knowing you were a man who cared about the truth. Well, where is the truth in this? Do you think she would be proud of what you're doing today?"

Her father brought his hands up and seized her wrists in an iron grip. "Don't you question what I'm doing. I'm trying to save the living of every rancher in this valley. If you can't understand that. . ." He thrust her away from him. "Now go to your room and stay there."

A band of fear tightened around her chest. "But I can't let—"

"Enough!" Her father's roar echoed through the room. "I told you to go to your room. Now get!"

twenty

Hallie lay across her bed, spent from the force of her crying. She stared dully at the sharp, ridged creases on her sheets where her hands had twisted them into knots.

Her pillow was a sodden lump beneath her cheek. Just when she thought she had used up all the tears left in her, a fresh wave of grief would wash over her to prove her wrong. But after an hour of weeping, the well had dried up. She pressed the tips of her fingers to her swollen eyelids and lay still, listening to the ragged sound of her breathing.

She had known grief when her mother died. But back then, she had her father to lean on. Now, the knowledge that he had turned away from her, bent on carrying out his heinous idea, plunged her into a depth of despair she couldn't have imagined before today.

Hallie rolled to her side and brushed her hand across her face. Damp strands of hair trailed across her cheek, glued to her skin by her own tears.

The meeting ended some time ago. She had heard the clomp of the men's boots on the front porch, then listened to the sound of hoofbeats fading into the distance. Wilson and Moore were gone, off to spread the word about a meeting that would stir up more trouble than this valley had ever seen—and ruin her father's life in the process.

"Hallie?" Her father's voice rumbled on the other side of her bedroom door.

She wrapped her arms around the tear-soaked pillow and

held it against her chest. He could send her to her room; he couldn't force her to talk to him.

"Hallie?" he called again. "I'm going after Pete and the rest of the boys." He paused, then tapped uncertainly on the door.

Another pause, then: *"Hallie!"* His pounding shook the walls and set her hairbrush vibrating on the top of her dresser.

She bit her lip until she tasted blood. Not for anything would she give him the satisfaction of a reply.

"All right." His voice carried a note of barely suppressed fury. "Have it your way. If you want to keep your door closed, then it'll stay closed until I get back."

Hallie heard a *snick* in the lock, then her pa's heavy footsteps pounding across the floor.

The front door slammed. Hallie waited until she felt sure he wouldn't be coming back, then she slipped out of bed and crossed the room. She gripped the knob and jiggled it. *No. He wouldn't. . .*

She grabbed the knob with both hands and twisted it with all her might. When that had no effect, she shook it back and forth until the door rattled in its frame. It didn't give.

He did. Hallie stared at the locked door, feeling like she had received a final blow. The strength drained from her limbs, and she tottered back to sprawl across the bed. Realization settled over her like a heavy cloak. She was a prisoner in her own room.

The tears flowed afresh.

੨ਾ

A hot, stuffy feeling replaced the morning coolness inside the house, reminding Hallie of how much time had passed. What was happening out there beyond the confines of her prison?

Had Edgar Wilson and Lee Moore had time to get back to their respective ranches? Hallie could picture them gathering their riders and sending them to bear their message of vengeance and death across the valley. And her own pa. . .

A shuddering moan rose from deep within when she thought of what he intended to do. What had happened to the father she had loved all her life? *Jacob was right, Pa. You need to forgive. Your anger and bitterness have turned you into a stranger, someone I don't want to know.*

Hallie pushed herself up to sit on the edge of her bed. What were the nesters doing at this moment? She could imagine them going about their usual routine, never dreaming that this day would be their last, that in a few hours death would descend on them in the form of grim-faced vigilantes.

Would they scatter and run or stand and fight? When would they realize there would be no escape, that the only future left to them involved a tree branch and a rope?

"Nooo!" The scream tore from Hallie's throat. She clutched at her hair with both hands. "Dear Lord, don't let my father's bitterness turn him into a murderer!"

Someone had to stop this madness, but there was no one.

Except her. Hallie stumbled to her feet and flung herself at the door. She pounded on it with both fists, but to no avail. Bracing herself, she raised her foot and kicked at the bottom panels.

Nothing happened.

Hallie shrieked in an agony of frustration. She clawed at the door, knowing it was futile, yet unable to stop herself. She had to get out. There had to be a way.

What about the window? Feeling foolish for not thinking of it before, she lifted her voice in a prayer of thanks and rushed across the room. She shoved the window wide open, then gathered her skirt and climbed onto the sill.

She teetered there for a moment, knowing she had reached

the point of no return. Once she left the house in defiance of her father's orders, she would cross a line from which she could never turn back. *Be with me, Lord. I have to save those nesters.*

I have to save my father. Hallie pushed herself out away from the sill and dropped to the ground.

She edged along the back of the house, then peered around the corner. She looked around the yard, halfway expecting her father to appear at any moment.

"He's gone." She said the words aloud, as if hearing the words spoken would provide added reassurance. "You've been given a gift of time. Make the most of it."

It took several attempts to saddle Gypsy. Hallie's fingers felt like wooden blocks as she fumbled to pull the cinch strap under the mare's belly, then buckle it in place. Finally the task was finished.

She led the horse outside the barn and swung up into the saddle. Which way should she go? Panic seized her. If she ran into her father, she didn't want to think about what would happen. Worse yet, what if she came across Pete, alone and unprotected?

Hallie forced herself to think. Her father had gone after Pete. Which way had he ridden? She squeezed her eyes shut tight to help her concentrate, then remembered her pa saying something about the hands all being up on the north range.

The decision had been made for her. She turned Gypsy toward the south and dug her heels in the mare's sides. She had to get to Jacob before it was too late.

❧

Once out of sight of the house, she realized the utter impossibility of the task she had set for herself. The valley itself covered a large territory, and the boundaries of Jacob's jurisdiction extended many miles beyond that in all directions. He was out there somewhere in that vast land; that much she knew. But where? Covering the whole area would take days.

Maybe she ought to acknowledge it as a fool's errand and turn back now. She started to rein Gypsy around, then froze. What if she didn't make it back to the house before her father discovered she was missing? The thought was enough to change her mind. She had no choice now but to go on.

Hallie looked overhead and marked the sun's position, just past its zenith. She had less than four hours to locate Jacob and get back to the house in time to stop her father.

"Where is he, Lord? Please help me to find him." If she had been able to choose freely, she would have ridden to the T Bar. If Jacob wasn't there, Dan O'Roarke might have some idea as to his whereabouts. And even if not, she knew Dan would not hesitate to saddle up and help her look for Jacob— or ride down to the Broken Box and help stand off the vigilantes himself.

But Pete was somewhere up on the north range, between her and the T Bar. No telling which part of the range he might be on. He could well be several miles away from the route that would take her to the O'Roarkes' home, but she couldn't rely on that.

With that option eliminated, Hallie breathed a quick prayer and set off toward the southwest. She needed to avoid the nearest ranches as much as possible. Wilson's and Moore's messengers would have started stirring things up already. Even now, riders from the other ranches might be on their way to the Broken Box with bloodlust in their hearts. It wouldn't pay to put herself in their way.

Not only that. Hallie groaned when she realized the other side of her dilemma. The gossip level of some of the cowboys would put a contingent of little old ladies to shame. Some of them had surely heard of her isolation from Jacob by now. If they caught her out there on her own, they might well feel duty-bound to return her to her father. And that meant. . .

Hallie's lips tightened. It meant she would have to stay away from everyone. She had no way of knowing who would help or hinder her until it was too late. She kept to the washes and other low areas, as intent on hiding her tracks as she was on finding Jacob.

The sun continued its inexorable march across the sky. An hour passed. Then another. Hallie crisscrossed the area to the west and south of the Broken Box. She never saw a living soul, not even cowhands traveling to join her father in his deadly foray. Hallie stood in her stirrups and gazed from one side of the valley to the other. *Where, Lord?*

The T Bar. She had to risk it. It was the only place she could approach in safety. Surely by now Pete and her father would be back at the house, waiting for the others. She guided Gypsy north, keeping a line of low hills between herself and the open valley.

The distance seemed interminably long, but at last she clattered into the yard, barely able to stay in her saddle. "Help!" she cried. "Is anyone home?"

The commotion brought Amy rushing outside. She leaped down the steps, her face etched with worry. "Hallie! What on earth—"

Hallie cut her off. "Jacob. Is he here?"

"What's wrong, Hallie? Let me help you down. We've got to get you inside."

She reached up, but Hallie pulled away. "There's no time. Amy, tell me quickly, do you know where Jacob is? I must find him."

"I heard him talking to Dan earlier. He said something about scouting out an area about an hour east of here."

"You're sure?" Hallie pulled her weary body upright and braced herself for the next leg of her search.

Amy caught at the reins. "You're in no condition to ride. Let me send one of the men out after him, if it's that important."

"There's no time. I'll explain it to you later." Hallie urged Gypsy into as fast a pace as she dared, praying all the way. An hour would be too late.

Thirty minutes later, she spotted a rider outlined against a low hill. She pulled up, wondering whether she should head for cover. Something about him, though. . .

He turned his head, and she caught a clear view of his profile. "Oh, thank You, Jesus!" She spurred Gypsy on and raced toward him.

When she had closed half the distance, Jacob caught sight of her. He gave an exuberant wave and rode toward her at a gallop.

twenty-one

At first Jacob thought his eyes were playing tricks on him. Growing up in Tucson, he'd seen mirages himself and heard plenty of stories of prospectors stranded in the desert heat, crawling toward shimmering pools of water that existed only in their imaginations. Had his own mind created an image of the woman he loved, an illusory vision that would disappear the moment he drew near?

The echo of galloping hoofbeats decided him. A mirage wouldn't affect his ears as well as his eyes. Joy welled up in him until he thought he would burst. This was no illusion. It was Hallie!

Cap didn't hesitate when Jacob dug his heels in. The steel-dust launched himself straight down the slope, closing the gap between them with amazing speed.

Jacob leaned over the gelding's neck, yearning for a closer view of that beloved face. How did she come to be out here? Had she persuaded her father to lift his ban on their being together?

It didn't matter. They could sort the details out later. All he cared about now was seeing Hallie, gazing into her sweet face, and taking her in his arms.

The gap narrowed to fifty yards. Twenty. Jacob felt a ripple of concern at the way Hallie slumped in the saddle. What happened to her usual easy grace?

At ten yards, worry built a knot in his throat. As he drew abreast of her, he took in her sharpened features, the way her clothes hung loose. *How much weight has she lost? Has she been sick, Lord, and I didn't know it?*

Hallie pulled Gypsy to a halt and braced her arms against the saddle horn as if it were the only way she could hold herself erect. Tear streaks stained her cheeks and strands of hair straggled along the sides of her face.

The knot in Jacob's throat threatened to choke him. *Hallie, sweetheart, what has he done to you?*

He opened his mouth to speak, but she cut him off before he could say a word. "You've got to stop them before they kill someone."

Whatever he had expected, it wasn't this. "Take a breath and slow down, Hallie. I don't understand."

"My father and some of the other ranchers. They're forming a vigilante group. They're riding out today, going after the nesters." Her mouth twisted and a sob erupted from her throat. "Jacob, they're going to hang them!"

His mouth went dry. "When? Where?"

"They're supposed to meet at our place, sometime between four and five o'clock." They glanced up toward the sun at the same moment, then Hallie turned toward him, her face set in a tragic expression. "It's almost four now. I don't know if we can get there in time."

"We can try." He looked at her doubtfully. "Are you up to it?"

Hallie gathered the reins in her trembling hands. "I'll make it. And if I don't, keep on going. You've got to stop them."

He didn't have time to argue her out of it. He ducked his head. "All right. Let's ride."

❧

Hallie bent low over Gypsy's neck, feeling the mare's power as she raced to keep pace with Cap. The wind whipped against Hallie's face and tore at her hair. She ducked her head lower and urged Gypsy on.

"Come on, girl, you can make it. We have to get there." By her calculations, it must be just past four o'clock. If all the men her father called had shown up on time or even early, the vigilantes could be gone already.

The miles Gypsy had run already that day began to take their toll, as Hallie felt the horse falter and heard her labor for breath. Jacob glanced over his shoulder. A frown crossed his face when he saw them falling behind. Hallie waved at him to go on. More important than their arrival together was Jacob getting there in time to keep her father from making the worst mistake of his life.

"Don't let it happen, Lord. Find a way to stop them, please." She couldn't let her father become a murderer. She *wouldn't*, as long as there was still breath left in her body.

The house and barn appeared as dots on the horizon, growing larger with every stride Gypsy made. Hallie squinted her eyes against the rushing wind and strained to see the yard. "Please let them be there. Please!"

Cap put on a burst of speed and increased the distance between them. Hallie felt Gypsy's pace slacken still more. She wanted to scream out her frustration, but bent all her concentration on staying in the saddle instead. She felt almost as exhausted as Gypsy. It wouldn't help matters for either one of them to become injured.

Ahead, she could see the dust rise as Jacob rode into the yard at a dead run. Hallie lost him from view when he passed around the far side of the barn. Was he even now confronting the band of vigilantes or waiting to break the news to her that they had been too late?

Hold on, hold on. You'll know in just a few moments. Uncertainty stretched her nerves to the breaking point.

It seemed like hours passed before Gypsy reached the barn. The mare stopped and stood with her head drooping between her front legs, her sides heaving in great gulps of air. Dreading what she might find, Hallie slipped from the saddle and rounded the corner on foot.

The sight she beheld stopped her in her tracks. Jacob stood facing a dozen mounted men. Every one of them stared back at him with stony contempt. Jacob's right hand rested on the grip of his pistol, but he spoke in a low, matter-of-fact tone.

"You have no proof, nothing more than mere speculation."

A hard-faced cowboy on a long-legged dun rode forward until his mount towered over Jacob. "We have all the proof we need. These nesters have been causing trouble all over the territory for years. It's time we were rid of this bunch. It might make others think twice before they try the same thing."

A rumble of assent came from the group, but Jacob didn't flinch. "What you're doing is wrong. Deep down in your hearts, I think you know that. You're all angry about losing your stock, and you have every right to be. Most of you are angry at me for not catching the men responsible, and I don't blame you for that, either."

He paused, and Hallie studied their faces intently. Jacob's last comment seemed to take some of the men by surprise. They watched him with guarded expressions.

"Now you've decided there's someone you can blame, and the idea of venting that anger sounds mighty appealing."

"You're right about that," Edgar Wilson called. "It's high time we took action. Some of us have felt all along that the nesters were responsible."

"Then why didn't you do anything about it before?" Jacob challenged him. "Why wait until now? Ask yourselves why it's easier to think about doing this as part of a group. Is it because it takes away the responsibility you'd feel if you acted alone? Because your consciences have been drowned out by the voices of a mob? That's what you are, gentlemen, if you'll just stop and think about it. Nothing but a mob."

"Enough!" Hallie's father rode forward, a look of loathing on his face. "We've been sitting on our backsides long enough. It's time to put an end to this, once and for all. If it takes more than one man to get rid of these thieves, then I say that's what is needed." He raised the coil of rope he held in his fist and shook it at Jacob. "I call it justice."

Jacob stood his ground. "The law calls it murder."

An uneasy silence settled over the group.

"If you go ahead with this fool scheme, you'll be breaking the law every bit as much as the men who have been rustling your stock. We still don't know who they are, but I can name every one of you."

The silence deepened. From the rear of the group, Lee Moore challenged, "Are you trying to say you'd go against the whole lot of us like that?"

The man beside Moore snorted. "I was there at the roundup, same as you and all the rest. If he felt that strong about a misbranded calf, what do you think he'll do about a thing like this?"

Moore drew back as if he'd been slapped. "Maybe you're right," he muttered. "This whole idea is starting to taste pretty sour to me. I'm going home." He signaled his men, and they rode off without further comment.

One by one, the other men followed suit until only the Broken Box riders were left. Finally, even they dismounted and began to unsaddle their horses. Pete Edwards paused in the act of loosening his cinch. Leaving his horse ground tied, he disappeared into the barn.

Hallie's father turned to Jacob. Fury smoldered in his eyes. "Well, you've driven off all my help. I guess you're mighty proud of yourself, aren't you?" He advanced a step and clenched his beefy fists. "Funny how you're so convincing as far as protecting these rustlers. How am I supposed to know you aren't in cahoots with them?"

"Pa!" Hallie spoke for the first time since her wild ride into the yard. "Stop and think what you're saying. He's saving you from going to prison, maybe worse."

Her father waved his arm through the air as though shooing away a troublesome fly and kept his gaze fixed on Jacob. "You've ruined this necktie party. But as soon as I know for sure who's doing it, as soon as I have that proof you keep talking about, they're going to pay. I don't care what you say."

Jacob's fingers curled into white-knuckled knots, then opened again. "You need to cool off," he stated in a flat tone. "So do I. So do our horses, for that matter." He walked back to where Cap and Gypsy stood, caught up their reins, and led them around toward the water trough.

With a muttered oath, Hallie's father stomped toward the house. He slammed the door so hard behind him, Hallie felt sure the wood would splinter. *Thank You, Lord. It's over.* Reaction set in, and she felt her whole body start to shake.

Pete strode out of the barn, carrying his saddlebags. *The last person I want to see,* Hallie thought. She gave him a wide berth as she circled around him to go join Jacob. Then something about his manner caught her attention.

She watched as Pete walked over to his horse and slung the saddlebags behind the cantle, then tightened the cinch.

All the others have put their horses up. Why would he be doing that, unless. . .

"You're leaving?" The words sprang out before she could stop them.

Pete glanced up, his features set in a surly expression. "You needn't sound so hopeful." He yanked the cinch. "Yes, I'm leaving. I've had all I can take. This whole business of turning vigilante is more than I signed on for."

Hallie wondered if he could sense her unbridled joy. "I'll wish you a good journey, then." *A long journey, as far from here as you can possibly go.* She turned to join Jacob around the side of the barn.

"Wait." Pete closed the distance between them with long strides. "I know we've had our differences, but all I ever wanted was for you to feel the same way about me as I do about you." He circled her upper arm with his fingers. "Why don't you come with me?"

twenty-two

"Let go of me." She wrenched her arm away and stepped back.

"I mean it, Hallie. You don't belong with Garrett. You belong to me; you always have." He lunged forward and gripped her shoulders with both hands. "Come away with me. We can make each other happy."

Hallie kicked out and caught him on the shin. He sucked in a quick breath and tightened his hold. "I told you this day would come. I thought I'd be around here long enough to make you see things my way. But it's time for me to leave, and you're coming with me." He shifted his hands to encircle her waist and dragged her toward his horse.

"Jacob!" she screamed. She dug in her heels and fought with all her might.

She heard hurried footsteps on the other side of the barn, and Jacob rounded the corner, his face dark with worry. He stopped abruptly. "Let her go," he ordered.

Pete swung Hallie around in front of him and clamped his arm across her throat. "Maybe she doesn't want me to. She's leaving with me, Garrett."

Jacob's eyes flicked back and forth from Pete to Hallie, then to Pete's holster. Hallie saw his jaw tighten and his hand settle on the pistol grip. Pete must have noticed it, too. He tightened his hold, pulling her closer to him.

"Don't!" she cried. The confusion in Jacob's eyes tore at her heart. "I've spent this day trying to stop bloodshed. I don't want

163

to be the reason for any being spilled." *Especially if it's yours.*

Pete chuckled. "See? I told you. She wants to go with me." He dragged her back another step. "Come on, Hallie. It's time to mount up."

Jacob sprang forward, putting himself beside Pete in a single leap. "I said, let her go!" He grabbed Pete by the collar and swung him around. The whiplike action broke Pete's grip and sent Hallie flying. She landed on her hands and knees, with her palms skidding across the rough ground.

❧

Breathing heavily, Jacob turned loose of Pete's shirt and stepped back. He had seen Hallie fall, but he didn't dare take his gaze off Pete to make sure she was all right. He moved forward a step, forcing Pete back closer to his horse.

"You said you were leaving. You'd better go now. Get on your horse and don't stop until you get to wherever it is you're headed."

Pete stood stock still for a moment, then he let out a string of curses and swung his fist.

The blow connected with Jacob's ribs. He caught his breath in a quick gasp and widened his stance. *I wasn't ready that time. I won't make the same mistake again.*

Pete threw another punch. This time, Jacob blocked it easily with his forearm. He pushed Pete away. "All right, we've settled things now. Let's call it quits."

"That's where you're wrong." Pete settled into a crouch. "This ain't over, not by a long shot." He rushed at Jacob, arms spread wide.

Jacob sidestepped and thumped Pete on the back of the head with his fist when he stumbled past. Maybe he could knock enough sense into the man to make him understand this fight was pointless.

Pete hit the ground on his knees, then staggered to his feet and turned to face Jacob. Pure hatred gleamed from his eyes. "When I get my hands on you, I'll beat you so bad nobody will want to look at your face, not even her." He jerked his head toward Hallie.

"There isn't any sense to this. You're ready to leave, so leave. Just pack up and go. But you're going alone."

Pete lowered his head and ran at Jacob, swinging his fists.

Enough. Jacob blocked the punches and responded with some of his own. *Sometimes there just doesn't seem to be any other answer.* They stood trading punches, then Jacob moved forward, gaining ground with every blow.

Pete stumbled backward and scrambled to regain his footing. The move brought him up next to his horse. The wide-eyed animal snorted and danced skittishly.

Pete glanced behind him, appearing to realize he was trapped. He feinted to the right, then the left, but Jacob blocked his escape. Pete turned as though to take his horse's reins. Then he whirled around, landing a savage kick on Jacob's right thigh, inches away from where he had been shot.

Jacob's vision turned dark and stars shot across the blackness. He had to end this now. He wouldn't be able to take another blow like that. Putting most of his weight on his left leg, he crouched slightly, then delivered a punch that started down at his knees.

His fist cracked against Pete's jaw, slamming him back against his horse. The gelding shied and whinnied. Pete slumped to the ground, out cold.

His saddlebags slid off the horse and flopped to the earth a few feet away, spilling their contents on the ground.

Jacob stood over the unconscious man, chest heaving and fists clenched, ready to deal with him again if he were playing possum. He watched Pete closely, waiting for him to move.

"Jacob?"

He shot a quick look over his shoulder. Hallie stood behind him, staring at a handful of papers.

"What is it?"

"These fell out of Pete's saddlebag. I think you'd better take a look."

"Later. I need to make sure he doesn't take a notion to start things up again when he comes around."

"I really don't think you want to wait." She moved closer and handed him the papers.

Jacob glanced at them quickly, then blinked and took a closer look. Bills of sale for small bunches of cattle, all dated within the past few months, and all listing Pete Edwards as the owner. Jacob looked up at Hallie and their gazes locked.

"Do you realize what this could mean?" he asked.

"Mm-hm. Look what else fell out." Hallie held out her other hand.

Jacob stared at a roll of bills big enough to choke a horse. "Where would a cowboy get that much money?"

"Not from working for my father, that's for sure."

As if on cue, Burke Evans threw open the front door and ran down the porch steps.

"What's all the commotion? What are you doing?" He stared at Pete's still figure and jerked his gaze back up to direct a menacing glare at Jacob. "You come here with all your talk about leaving people in peace, then you go and do something like this?"

Jacob held out the papers and nodded toward the money still in Hallie's hand. "Any idea where he'd come by that amount of cash?"

Burke gaped at the wad of money, then flipped through the

bills of sale Jacob handed him. His features hardened. "No, but we're going to find out." He prodded Pete with his boot. "Wake up. We've got some talking to do."

Pete rolled his head to one side and moaned. Burke reached down and pulled him up by the front of his shirt. "Wake up," he repeated. He shook the groggy man and waved the papers in his face. "What do you have to say about this?"

Pete shook his head and blinked. His gaze lit on the papers in Burke's hand, and his eyes seemed to snap back into focus. He stiffened and shifted his gaze from side to side like a trapped coyote. Seeing no way of escape, he swung around and turned to Jacob.

"Don't let him hang me," he said.

ra

The sun hung low in the western sky. Hallie waited outside the barn door while Jacob and her father tied Pete securely in one of the stalls. Even though Jacob assured him he would be taken back to Prescott for trial, the sight of Burke Evans carrying a rope had been enough to frighten the cowboy into rattling off all the details of the rustling operation he had spearheaded.

Jacob had the names he needed now and enough physical evidence in the form of the bills of sale and ill-gotten money to bring the guilty men to justice. In the morning, he could go after the rest of the lot and turn them over to Sheriff Ruffner along with their erstwhile leader.

Pete's sudden transformation from a blustering bully into a broken man shocked Hallie, but not as much as the plea he made while her father and Jacob dragged him into the barn. At the doorway he turned back toward her, his face pale and frightened. "You know I never would have hurt you, Hallie. I was going to let you go that day at the canyon, remember?"

His voice cracked, and a sharp push from her father hurried him out of her sight.

So Pete had been one of the men she'd surprised in the canyon. The one who knelt in the small of her back and pushed her face into the dirt? Probably. It would fit with his enjoyment of bullying anyone smaller and weaker than himself.

And he had been the one who promised to carry her off with him, she felt sure of that. The bandanna over his face, coupled with the shock of finding her there, had distorted his voice enough to keep her from recognizing it. Besides, she had been so sure he was at the other end of the range that fateful day.

The creak of the barn door brought her out of her reverie. Jacob watched her father drop the heavy bar into place. "Thanks for your help. That should hold him until I'm ready to leave for town."

Her father nodded, then looked down at his feet. "I guess I owe you an apology. You kept me from doing something I would have regretted for the rest of my days."

Hallie could see the effort it cost him to reach his hand out toward Jacob, who took it in a firm grip.

"Apology accepted," he said. "We'll let this stay in the past, where it belongs. And I'm glad to think we're starting over fresh. There's something I want to talk to you about." He walked over to Hallie and stopped beside her.

Her father's mouth dropped open, then he pressed his lips together in a thin line. "If you're thinking about the kind of talk I suspect you are, you can just forget it." He looked straight at her. "Hallie, get in the house."

"Wait." Jacob stepped closer and put his arm around her shoulders. Hallie let his warmth flow through her and give her strength. "I love your daughter, Mr. Evans. I'd like your permission to ask her to marry me."

Please, Pa. Say yes. Hallie turned a hopeful gaze upon him.

He stared at them for a long moment, then gave his head a decisive shake. "No. You can put that notion right out of your mind. I'll lock her up again if I have to."

"How much good did it do you to lock me in my room today?" Hallie stepped forward, leaving the security of Jacob's touch. Her lips trembled so, she could barely speak.

She took a deep breath to keep her voice from shaking and plunged ahead. "My birthday is in August, remember? I'll be twenty-one in just a few weeks. You can order me to obey you, and I will. . .for now. But you can't keep a hold on me forever, Pa. Once I reach majority, I'll do whatever needs to be done to be with Jacob."

She stepped back and put her arm around Jacob's waist. Lifting her chin, she said, "I love him, Pa. Nothing you can do is going to change that."

୬ଈ

Jacob watched Burke and saw a flicker of uncertainty in his eyes. He decided to press their advantage. "Do you really want Hallie at your beck and call because you demand it? Or would you rather she gave her affection to you freely?" He wrapped his arm around her shoulders and drew her close.

Burke kept silent, studying the two of them. Finally he turned toward the house. "Hallie, you come inside." His mouth turned up in a wry smile. "Whenever you're of a mind to."

"Oh, Pa!" Hallie ran to her father and wrapped her arms around his waist. "Thank you. I'll never stop loving you, you know that, don't you?"

Burke stroked her hair with his work-hardened hand, and a tender expression lit his face. "I know that. I guess I always have." He dropped a kiss on her forehead, then looked up and leveled a stern gaze at Jacob.

"You take care of her, do you hear? I shot you once. I can do it again if you don't treat her right." With that, he turned on his heel and walked away.

Hallie pressed her lips together and drew in a shaky breath. "Coming from him, that's practically a blessing."

"I know." Jacob chuckled, then pulled her to him and tilted her head back so he could look straight into her eyes. "Hallie, I need to make it official. Will you do me the honor of becoming my wife?"

She cupped her hand around his face and traced the line of his jaw with her fingers. Her soft breath caressed his cheek. "God has answered all my prayers," she said simply.

"Even if it meant me getting shot?" Jacob tried to look stern, but he couldn't hold back a smile.

"Yes, Jacob." He stiffened, and Hallie looked puzzled. Then she laughed. "I mean, yes, I will be your wife."

Jacob's laughter mingled with hers. "God has brought us through heartbreak to joy." He slid his arms around her and cradled her head against his chest. "Who knows what He has in store for us along the road ahead?"

Hallie tilted her head to one side. Her breath came out in a soft sigh. "I have no idea what is going to come our way. But whatever it is, I know I can get through it as long as I have Him." She lifted her face and closed her eyes.

"And you," she whispered, just before his lips touched hers.

A Letter To Our Readers

Dear Reader:

In order that we might better contribute to your reading enjoyment, we would appreciate your taking a few minutes to respond to the following questions. We welcome your comments and read each form and letter we receive. When completed, please return to the following:

Fiction Editor
Heartsong Presents
PO Box 719
Uhrichsville, Ohio 44683

1. Did you enjoy reading *Road to Forgiveness* by Carol Cox?
   ❏ Very much! I would like to see more books by this author!
   ❏ Moderately. I would have enjoyed it more if

   _____

   _____

   _____

2. Are you a member of **Heartsong Presents**? ❏ Yes ❏ No
   If no, where did you purchase this book? _____

   _____

3. How would you rate, on a scale from 1 (poor) to 5 (superior), the cover design? _____

4. On a scale from 1 (poor) to 10 (superior), please rate the following elements.

   ____ Heroine   ____ Plot
   ____ Hero   ____ Inspirational theme
   ____ Setting   ____ Secondary characters

5. These characters were special because?_____

_____

_____

6. How has this book inspired your life?_____

_____

_____

7. What settings would you like to see covered in future **Heartsong Presents** books? _____

_____

_____

8. What are some inspirational themes you would like to see treated in future books? _____

_____

_____

9. Would you be interested in reading other **Heartsong Presents** titles? ❑ Yes   ❑ No

10. Please check your age range:

    ❑ Under 18   ❑ 18-24

    ❑ 25-34   ❑ 35-45

    ❑ 46-55   ❑ Over 55

Name_____

Occupation _____

Address _____

City_____ State_____ Zip_____

COLORADO

4 stories in 1

Taming the frontier is a daunting task—one that can't be burdened by the luxuries of life, including romance. Four settlers take the challenge and are surprised when love springs up beside them along the way.

Four complete inspirational romance stories by author Rosey Dow.

Historical, paperback, 464 pages, 5 ³/₁₆" x 8"

Presents

Great Inspirational Romance at a Great Price!

Heartsong Presents books are inspirational romances in contemporary and historical settings, designed to give you an enjoyable, spirit-lifting reading experience. You can choose wonderfully written titles from some of today's best authors like Peggy Darty, Sally Laity, DiAnn Mills, Colleen L. Reece, Debra White Smith, and many others.

When ordering quantities less than twelve, above titles are $2.97 each.
Not all titles may be available at time of order.

JEARTSONG ❤ PRESENTS

Love Stories
Are Rated G!

That's for godly, gratifying, and of course, great! If you love a thrilling love story but don't appreciate the sordidness of some popular paperback romances, **Heartsong Presents** is for you. In fact, **Heartsong Presents** is the premiere inspirational romance book club featuring love stories where Christian faith is the primary ingredient in a marriage relationship.

Sign up today to receive your first set of four, never-before-published Christian romances. Send no money now; you will receive a bill with the first shipment. You may cancel at any time without obligation, and if you aren't completely satisfied with any selection, you may return the books for an immediate refund!

Imagine. . .four new romances every four weeks—two historical, two contemporary—with men and women like you who long to meet the one God has chosen as the love of their lives. . .all for the low price of $10.99 postpaid.

To join, simply complete the coupon below and mail to the address provided. **Heartsong Presents** romances are rated G for another reason: They'll arrive Godspeed!